Anonymus

Report on District, Local and Private Lunatic Asylums in Ireland

With appendices

Anonymus

Report on District, Local and Private Lunatic Asylums in Ireland
With appendices

ISBN/EAN: 9783742810366

Manufactured in Europe, USA, Canada, Australia, Japa

Cover: Foto ©Suzi / pixelio.de

Manufactured and distributed by brebook publishing software
(www.brebook.com)

Anonymus

Report on District, Local and Private Lunatic Asylums in Ireland

LUNATIC ASYLUMS.—IRELAND.

THE

THIRTY-FIFTH REPORT

OF THE

DISTRICT, CRIMINAL, AND PRIVATE LUNATIC ASYLUMS IN IRELAND;

WITH APPENDICES.

Presented to both Houses of Parliament by Command of Her Majesty.

DUBLIN:
ALEX. THOM & CO. (LIMITED), 87, 88, & 89, ABBEY-STREET,
THE QUEEN'S PRINTING OFFICE.

To be purchased, either directly or through any Bookseller, from any of the following Agents, viz.:
Messrs. HANSARD, 13, Great Queen-street, W.C., and 32, Abingdon-street, Westminster;
Messrs. EYRE and SPOTTISWOODE, East Harding-street, Fleet-street, and Sale Office, House of Lords;
Messrs. ADAM and CHARLES BLACK, of Edinburgh;
Messrs. ALEXANDER THOM and Co. (Limited), or Messrs. HODGES, FIGGIS, and Co., of Dublin.

1886.

CONTENTS.

APPENDICES.

APPENDIX A.—INSANE PERSONS IN UNION WORKHOUSES, IRELAND.

APPENDIX B.—CENTRAL LUNATIC ASYLUM, DUNDRUM, RETURNS, 1885.

A 2

Table. Page

APPENDIX C.—RETURNS OF DISTRICT ASYLUMS FOR THE YEAR ENDING 31ST DECEMBER, 1885.

APPENDIX D.—LUNATICS IN GAOLS, 1885.

APPENDIX E.—CONVICTS, 1885.

APPENDIX F.—PRIVATE LICENSED HOUSES, 1885.

APPENDIX G.

THIRTY-FIFTH REPORT

ON THE

DISTRICT, CRIMINAL,

AND

PRIVATE LUNATIC ASYLUMS

IN IRELAND.

TO HIS EXCELLENCY JOHN CAMPBELL, EARL OF ABERDEEN,

LORD LIEUTENANT-GENERAL AND GENERAL GOVERNOR OF IRELAND.

24th June, 1886.

MAY IT PLEASE YOUR EXCELLENCY:

We have the honour to submit our Thirty-fifth Annual Report on the Lunacy Department of this country during the past year for presentation to Parliament. The statistical tables supplied in minute detail in the Appendices to the present Report, differ but little, on some points, from those given in the preceding—that for 1884.

The distribution of the insane both in public and private in- Statistics
stitutions on the 1st of January, 1885, was as follows:—In district asylums, especially intended for the poorer classes, there were 9,687—5,322 being males and 4,365 females; in the Dundrum or Criminal Asylum, 178, 146 men and 32 women;—in houses licensed under the 5th & 6th Vic., cap. 123, 639 persons were located, comprising 245 males and 394 females, belonging to the better classes of society, and paying various stipends for their care and maintenance; while in poor law unions there were no less than 3,775, of whom a perceptible majority, or 2,257, were females. From the preceding data it would appear as regards the accommodation of the insane poor in Ireland, that while each sex is almost identical in the population at large, the male inmates of district asylums are 7 per cent. over the female, whereas females in poorhouses are 23 per cent. more numerous than males. A further disparity may be added, namely, that moral causes of lunacy are a third more prevalent among women than men, with whom physical causes stand nearly in a two fold excess.

A total of 14,279 persons were registered as being mentally affected in some form or other at the beginning of last year; in

Admissions.

the course of which, independent of the 9,687 above adverted to as being in district asylums, 2,850 cases were admitted, constituting an aggregate of 6,798 males, and 5,739 females, as the full number treated in these establishments on a daily average of 9,781. Of the admissions, 2,240 were cases of first attack, and 610 relapses, the intervals of recovery in the latter varying from months to years; a fact indicative of the fixity of mental disease in some constitutions, awaiting only, as it were, an opportunity for its re-development.

With reference to these admissions, we cannot but think, from personal observation on visits of inspection to asylums, and the opinions of resident physicians in them, that in the past year, much more than previously, acute attacks of insanity were caused by a want of nutritious food, and at the same time by a continuous indulgence in raw spirituous liquors of bad quality. The patients so affected, and physically of good frame, were recognisable from their pallid, emaciated features, extreme irritability, waywardness, and disposition to violence. Some few cases proved speedily fatal.

Discharges.

The discharges cured in 1885 were returned at 1,196, and of relieved at 510; 89 were taken home on probation, for the most part by their relatives, mentally little improved, though tranquil and inoffensive—a change which, not alone on the grounds of humanity, but as likely to prove beneficial, we could desire to be more general, particularly among the better circumstanced in society. Eight persons continuing insane were relegated to other institutions.

Recoveries.

The proportion of recoveries on the daily average of patients in 1885 was 12, and of improvements 5½ per cent; between both it would thus appear that about 18 individuals in each 100 directly benefited in a curative or ameliorative point of view from district asylum treatment. Were recoveries, however, estimated as is ordinarily done, on the basis of admissions, they would stand much higher or about 53 per cent. In either case an opinion is, nevertheless, prevalent, the justness of which may be fairly questioned, that the utility of hospitals for the insane is not equivalent to the large outlay on their primitive establishment and current cost of maintenance. But, it should be borne in mind, as already on principle upheld by us, that lunatics deprived of liberty and personal privileges, from the character of their affliction, not only have peculiar claims on the public, but require for their own, and alike for the protection of society, the unremitting care that can only be afforded in establishments specially adapted to their detention, in a curative and protective point of view.

Deaths.

The deaths, in all 856, were somewhat lower than those which occurred in the previous year—four were suicidal, but not from any culpability on the part of attendants in charge, according to the verdicts returned in each case at a coroner's inquest. The stealthy and studied ingenuity of a person bereft of reason, when bent on self-destruction, or as the result of a sudden impulse in the feelings of a lunatic though seemingly quite contented with his surroundings, cannot be well obviated on some occasions. We ourselves are familiar with instances in private life where sanity itself was persistently feigned in order to obtain the deplorable opportunity. No life was lost from accident, and only two effected a permanent escape. Deaths.

With respect to the interior organization of district asylums in Ireland, progressing from year to year under the judicious control of their Medical Superintendents, as well as to their order, regularity, and cleanliness, we feel justified in reporting favourably to your Excellency. The subordinate resident staffs attached to them fulfil their duties on the whole in a very praiseworthy manner, notwithstanding that in some, many of the employed are dissatisfied with their pay and allowances, still more at "hopes deferred." On a full inquiry we cannot but feel that their position admits of a more liberal consideration, taking into account the irksome, responsible, and not unfrequently dangerous occupations in which they are unceasingly engaged. Organization and Staffs.

A more encouraging system prevails in England, where Boards, contrasting, in their different localities, from personal observation and experience, the relative value of money with services rendered, can requite the latter accordingly. Thereby a superior or at all events a more educated class of servants and attendants can be procured; not one, however, we are bound to say, more humane, better conducted, or more faithful, than to be found in this country where, out of a total of nearly 1,000, very few indeed were dismissed for impropriety of conduct, or legal offences during the last year. Fines, however, were occasionally inflicted, the total amount scarcely exceeding thirty pounds. System in England.

Adding to the Insane accommodated in district asylums on the 31st December, 1884, those admitted during the subsequent twelvemonth, a total is made up of 12,537; abstracting from which ordinary discharges, deaths, escapes, and transferences, 9,872—5,402 males and 4,470 females remained under treatment. Patients under treatment.

In 1884, with a daily average in public asylums of 9,614, the expenditure on their maintenance, including incidental expenses, save those connected with structural enlargements or the purchase of land (repayable as a rule within fourteen years), reached the sum of £221,753 17*s.* 7*d.*, being at a capitation rate of £23 0*s.* 11*d.* Deducting the Government rate in aid of £10 8*s.* per head annually, and with it a lump sum of £5,497 received for patients wholly or partially paying for their support, besides some minor items, the balance chargeable to local taxation was reduced to £117,645 4*s.* 5*d.* Audited expenditure.

In 1885, under parallel circumstances, with a population of 9,793, an increase of 162 on the average of patients, and of 26 Expenditure.

additional servants, the cost of supporting district asylums was £216,709 17*s.* 4*d.*—£4,954, less than that of the preceding year, (the difference of £1 1*s.* 6*d.* per head, being in favour of 1885), or £21 10*s.* 5*d.* as against £23 0*s.* 11*d.* in 1884; a decrease referable in part to cheaper contracts as authorized by the Inspectors, and to more economical domestic arrangements.

Audit.

With reference to the audit of accounts as directed by the 31st & 32nd Victoria, cap. 97, they were passed without reduction or disallowances by the ten Government officials employed collectively for seventy-eight days at their several investigations.

The preceding statement, bearing on the mode in which the fiscal business of public institutions for the Insane has been conducted, is satisfactory, still more as being in character almost invariably with reports made since the passing of the Act. It could not well be otherwise, looking to the social position of Governors appointed by the Executive, who, in the control of these establishments, devote much time, and not unfrequently at personal inconvenience, to self imposed duties.

Government grant.

We would, however, allude to one result of the parliamentary rate in aid, which was granted perhaps, not so much to keep down local taxation, as to ensure a more liberal treatment of the Insane. It is evinced in a disposition at some Boards occasionally, to reduce asylum expenditure by it, to an approximate equality, it may even be lower than that in poorhouses, which the destitute are at liberty to enter or leave as they please. To this theory we have invariably objected, impressed with the conviction that the boon in question was exclusively intended for the individuals themselves, their comforts and well-being, so as to increase thereby every hope of recovery or improvement, as well as, from compassionate motives, to make amends for a want of freedom.

Farm produce and expenses.

Adverting to the quantity of land attached to the twenty-two district asylums of this country, and amounting to 978 statute acres—697 were under spade cultivation or in grass, and 281 occupied by buildings, pleasure grounds, airing courts, and gardens. The value of produce consumed, at ordinary current prices, inclusive of animal food, was £8,211 5*s.* 7*d.*, while that for produce sold reached £2,423 13*s.*, as passed at audit. It is, however, to be observed that interest on the primitive cost of purchased estates is omitted in the calculation, as well as on that for farm buildings. The approximate gain per acre, after an expenditure of £4,822 7*s.* 7*d.* may be represented on the total quantity of land at £5 19*s.* 7*d.*—and the value of assets on hand, at £6,739 6*s.* 5*d.*

Employment.

It is to be regretted that the farms, on the score of their economical working through unpaid labour, and averaging one with another thirty-two acres, are not larger, so as to afford means of occupation for double the number of those now employed out of doors.

As a counter-part to the deficiency of cultivated land, we are gratified to observe that useful employments are perceptibly on the increase in regard to handicraft work and trades, as well as ordinary domestic services—while amusements of various kinds in the open air and recreation halls are liberally afforded. Some institutions have musical bands of fair pretensions. Employments.

A special return having been presented to the House of Commons last January by the Board of Control, (of which we form two of the five constituent members), "showing moneys ordered to be expended on sites and buildings of lunatic asylums in Ireland for a period of twenty years to January, 1885, as well as the dates of Orders in Council for sanctioned increases of additional land," it is unnecessary to advert to them in the present report. The indebtedness of each district for advances from the Treasury was also exhibited therein. Cost of Buildings.

In the annexed appendices ample information is supplied in tabular forms, not only of general expenditure during the past year in its various items, but of all matters connected with the domestic economy of district asylums, and so arranged that a comparison with respect to each is readily afforded.

POORHOUSES.

The aggregate number of persons mentally affected in the above named institutions (153 in number), on the 31st December last amounted to 3,733, being 42 less than at a like date in the preceding year. It was composed of lunatics, aged, utterly demented, and tranquil—714 being males, 1,182 females; and of idiots and epileptic imbeciles between both sexes, 1837—786 males, 1,051 females. Unfit to associate with ordinary paupers, they are separately provided for in each workhouse. If the 3,733 were equally divided every union would average 25, but such is far from the case, as the proportion in them varies from two and three individuals to as many hundred, their number being greatest in the vicinity of cities and large towns such as Dublin, Cork, Limerick, Belfast, &c. Classification of Inmates.

Latterly at some Union Boards, a strong feeling has been expressed that the insane of all denominations should be transferred to District Asylums—a scheme which, if carried out, would entail a large outlay on new buildings, or on extensive additions to the existing ones, independent of an increased local taxation and a fresh call on the Government rate in aid. We have uniformly expressed the opinion that it is quite inexpedient to erect costly institutions as abodes for a class of our fellow-creatures whose well-being and comfort we would not the less sedulously consult, however incapable the great majority of them might be to ap- Removal to Asylums.

preciate the increased advantages afforded by this expenditure; or, in a curative point of view, however unlikely to benefit therefrom. Some thirty years ago it was proposed to erect large provincial receptacles for idiots, epileptics, and demented lunatics, but on examination the project was abandoned from the likelihood, if not certainty, of its failure. We reported to the Executive our objection to these depôts as, independent of the outlay for their construction, the number of counties and cities attached to them would cause much embarrassment in their working, with continuous and unavoidable expenses and inconveniences, consequent upon the conveyance and return of patients, at the desire of their friends, to and from remote localities, distant perhaps 100 or 130 miles. The full establishment cost of each for 600, or 1,000 inmates might be reasonably estimated at from £25,000 to £30,000.

Provincial Depôts.

Suggestion as to accommodation.

Experience from year to year convinces us the more that economy and practical utility can be best combined by the conversion of an unrequired poorhouse, if one existed, with some acres of land attached to it, in each district, for the reception of the exceptional classes under immediate consideration. And further, that such poorhouse should be commodiously adapted to its new object, both by additions and alterations, and be supported altogether out of a Union taxation, as at present maintained. What has been so satisfactorily adopted at Belfast may well serve as an example. The Guardians there met the difficulty in a business-like way. The poorhouse at large was much overcrowded with idiots, imbeciles, epileptics, and the like, not a few of them living in common with the pauper population. The attention of the Local Board was specially directed by the Inspectors to this unsatisfactory state of things, as has that of other Poor-Law Boards in like circumstances, but not with a similar success. The result at Belfast being the erection of a suitable, commodious, and well-furnished structure for 350 inmates, on an open and elevated site close to the main buildings at a total cost of £6,600.

Metropolitan Poorhouses.

As regards the accommodation for insane paupers at the North and South Dublin poorhouses, few in Ireland are more unfavourably circumstanced. The inmates between both, amounting to 320, should, in our opinion, be transferred to the one establishment in a healthful situation; a similar suggestion extends to other urban localities. In England, or rather within the metropolitan counties, intermediate establishments between regularly organized hospitals for lunatics and ordinary institutions for the destitute poor, have been provided, suited to the reception of chronic or hopeless cases of insanity, as also for imbeciles and persons affected with epilepsy of a marked but not dangerous character. Thereby some large asylums have been disembarrassed to a considerable extent of persons not requiring a special, or more expensive, mode of treatment, and being conducted by smaller and much less expensive staffs, effect a considerable saving to the public rates. What we would advocate is a somewhat similar system, but practically rendered more economical by taking advantage, where available, of poorhouses in separate districts, and fitting them up becomingly to their intended purpose.

With reference to the treatment of the mentally affected in poorhouses throughout the country at present, and making due allowance for the manifold deficiencies in them as means to an end, we are quite disposed, on the whole, to record from personal knowledge a not unfavourable judgment. In the almost uniform absence of paid and responsible attendants, well conducted and kindly disposed paupers, rewarded only by somewhat more liberal dietary allowances, have charge of the insane. We find too that the principal resident officials, masters and matrons, do not overlook their well-being. The insane, as a rule, are on the best scale of food, and visited daily by the Union physicians. The bedding in the "idiot wards," for such is the general denomination of the department assigned to the classes in question, is on the whole good, and the wearing apparel passable; but facilities for washing and bathing are very meagre, while the rooms inhabited by day are dark, gloomy, restricted, and opening into very circumscribed and walled-in yards, which, generally speaking, constitute the sole exercise or airing courts. Nevertheless, improvements, slight though they be, are noticeable from year to year, and notwithstanding all the wants and drawbacks above adverted to, neither the health nor mortality of the insane resident in Irish poorhouses contrasts unfavourably with what elsewhere obtains. All circumstances considered, their condition in fact presents an anomaly as regards result of their treatment, and that of patients in asylums who, as a rule, notwithstanding a studied attention to their wants and wishes are discontented, ever seeking to be liberated, whereas in poorhouses they seem to be satisfied with their position, scarcely ever thinking of its amelioration or their own freedom. Thus, philanthropy in their regard is altogether a gratuitous sentiment in public feeling. General treatment in Workhouses.

We are unable to name any definite sum, per head, as the annual current cost of the mentally affected in poorhouses. It might, however, be set down on an average at £11 12s., while that in district asylums is £22; the difference between both being made up by the Government rate in aid to the latter. Exclusive of the cost of enlargement and alterations it may, we think, be accepted that an increase for the current maintenance of lunatics as a body, under the improved system advocated by us, would be covered for the demented in poorhouses by £11,000 a year, or about £3 on a capitation scale. Cost in Workhouses.

CENTRAL ASYLUM AT DUNDRUM.

The progressive condition of this Institution, has been so fully brought under the notice of Government from year to year since its establishment in 1850, with the results of its management, that the furnishing of details, beyond those indicative of its working during the past twelvemonth, would be in great measure a repetition of previous statements. It continues to fulfil, on the whole, very satisfactorily, the double object of its creation, viz., as a place for segregating certain classes of the insane, charged with serious offences, from the vast majority of inmates to be found in ordinary asylums, altogether untainted by crime;—and at the same time, while providing for their safe custody, does not debar them from social comforts and the full opportunity of a restoration to health. We advert specially to the latter fact for two reasons—first, because it has been lately advanced that the main and primitive object of a criminal asylum was, and should be, a strict confinement of its inmates, and consequently that it ought to be regarded essentially as a gaol—thus rendering curative treatment secondary to secure incarceration. From this doctrine we dissent, our contention being that any person labouring under an aberration of mind, who may have broken the law while so affected, or who after a criminal act becomes insane, ought to be treated as a lunatic; for in the first instance insanity condones the offence however punishable of itself, and in the second, entails a condonation during its existence—thus excluding such a convict from the category of common prisoners undergoing punishment after conviction. Hence it devolves on the Executive, while looking to the safe custody of these afflicted parties, to treat them in every way conducive to their comfort, and, above all, to their recovery—selecting as the place of detention one thoroughly calculated to the latter purpose.

Treatment of Criminal Lunatics.

Advantages of a special Asylum.

If, however, invalid prisons, as they are denominated, with all their appurtenances, erected on small confined areas, and encircled by lofty walls, are to be converted into depôts for the insane, and at the same time made the abode of convicts labouring under physical disorders, as well as of malingerers, nothing in our estimation could be more incongruous, and nothing more calculated from association, to make the latter proficient in the art of deception. The logic of facts, no less than the bias of public opinion is against retrogression, and thus it seems highly improbable that a well devised and benevolent legislation dating from early in the present century will be superseded towards its close on the plea of almost imperceptible savings. The Asylum at Dundrum has hitherto partaken of the characteristic attributes of a district hospital for the insane, from the openness of its site, unprison-like surroundings, and the extent of land belonging to it.

It may not be uninteresting to afford here a brief summary of its operation up to the present date, or during a period of thirty-six years. The admissions between both sexes amounted to 706—502 males and 204 females—of them 149 men and 47 women were charged with murder or homicide—209 with assaults of a malevolent character, and the remainder either with burglary, robbery, infraction of military law, arson, or felonies of various kinds involving for the most part penal servitude. Brief reference to its operation.

The total number of patients located in the institution on an average annual calculation of 140, amounted to 5,040. The discharges have been 325—partly on recovery, and partly on the termination of sentences—escapes 10, suicides 2—1 homicide, and 184 natural deaths. The mortality one year with another was 3 per cent. Of the above large number of discharges no case was attended by an unfavourable result.

Dealing immediately with the statistics of the past year:—On the 1st of January, 1885, there were 178 patients in confinement. During the following twelvemonth, out of 102 cases submitted to our consideration for removal from prisons to Dundrum, 30 only were so transferred—26 males and 4 females; a fact indicating the care taken by us in the selection of appropriate persons. Of these, 9 were charged with murder (8 men and 1 woman), 9 males for violent assault and burglary, 6 for breach of the articles of war, a State offence, and 6 for minor crimes; the remainder being sent to district institutions. Thus a total of 208 was under treatment, of which number 24 were discharged—10 recovered, and 14 still insane transferred to district asylums, their period of servitude having terminated—11 died, one only being a female. On the 1st of January, 1886, there consequently remained 173, composed of 65 males and 14 females indicted for murder; 40 males and 4 females for dangerous assaults, burglary, or arson; 5 for State offences, and 36—25 males and 11 females—for lesser crimes committed by individuals previously of a bad or vicious character. Statistics for past year.

Classifying the present patients at Dundrum under different heads, we find the married and widowed to be 41, as against 126 single—the illiterate to be a third in proportion to those who are well educated, or can read and write; 133 of the total, or about four-fifths, are quiet and orderly, much about what obtains in ordinary asylums. Nearly one-half are of the agricultural class, and next to them, numerically, are 15 soldiers and pensioners. The incurable, between both sexes, may be estimated at 132, while the average number of males usefully employed is 50, and of females 24. Classification.

Towards the close of last year two Commissioners, after an inquiry of many weeks, reported on the condition of the asylum, the result being that various improvements which we had long deemed essential, and to which in Parliamentary and other papers we had directed attention, were fully recognised by them, notably the elevation and repairing of the boundary walls, the lowness of Visit of Commission.

which, as remarked by us, encouraged and facilitated attempts to escape. The deficiency of attendants and warders, two-fifths at least under those at Broadmoor, and the prison at Perth—the circumscribed size of the dining-hall, scarcely one-half large enough, and the generally limited accommodation at the male side. The sleeping and day room provision for men, as suggested to be met by the Commissioners, not appearing to us advisable, we proposed a different and simpler scheme, viz., to erect new buildings altogether, of ample size, and fully adapted to their object. Our recommendation having been approved of by Government, and the expense sanctioned by the Treasury, we trust they may be speedily commenced, and the more so as not interfering with present arrangements, they would afford increased facilities for future discipline. It is unnecessary to advert to other points of minor importance, suggested by us to the Executive for consideration.

In the appendices the usual Report of the Resident Physician and Governor to the Inspectors is furnished, together with a variety of statistical tables and returns, bearing on the criminal asylum. Amongst the latter is one by desire of the Under Secretary, Sir R. Hamilton, and having reference to the case of each patient admitted during the year.

PRIVATE ASYLUMS.

These establishments are twenty-two in number. Three of them being on charitable foundations—namely, St. Patrick's or Swift's Hospital, the "Friends'" Retreat, near Dublin, and the Stewart Institution, pay no licenses. On the 31st of December, 1885, they contained amongst them 632 patients—243 males and 389 females, or seven less, between both sexes, than at a like date in 1884. It is remarkable that for many years a very slight variation has been perceptible in the number of inmates under treatment in each—not 2 per cent.

The admissions into private asylums during the past year amounted to 172; 136 of them—73 males, and 63 females, being cases of first attack, and 36 relapses—18 of either sex. The total number of patients under treatment in the twelvemonth was 811, of whom 71 were sent out cured, 25 improved, and 24 unimproved: 59 died. Relatively speaking, as between public and private asylums, the latter, in regard to recoveries and improvements, are fully on a par with the former, while as to deaths there is an excess in them of nearly 1 per cent.

With respect to social condition, the married number 69, the widowed 57, and the single no less than 506.

Of the aggregate just given, on the 31st of December last 52 were under 20 years of age; from 20 to 60, 446; and over 60, 134. There were 21 only belonging to the agricultural classes, as against 12 students, 22 army officers, 17 clergymen, 9 lawyers, 5 physicians, and 82 in trade. The remainder, 464, had been previously unoccupied.

Private asylums on the whole in this country are well conducted, some of them in a very superior manner, and affording all domestic requirements suitable to the higher classes of society. A few of them, however, are not so satisfactorily circumstanced as we could desire, still allowances are to be made, when want of means to meet payments for maintenance due by the friends of the patients, is in question. We have no reason to attribute neglect or unkindness on the part of proprietors, and we may add that complaints are very rarely justified by facts. With reference to illegal admissions, and consequently undue detentions, we have had no instances before us during the past year, although technical irregularities, of prompt and easy amendment, may have occurred. Management

Our visits to these institutions are not only frequent, but at uncertain intervals, and at all times patients have liberty to communicate directly with us.

Houses on charitable foundations are commendable in every respect, and none more so than the institution for imbeciles at Palmerstown, close to the metropolis, Swift's Hospital, and St. Vincent's conducted by a religious community of ladies.

Most respectfully submitting the preceding Report to your Excellency,

We have the honour to subscribe ourselves,

Your Excellency's obedient servants,

J. NUGENT.

GEO. W. HATCHELL.

APPENDIX.

APPENDIX:—A.—Insane Persons in

No. 1.—Return showing the Number of Idiots in Union Workhouses,

Names of Unions.	Simple Idiots, under 14 years of age.			Epileptic Idiots, under 14 years of age.			Total of the two preceding Classes.			Simple Idiots, 14 years and under 20.			Epileptic Idiots, 14 years and under 20.			Total of the two preceding Classes.		
	M.	F.	T.	M.	F.	T.	M.	F.	T.	M.	F.	T.	M.	F.	T.	M.	F.	T.
ULSTER.																		
Co. Antrim:																		
Antrim,	1	–	1	–	–	–	1	–	1	1	5	6	–	–	–	1	5	6
Ballycastle,	–	–	–	–	–	–	–	–	–	1	2	3	–	–	–	1	2	3
Ballymena,	1	1	2	–	1	1	1	2	3	5	4	9	–	–	–	5	4	9
Ballymoney,	–	–	–	–	–	–	–	–	–	3	1	4	–	1	1	3	2	5
Belfast,	–	4	4	1	1	2	1	5	6	6	7	13	4	5	9	10	12	22
Larne,	–	–	–	–	–	–	–	–	–	1	3	4	–	–	–	1	3	4
Lisburn,	–	1	1	–	–	–	–	1	1	2	2	4	–	1	1	2	3	5
Co. Armagh:																		
Armagh,	1	–	1	–	–	–	1	–	1	1	1	2	–	–	–	1	1	2
Lurgan,	–	–	–	–	–	–	–	–	–	3	2	5	1	1	2	3	4	7
Co. Cavan:																		
Bailieborough,	–	–	–	–	–	–	–	–	–	1	4	5	–	–	–	1	4	5
Bawnboy,	–	–	–	–	–	–	–	–	–	–	–	–	–	–	–	–	–	–
Cavan,	–	–	–	–	–	–	–	–	–	3	2	5	–	2	2	3	4	7
Cootehill,	–	–	–	–	–	–	–	–	–	–	1	1	–	–	–	–	1	1
Co. Donegal:																		
Ballyshannon,	–	–	–	–	–	–	–	–	–	–	–	–	–	–	–	–	–	–
Donegal,	1	–	1	–	–	–	1	–	1	–	–	–	–	–	–	–	–	–
Dunfanaghy,	–	–	–	–	–	–	–	–	–	–	–	–	–	–	–	–	–	–
Glenties,	–	–	–	–	1	1	–	1	1	1	–	1	–	–	–	1	–	1
Inishowen,	–	–	–	–	–	–	–	–	–	–	1	1	–	–	–	–	1	1
Letterkenny,	–	–	–	–	–	–	–	–	–	–	–	–	–	–	–	–	–	–
Milford,	–	–	–	–	–	–	–	–	–	–	–	–	–	–	–	–	–	–
Stranorlar,	–	–	–	–	–	–	–	–	–	–	–	–	–	–	–	–	–	–
Co. Down:																		
Banbridge,	1	1	2	–	–	–	1	1	2	5	1	6	–	1	1	5	2	7
Downpatrick,	1	–	1	–	–	–	1	–	1	1	1	2	–	–	–	1	1	2
Kilkeel,	–	–	–	–	–	–	–	–	–	–	–	–	–	–	–	–	–	–
Newry,	–	–	–	–	–	–	–	–	–	3	2	5	–	–	–	3	2	5
Newtownards,	1	2	3	–	–	–	1	2	3	6	3	9	–	2	2	4	7	11
Co. Fermanagh:																		
Enniskillen,	2	–	2	–	–	–	2	–	2	1	1	2	–	–	–	1	1	2
Irvinestown,	–	–	–	–	–	–	–	–	–	–	1	1	–	–	–	–	1	1
Lisnaskea,	–	–	–	–	–	–	–	–	–	–	1	1	–	–	–	–	1	1
Co. Londonderry:																		
Coleraine,	–	–	–	–	–	–	–	–	–	–	2	2	–	–	–	–	2	2
Newtownlimavady,	1	–	1	–	–	–	1	–	1	1	–	1	–	–	–	1	–	1
Londonderry,	–	1	1	–	–	–	–	1	1	1	2	3	1	1	2	2	3	5
Magherafelt,	–	–	–	–	–	–	–	–	–	3	1	4	2	1	3	5	2	7
Co. Monaghan:																		
Carrickmacross,	–	1	1	–	–	–	–	1	1	–	–	–	–	–	–	–	–	–
Castleblayney,	1	–	1	1	–	1	2	–	2	3	4	7	–	–	–	3	4	7
Clones,	1	–	1	–	–	–	1	–	1	1	–	1	2	–	2	3	–	3
Monaghan,	–	–	–	–	1	1	–	1	1	–	2	2	–	–	–	–	2	2
Co. Tyrone:																		
Castlederg,	–	–	–	–	–	–	–	–	–	–	–	–	–	–	–	–	–	–
Clogher,	1	–	1	–	–	–	1	–	1	2	–	2	–	–	–	2	–	2
Cookstown,	–	–	–	–	–	–	–	–	–	–	1	1	1	–	1	1	1	2
Dungannon,	–	–	–	–	–	–	–	–	–	2	–	2	–	–	–	2	–	2
Gortin,	–	–	–	–	–	–	–	–	–	–	1	1	–	–	–	–	1	1
Omagh,	–	–	–	–	–	–	–	–	–	–	1	1	–	–	–	–	1	1
Strabane,	–	–	–	–	–	–	–	–	–	–	–	–	–	–	–	–	–	–

Union Workhouses, Ireland.

Ireland, on the 31st December, 1885, classified under the following heads:—

Simple Idiots, 20 years, and upwards.			Epileptic Idiots, 20 years, and upwards.			Total of the two preceding Classes.			Total Simple Idiots.			Total Epileptic Idiots.			Gross Total of Simple and Epileptic Idiots.			Name of Unions.
M.	F.	T.	M.	F.	T.	M.	F.	T.	M.	F.	T.	M.	F.	T.	M.	F.	T.	
																		ULSTER.
																		Co. Antrim:
[illegible]	–	2	–	2	2	2	[illegible]	4	[illegible]	5	[illegible]	–	[illegible]	2	[illegible]	7	11	Antrim.
[illegible]	6	8	–	–	–	4	[illegible]	5	5	5	10	–	–	–	[illegible]	[illegible]	10	Ballycastle.
[illegible]	8	13	–	–	–	7	[illegible]	13	13	11	24	–	1	1	13	12	[illegible]	Ballymena.
[illegible]	1	3	–	–	–	[illegible]	1	[illegible]	[illegible]	2	[illegible]	–	1	1	5	3	8	Ballymoney.
[illegible]	5	14	1	1	[illegible]	9	7	16	14	17	31	6	7	13	20	24	44	Belfast.
[illegible]	7	11	2	–	[illegible]	6	7	13	5	10	15	2	–	[illegible]	7	10	17	Larne.
[illegible]	4	8	–	2	[illegible]	3	8	11	7	7	14	–	3	3	7	10	17	Lisburn.
																		Co. Armagh:
12	10	[illegible]	1	3	4	13	13	[illegible]	14	11	25	1	3	4	15	14	29	Armagh.
4	1	5	1	–	1	5	1	6	6	4	10	2	1	3	[illegible]	5	13	Lurgan.
																		Co. Cavan:
[illegible]	–	2	1	1	[illegible]	3	1	4	3	4	7	1	1	2	4	[illegible]	[illegible]	Bailieborough.
–	–	–	1	–	1	1	–	1	–	–	–	1	–	1	1	–	1	Bawnboy.
3	4	6	2	6	8	7	10	17	[illegible]	6	14	2	8	10	10	14	24	Cavan.
–	1	1	–	1	1	–	2	2	–	2	2	–	1	1	–	3	3	Cootehill.
																		Co. Donegal:
[illegible]	2	3	–	–	–	1	2	3	[illegible]	2	[illegible]	–	–	–	[illegible]	2	3	Ballyshannon.
[illegible]	2	3	–	–	–	1	2	3	2	2	4	–	–	–	[illegible]	2	4	Donegal.
–	–	–	–	–	–	–	–	–	–	–	–	–	–	–	–	–	–	Dunfanaghy.
[illegible]	3	7	–	1	1	4	4	8	5	5	[illegible]	–	2	2	[illegible]	5	10	Glenties.
[illegible]	1	3	–	–	–	2	1	3	2	2	4	–	–	–	2	2	4	Inishowen.
1	–	1	–	–	–	1	–	1	1	–	1	–	–	–	1	–	1	Letterkenny.
[illegible]	2	5	–	–	–	3	2	5	3	2	5	–	–	–	3	2	5	Milford.
[illegible]	1	3	–	–	–	2	1	3	2	1	3	–	–	–	2	1	3	Stranorlar.
																		Co. Down:
4	[illegible]	13	1	1	2	[illegible]	10	15	10	11	21	1	2	3	11	13	24	Banbridge.
[illegible]	[illegible]	[illegible]	–	–	–	[illegible]	[illegible]	[illegible]	[illegible]	[illegible]	[illegible]	–	–	–	[illegible]	[illegible]	[illegible]	Downpatrick.
[illegible]	[illegible]	[illegible]	–	–	–	[illegible]	[illegible]	[illegible]	[illegible]	[illegible]	[illegible]	–	–	–	[illegible]	1	[illegible]	Kilkeel.
[illegible]	[illegible]	9	–	1	1	[illegible]	[illegible]	10	5	5	11	–	[illegible]	1	[illegible]	10	15	Newry.
[illegible]	[illegible]	7	1	[illegible]	3	[illegible]	[illegible]	10	7	12	19	1	4	5	8	16	24	Newtownards.
																		Co. Fermanagh:
[illegible]	[illegible]	[illegible]	–	1	1	[illegible]	[illegible]	[illegible]	[illegible]	[illegible]	[illegible]	–	2	[illegible]	[illegible]	[illegible]	6	Enniskillen.
[illegible]	[illegible]	[illegible]	–	–	–	[illegible]	[illegible]	[illegible]	[illegible]	[illegible]	[illegible]	–	–	–	[illegible]	[illegible]	6	Irvinestown.
[illegible]	[illegible]	[illegible]	–	–	–	[illegible]	[illegible]	[illegible]	[illegible]	[illegible]	[illegible]	–	–	–	[illegible]	[illegible]	5	Lisnaskea.
																		Co. Londonderry:
[illegible]	[illegible]	6	–	–	–	[illegible]	[illegible]	[illegible]	[illegible]	[illegible]	[illegible]	–	–	–	[illegible]	[illegible]	8	Coleraine.
[illegible]	[illegible]	1	–	–	–	[illegible]	[illegible]	[illegible]	[illegible]	[illegible]	[illegible]	–	–	–	[illegible]	[illegible]	5	Limavady.
4	[illegible]	9	2	–	2	[illegible]	[illegible]	11	[illegible]	[illegible]	14	[illegible]	1	[illegible]	[illegible]	[illegible]	17	Londonderry.
–	[illegible]	1	–	1	1	–	[illegible]	[illegible]	[illegible]	3	[illegible]	2	2	[illegible]	[illegible]	[illegible]	9	Magherafelt.
																		Co. Monaghan:
2	–	2	–	–	–	[illegible]	–	[illegible]	[illegible]	1	[illegible]	–	–	–	[illegible]	[illegible]	3	Carrickmacross.
4	[illegible]	9	–	–	–	[illegible]	5	[illegible]	[illegible]	9	17	[illegible]	–	1	[illegible]	[illegible]	15	Castleblayney.
1	[illegible]	[illegible]	–	–	–	[illegible]	3	[illegible]	[illegible]	[illegible]	[illegible]	[illegible]	–	[illegible]	[illegible]	[illegible]	5	Clones.
–	9	9	–	1	1	–	10	[illegible]	–	11	11	–	2	[illegible]	–	13	13	Monaghan.
																		Co. Tyrone:
–	–	–	–	–	–	–	–	–	–	–	–	–	–	–	–	–	–	Castlederg.
5	[illegible]	8	–	–	–	[illegible]	3	[illegible]	[illegible]	3	11	–	–	–	[illegible]	[illegible]	11	Clogher.
3	[illegible]	6	–	–	–	[illegible]	3	[illegible]	3	[illegible]	7	1	–	1	[illegible]	[illegible]	8	Cookstown.
4	[illegible]	5	[illegible]	[illegible]	[illegible]	[illegible]	[illegible]	9	7	1	8	[illegible]	[illegible]	[illegible]	[illegible]	[illegible]	13	Dungannon.
–	[illegible]	1	–	–	–	–	1	1	–	[illegible]	[illegible]	–	–	–	–	[illegible]	[illegible]	Gortin.
[illegible]	[illegible]	8	[illegible]	[illegible]	[illegible]	[illegible]	6	10	[illegible]	5	7	[illegible]	[illegible]	[illegible]	[illegible]	[illegible]	11	Omagh.
–	–	–	–	–	–	–	–	–	–	–	–	–	–	–	–	–	–	Strabane.
113	126	239	17	28	45	130	154	284	161	198	379	30	47	77	210	243	456	Total, Ulster.

(continued.

No. 1.—Return showing the Number of Idiots in Union Workhouses,

Names of Unions.	Simple Idiots, under 14 years of age.			Epileptic Idiots, under 14 years of age.			Total of the two preceding classes.			Simple Idiots, 14 years and under 20.			Epileptic Idiots, 14 years and under 20.			Total of the two preceding classes.		
	M.	F.	T.	M.	F.	T.	M.	F.	T.	M.	F.	T.	M.	F.	T.	M.	F.	T.
MUNSTER.																		
Co. Clare:																		
Ballyvaghan,	–	–	–	–	–	–	–	–	–	–	1	1	1	–	1	1	1	2
Corofin,	–	–	–	–	–	–	–	–	–	–	–	–	–	–	–	–	–	–
Ennis,	–	–	–	–	–	–	–	–	–	2	1	3	1	–	1	3	1	4
Ennistymon,	–	–	–	–	–	–	–	–	–	1	2	3	1	1	2	2	3	5
Killadysert,	–	–	–	–	–	–	–	–	–	–	–	–	–	–	–	–	–	–
Kilrush,	–	–	–	–	–	–	–	–	–	–	3	3	–	2	2	–	5	5
Scariff,	–	–	–	–	–	–	–	–	–	–	[illegible]	[illegible]	–	–	–	–	[illegible]	[illegible]
Tulla,	3	1	4	–	–	–	3	1	4	–	[illegible]	[illegible]	2	–	2	2	[illegible]	[illegible]
Co. Cork:																		
Bandon,	–	–	–	–	–	–	–	–	–	1	–	1	–	–	–	1	–	1
Bantry,	–	–	–	–	–	–	–	–	–	1	–	1	–	–	–	1	–	1
Castletown,	–	–	–	–	–	–	–	–	–	–	–	–	1	–	1	1	–	1
Clonakilty,	–	–	–	–	–	–	–	–	–	1	–	1	–	1	1	1	1	2
Cork,	–	–	–	–	–	–	–	–	–	8	15	23	3	14	17	11	29	40
Dunmanway,	–	–	–	–	–	–	–	–	–	–	–	–	–	–	–	–	–	–
Fermoy,	–	–	–	2	–	2	2	–	2	4	[illegible]	[illegible]	–	–	–	4	4	[illegible]
Kanturk,	–	1	1	–	–	–	–	1	1	1	[illegible]	[illegible]	–	–	–	1	2	[illegible]
Kinsale,	–	–	–	–	–	–	–	–	–	–	–	–	–	–	–	–	–	–
Macroom,	–	–	–	–	–	–	–	–	–	1	–	1	1	1	2	2	1	3
Mallow,	–	1	1	1	–	1	2	1	3	[illegible]	[illegible]	[illegible]	–	[illegible]	[illegible]	[illegible]	[illegible]	[illegible]
Midleton,	–	–	–	–	–	–	–	–	–	[illegible]	[illegible]	[illegible]	–	–	–	[illegible]	[illegible]	[illegible]
Millstreet,	1	–	1	–	–	–	1	–	1	[illegible]	[illegible]	[illegible]	1	1	2	[illegible]	[illegible]	[illegible]
Mitchelstown,	–	1	1	–	–	–	–	1	1	[illegible]	–	[illegible]	–	–	–	[illegible]	–	[illegible]
Skibbereen,	–	–	–	–	–	–	–	–	–	[illegible]	1	[illegible]	–	1	1	1	[illegible]	[illegible]
Skull,	–	–	–	–	–	–	–	–	–	–	–	–	–	–	–	–	–	–
Youghal,	1	–	1	–	–	–	1	–	1	–	1	1	–	1	1	–	2	2
Co. Kerry:																		
Cahersiveen,	–	–	–	–	–	–	–	–	–	–	–	–	–	–	–	–	–	–
Dingle,	–	–	–	–	–	–	–	–	–	–	1	1	–	–	–	–	1	1
Kenmare,	–	–	–	–	–	–	–	–	–	–	1	1	–	–	–	–	1	1
Killarney,	1	–	1	–	–	–	1	–	1	[illegible]	2	[illegible]	[illegible]	–	[illegible]	[illegible]	[illegible]	[illegible]
Listowel,	1	–	1	–	–	–	1	–	1	[illegible]	[illegible]	[illegible]	–	2	[illegible]	[illegible]	[illegible]	[illegible]
Tralee,	1	–	1	1	–	1	2	–	2	[illegible]	[illegible]	[illegible]	–	–	–	[illegible]	[illegible]	[illegible]
Co. Limerick:																		
Croom,	–	–	–	–	–	–	–	–	–	–	–	–	–	–	–	–	–	–
Glin,	1	–	1	–	–	–	1	–	1	[illegible]	–	[illegible]	–	–	–	[illegible]	–	[illegible]
Kilmallock,	1	–	1	–	–	–	1	–	1	[illegible]	1	[illegible]	–	–	–	[illegible]	[illegible]	[illegible]
Limerick,	–	–	–	–	–	–	–	–	–	[illegible]	[illegible]	[illegible]	1	1	[illegible]	[illegible]	[illegible]	[illegible]
Newcastle,	–	–	–	1	1	2	1	1	2	1	–	1	–	–	–	[illegible]	–	[illegible]
Rathkeale,	–	–	–	–	–	–	–	–	–	[illegible]	1	[illegible]	–	–	–	[illegible]	[illegible]	[illegible]
Co. Tipperary:																		
Borrisokane,	–	–	–	–	–	–	–	–	–	–	–	–	–	–	–	–	–	–
Carrick-on-Suir,	–	–	–	–	–	–	–	–	–	–	1	[illegible]	–	1	[illegible]	[illegible]	–	[illegible]
Cashel,	–	[illegible]	[illegible]	–	–	–	–	1	1	[illegible]	[illegible]	[illegible]	–	2	[illegible]	[illegible]	[illegible]	[illegible]
Clogheen,	–	[illegible]	[illegible]	–	–	–	–	1	1	[illegible]	[illegible]	[illegible]	–	–	–	[illegible]	[illegible]	[illegible]
Clonmel,	–	–	–	–	–	–	–	–	–	[illegible]	[illegible]	[illegible]	1	–	1	[illegible]	[illegible]	[illegible]
Nenagh,	–	–	–	–	–	–	–	–	–	1	[illegible]	[illegible]	–	–	–	[illegible]	[illegible]	[illegible]
Roscrea,	–	–	–	–	–	–	–	–	–	–	[illegible]	[illegible]	–	–	–	–	[illegible]	[illegible]
Thurles,	–	–	–	–	–	–	–	–	–	[illegible]	[illegible]	[illegible]	–	–	–	[illegible]	[illegible]	[illegible]
Tipperary,	–	–	–	–	–	–	–	–	–	[illegible]	[illegible]	[illegible]	1	1	[illegible]	[illegible]	[illegible]	[illegible]
Co. Waterford:																		
Dungarvan,	–	–	–	–	–	–	–	–	–	3	[illegible]	[illegible]	[illegible]	3	[illegible]	[illegible]	[illegible]	10
Kilmacthomas,	–	1	1	–	–	–	–	1	1	–	1	1	–	–	–	–	[illegible]	[illegible]
Lismore,	–	–	–	–	–	–	–	–	–	–	1	1	1	–	1	1	[illegible]	[illegible]
Waterford,	–	1	1	–	–	–	–	1	1	4	10	14	[illegible]	2	[illegible]	7	12	[illegible]
Total, Munster,	10	6	16	4	1	[illegible]	14	[illegible]	24	62	83	145	[illegible]	37	[illegible]	84	120	204

Workhouses, Ireland—*continued.*

Ireland, on the 31st December, 1885, classified under the f

Simple Idiots, 20 years, and upwards.			Epileptic Idiots, 20 years, and upwards.			Total of the two preceding classes.			Total Simple Idiots.			Total Epileptic Idiots.			Grand To[tal] of Simp[le] and Epile[ptic] Idio[ts]	
M.	F.	T.	M.	F.	T.	M.	F.	T.	M.	F.	T.	M.	F.	T.	M.	F.

INSANE PERSONS IN UNION

No. 1.—RETURN showing the Number of Idiots in Union Workhouses,

NAMES OF UNIONS.	Simple Idiots, under 14 years of age.			Epileptic Idiots, under 14 years of age.			Total of the two preceding Classes.			Simple Idiots, 14 years and under 30.			Epileptic Idiots, 14 years and under 30.			Total of the two preceding Classes.		
LEINSTER.	M.	F.	T.	M.	F.	T.	M.	F.	T.	M.	F.	T.	M.	F.	T.	M.	F.	T.
Co. CARLOW:																		
Carlow,	1	–	1	–	–	–	1	–	1	3	–	3	–	2	2	3	2	5
Co. DUBLIN:																		
Balrothery,	–	–	–	–	–	–	–	–	–	1	–	1	–	–	–	1	–	1
Dublin, North,	–	–	–	–	–	–	–	–	–	6	5	11	–	1	1	6	6	12
Dublin, South,	–	–	–	1	–	1	1	–	1	2	–	2	–	–	–	2	–	2
Rathdown,	–	–	–	–	–	–	–	–	–	6	4	10	–	1	1	6	5	11
Co. KILDARE:																		
Athy,	–	–	–	–	–	–	–	–	–	–	2	2	–	2	2	–	4	4
Celbridge,	–	–	–	–	–	–	–	–	–	1	3	4	–	–	–	1	3	4
Naas,	–	2	2	–	–	–	–	2	2	7	1	8	–	1	1	7	2	9
Co. KILKENNY:																		
Callan,	–	–	–	–	–	–	–	–	–	2	1	3	–	–	–	2	1	3
Castlecomer,	–	–	–	–	–	–	–	–	–	–	–	–	–	–	–	–	–	–
Kilkenny,	–	1	1	–	–	–	–	1	1	1	1	2	–	2	2	1	3	4
Thomastown,	–	–	–	–	–	–	–	–	–	–	–	–	–	–	–	–	–	–
Urlingford,	1	–	1	–	–	–	1	–	1	–	–	–	–	–	–	–	–	–
KING'S CO.:																		
Edenderry,	1	–	1	–	–	–	1	–	1	–	–	–	–	–	–	–	–	–
Parsonstown,	–	–	–	–	–	–	–	–	–	–	–	–	–	1	1	–	1	1
Tullamore,	1	1	2	–	–	–	1	1	2	2	3	5	–	–	–	2	3	5
Co. LONGFORD:																		
Ballymahon,	–	–	–	–	–	–	–	–	–	–	–	–	–	–	–	–	–	–
Granard,	–	–	–	–	–	–	–	–	–	1	1	2	–	1	1	1	2	3
Longford,	–	–	–	–	–	–	–	–	–	2	4	6	1	1	2	3	5	8
Co. LOUTH:																		
Ardee,	–	1	1	–	–	–	–	1	1	–	2	2	–	–	–	–	2	2
Drogheda,	–	–	–	–	–	–	–	–	–	7	3	10	–	–	–	7	3	10
Dundalk,	–	–	–	–	3	3	–	3	3	2	4	6	1	–	1	3	4	7
Co. MEATH:																		
Dunshaughlin,	–	–	–	–	–	–	–	–	–	–	–	–	–	–	–	–	–	–
Kells,	1	–	1	–	–	–	1	–	1	3	–	3	–	2	2	3	2	5
Navan,	–	1	1	1	–	1	1	1	2	2	3	5	1	–	1	3	3	6
Oldcastle,	–	–	–	–	–	–	–	–	–	–	2	2	–	2	2	–	4	4
Trim,	–	–	–	–	–	–	–	–	–	1	–	1	1	1	2	2	1	3
QUEEN'S CO.:																		
Abbeyleix,	1	–	1	–	–	–	1	–	1	–	1	1	–	1	1	–	2	2
Donaghmore,	–	–	–	–	–	–	–	–	–	1	–	1	–	–	–	1	–	1
Mountmellick,	–	–	–	–	–	–	–	–	–	2	2	4	–	–	–	2	2	4
Co. WESTMEATH:																		
Athlone,	–	–	–	–	–	–	–	–	–	2	–	2	–	1	1	2	1	3
Delvin,	–	–	–	–	–	–	–	–	–	–	–	–	1	–	1	1	–	1
Mullingar,	–	–	–	–	–	–	–	–	–	2	1	3	1	1	2	3	2	5
Co. WEXFORD:																		
Enniscorthy,	–	2	2	–	–	–	–	2	2	–	4	4	1	–	1	1	4	5
Gorey,	–	–	–	–	–	–	–	–	–	1	1	2	–	1	1	1	2	3
New Ross,	1	–	1	–	1	1	1	1	2	2	–	2	1	–	1	3	–	3
Wexford,	–	–	–	1	2	3	1	2	3	3	2	5	1	1	2	4	3	7
Co. WICKLOW:																		
Baltinglass,	–	–	–	–	–	–	–	–	–	2	–	2	1	–	1	3	–	3
Rathdrum,	–	–	–	–	–	–	–	–	–	4	1	5	1	–	1	5	1	6
Shillelagh,	–	–	–	–	–	–	–	–	–	–	–	–	–	1	1	–	1	1
Total, Leinster,	7	8	15	2	6	8	10	14	24	68	50	118	12	23	35	80	73	153

Simple Idiots, 20 years and upwards			Epileptic Idiots, 20 years and upwards			Total of the two preceding Classes.			Total Simple Idiots.			Total Epileptic Idiots.			Grand Total of Simple and Epileptic Idiots.			Name of Union.
M.	F.	T.	M.	F.	T.	M.	F.	T.	M.	F.	T.	M.	F.	T.	M.	F.	T.	**LEINSTER.**
																		Co. Carlow:
3	5	8	–	2	2	3	7	10	7	5	12	–	4	4	7	9	16	Carlow.
																		Co. Dublin:
8	4	12	2	2	4	10	6	16	9	4	13	2	2	4	11	6	17	Balrothery.
3	4	7	1	–	1	4	4	8	9	9	18	1	1	2	10	10	20	Dublin, North.
2	–	2	–	–	–	2	–	2	4	–	4	1	–	1	5	–	5	Dublin, South.
–	12	12	–	1	1	–	13	13	6	16	22	–	2	2	6	18	24	Rathdown.
																		Co. Kildare:
3	3	6	2	–	2	5	3	8	5	4	9	2	2	[illegible]	5	7	12	Athy.
–	3	3	–	–	–	–	3	3	1	6	7	–	–	–	1	6	7	Celbridge.
6	9	15	–	1	1	6	10	16	13	12	25	–	2	2	13	14	27	Naas.
																		Co. Kilkenny:
1	1	2	–	4	4	1	5	6	3	2	5	–	4	4	3	6	9	Callan.
–	–	–	–	–	–	–	–	–	–	–	–	–	–	–	–	–	–	Castlecomer.
3	1	4	1	2	3	4	3	7	4	3	7	1	4	5	5	7	12	Kilkenny.
3	1	4	1	2	3	4	3	7	[illegible]	[illegible]	[illegible]	1	2	3	4	3	7	Thomastown.
2	4	6	–	–	–	2	4	6	3	4	7	–	–	–	3	4	7	Urlingford.
																		King's Co.:
1	1	2	–	2	2	1	3	4	2	1	3	–	2	2	2	3	5	Edenderry.
7	6	13	–	–	–	7	6	13	7	8	15	–	1	1	7	7	14	Parsonstown.
7	3	10	–	1	1	7	4	11	10	7	17	–	1	1	10	8	18	Tullamore.
																		Co. Longford:
–	1	1	–	1	1	–	2	2	–	1	1	–	1	1	–	2	2	Ballymahon.
3	6	9	–	–	–	3	6	9	4	7	11	–	1	1	4	8	12	Granard.
1	3	4	2	1	3	3	4	7	3	7	10	3	2	5	6	9	15	Longford.
																		Co. Louth:
8	5	13,	[illegible]	1	[illegible]	6	10	16	[illegible]	12	16	[illegible]	1	[illegible]	6	13	19	Ardee.
10	5	15	[illegible]	4	[illegible]	16	6	22	20	[illegible]	25	[illegible]	4	7	22	9	32	Drogheda.
1	4	5	1	1	2	2	5	7	3	7	10	3	4	7	6	11	17	Dundalk.
																		Co. Meath:
1	3	4	–	1	1	1	4	5	1	3	4	–	1	1	1	4	5	Dunshaughlin.
8	5	13	–	–	–	8	5	13	12	5	17	–	2	2	12	7	19	Kells.
5	6	11	–	–	–	5	6	11	7	10	17	2	–	2	9	10	19	Navan.
2	–	2	–	–	–	2	–	2	2	2	4	–	2	2	2	4	6	Oldcastle.
3	5	8	–	1	1	2	7	9	3	6	9	1	2	3	4	8	12	Trim.
																		Queen's Co.:
4	6	10	1	–	1	5	6	11	5	7	12	1	1	2	6	8	14	Abbeyleix.
7	3	10	–	–	–	7	3	10	8	3	11	–	–	–	8	3	11	Donaghmore.
1	6	7	–	1	1	1	7	8	3	8	11	–	1	1	3	9	12	Mountmellick.
																		Co. Westmeath:
–	3	3	–	3	3	–	6	6	2	3	5	–	4	4	2	7	9	Athlone.
2	–	2	–	–	–	2	–	2	2	–	2	1	–	1	3	–	3	Delvin.
4	3	7	2	2	4	6	5	11	6	4	10	3	3	6	9	7	16	Mullingar.
																		Co. Wexford:
4	8	12	2	5	7	6	13	19	4	15	19	3	3	6	7	19	26	Enniscorthy.
[illegible]	[illegible]	6	–	–	–	[illegible]	1	6	[illegible]	[illegible]	[illegible]	–	1	1	6	[illegible]	[illegible]	Gorey.
10	11	21	1	–	1	11	11	22	13	11	24	2	1	3	15	12	27	New Ross.
[illegible]	[illegible]	7	–	1	1	[illegible]	6	8	6	6	12	[illegible]	[illegible]	7	8	11	19	Wexford.
																		Co. Wicklow:
–	–	–	1	9	10	1	9	10	2	–	2	2	9	11	4	9	13	Baltinglass.
5	5	10	1	1	2	6	6	12	9	6	15	2	1	3	11	7	18	Rathdrum.
4	9	13	1	2	3	4	11	15	3	9	12	1	3	4	4	12	16	Shillelagh.
37	161	298	34	39	74	161	213	371	212	219	431	29	81	120	231	300	531	Total, Leinster.

INSANE PERSONS IN UNION

No. 1.—RETURN showing the Number of Idiots in Union Workhouses,

Names of Unions, &c.	Simple Idiots, under 14 years of age.			Epileptic Idiots, under 14 years of age.			Total of the two preceding Classes.			Simple Idiots, 14 years and under 25.			Epileptic Idiots, 14 years and under 25.			Total of the two preceding Classes.		
CONNAUGHT.	M.	F.	T.	M.	F.	T.	M.	F.	T.	M.	F.	T.	M.	F.	T.	M.	F.	T.
Co. Galway:																		
Ballinasloe,	–	–	–	–	–	–	–	–	–	–	–	–	–	2	2	–	2	2
Clifden,	–	–	–	–	–	–	–	–	–	–	1	1	–	1	1	–	2	2
Galway,	1	–	1	–	–	–	1	–	1	1	2	3	–	–	–	1	2	3
Glennamaddy,	1	1	2	–	–	–	1	1	2	2	1	3	–	–	–	2	1	3
Gort,	–	–	–	–	–	–	–	–	–	1	–	1	–	–	–	1	–	1
Loughrea,	–	–	–	–	–	–	–	–	–	–	2	2	–	–	–	–	2	2
Mount Bellew,	–	–	–	–	–	–	–	–	–	–	3	3	–	1	1	–	4	4
Oughterard,	–	–	–	–	1	1	–	1	1	–	–	–	–	–	–	–	–	–
Portumna,	–	–	–	–	–	–	–	–	–	–	–	–	–	–	–	–	–	–
Tuam,	–	–	–	–	–	–	–	–	–	–	–	–	–	–	–	–	–	–
Co. Leitrim:																		
Carrick-on-Shannon,	–	–	–	–	–	–	–	–	–	–	1	1	–	–	–	–	1	1
Manorhamilton,	1	–	1	–	–	–	1	–	1	1	3	4	–	–	–	1	3	4
Mohill,	1	1	2	–	–	–	1	1	2	1	–	1	1	1	2	2	1	3
Co. Mayo:																		
Ballina,	–	–	–	–	–	–	–	–	–	–	–	–	–	–	–	–	–	–
Ballinrobe,	–	–	–	–	–	–	–	–	–	2	–	2	–	–	–	2	–	2
Belmullet,	–	–	–	–	–	–	–	–	–	–	2	2	–	–	–	–	2	2
Castlebar,	–	–	–	–	–	–	–	–	–	1	–	1	–	–	–	1	–	1
Claremorris,	–	–	–	–	–	–	–	–	–	2	1	3	–	–	–	2	1	3
Killala,	–	–	–	–	–	–	–	–	–	–	–	–	–	–	–	–	–	–
Newport,*	–	–	–	–	–	–	–	–	–	–	–	–	–	–	–	–	–	–
Swineford,	3	1	4	–	1	1	3	2	5	2	4	6	1	–	1	3	4	7
Westport,	–	–	–	–	–	–	–	–	–	–	2	2	–	–	–	–	2	2
Co. Roscommon:																		
Boyle,	–	–	–	–	–	–	–	–	–	2	1	3	–	–	–	2	1	3
Castlerea,	1	–	1	–	–	–	1	–	1	3	6	9	4	8	12	7	14	21
Roscommon,	–	1	1	–	–	–	–	1	1	–	–	–	–	1	1	–	1	1
Strokestown,	–	–	–	–	–	–	–	–	–	–	–	–	–	–	–	–	–	–
Co. Sligo:																		
Dromore West,	–	–	–	–	–	–	–	–	–	–	–	–	–	–	–	–	–	–
Sligo,	–	–	–	–	–	–	–	–	–	1	1	2	1	–	1	2	1	3
Tobercurry,	–	–	–	–	–	–	–	–	–	–	3	3	–	1	1	–	4	4
Total, Connaught,	8	4	12	–	2	2	8	6	14	19	33	52	7	15	22	26	48	74

* Not amalgamated.

SUMMARY OF

Ulster,	13	11	24	2	4	6	15	15	30	55	61	116	11	15	26	66	76	142
Munster,	10	8	18	5	1	6	15	9	24	62	83	145	22	37	59	84	120	204
Leinster,	7	8	15	3	6	9	10	14	24	65	50	115	12	23	35	80	73	153
Connaught,	8	4	12	–	2	2	8	6	14	19	33	52	7	15	22	26	48	74
Total, Ireland,	38	31	69	10	13	23	48	44	92	204	237	131	62	80	142	256	317	573

WORKHOUSES, IRELAND—*continued.*

Ireland, on the 31st December, 1885, classified under the following heads:—

Simple Idiots, 20 years and upwards.			Epileptic Idiots, 20 years and upwards.			Total of the two preceding Classes.			Total Simple Idiots.			Total Epileptic Idiots.			Grand Total of Simple and Epileptic Idiots.			Names of Unions, &c.
M.	F.	T.	M.	F.	T.	M.	F.	T.	M.	F.	T.	M.	F.	T.	M.	F.	T.	CONNAUGHT.
																		Co. Galway:
–	–	–	1	–	1	1	–	1	–	–	–	1	2	3	1	2	3	Ballinasloe.
–	–	–	–	–	–	–	–	–	–	1	1	–	1	1	–	2	2	Clifden.
–	–	–	–	–	–	–	–	–	2	2	4	–	–	–	2	2	4	Galway.
1	6	7	3	–	3	4	6	10	4	8	12	3	–	3	7	8	15	Glennamaddy.
2	1	3	–	–	–	2	1	3	3	1	4	–	–	–	3	1	4	Gort.
2	3	5	–	–	–	2	3	5	2	5	7	–	–	–	2	5	7	Loughrea.
2	6	8	1	–	1	3	6	9	2	9	11	1	1	2	3	10	13	Mount Bellew.
1	1	2	1	–	1	2	1	3	1	1	2	1	1	2	2	2	4	Oughterard.
–	–	–	–	–	–	–	–	–	–	–	–	–	–	–	–	–	–	Portumna.
1	3	4	1	1	2	2	4	6	1	3	4	1	1	2	2	4	6	Tuam.
																		Co. Leitrim:
1	1	2	–	–	–	1	1	2	1	2	3	–	–	–	1	2	3	Carrick-on-Shannon.
2	6	8	–	–	–	2	6	8	4	9	13	–	–	–	4	9	13	Manorhamilton.
2	3	5	2	1	3	4	4	8	5	3	8	3	2	5	8	5	13	Mohill.
																		Co. Mayo:
2	1	3	–	–	–	2	1	3	2	1	3	–	–	–	2	1	3	Ballina.
1	–	1	–	–	–	1	–	1	3	–	3	–	–	–	3	–	3	Ballinrobe.
–	–	–	–	–	–	–	–	–	–	2	2	–	–	–	–	2	2	Belmullet.
2	2	4	1	1	2	3	3	6	3	2	5	1	1	2	4	3	7	Castlebar.
2	5	7	1	–	1	3	5	8	4	6	10	1	–	1	5	6	11	Claremorris.
–	1	1	–	–	–	–	1	1	–	1	1	–	–	–	–	1	1	Killala.
–	–	–	–	–	–	–	–	–	–	–	–	–	–	–	–	–	–	Newport.*
–	1	1	–	2	2	–	3	3	5	6	11	1	3	4	6	9	15	Swineford.
2	2	4	–	–	–	2	2	4	2	4	6	–	–	–	2	4	6	Westport.
																		Co. Roscommon:
3	3	6	–	1	1	3	4	7	5	4	9	–	1	1	5	5	10	Boyle.
–	–	–	–	–	–	–	–	–	4	6	10	4	8	12	8	14	22	Castlerea.
3	5	8	–	1	1	4	6	10	4	6	10	–	2	2	4	8	12	Roscommon.
2	2	4	1	–	1	2	2	4	1	2	3	1	–	1	2	2	4	Strokestown.
																		Co. Sligo:
2	2	4	2	–	2	4	2	6	2	2	4	2	–	2	4	2	6	Dromore West.
6	9	15	–	1	1	8	8	16	9	8	17	1	1	2	10	9	19	Sligo.
1	5	6	–	1	1	1	6	7	1	8	9	–	2	2	1	10	11	Tobercurry.
43	65	108	14	9	23	57	74	131	70	102	172	21	26	47	91	128	219	Total, Connaught.

* with Westport Union.

PROVINCES.

M.	F.	T.	M.	F.	T.	M.	F.	T.	M.	F.	T.	M.	F.	T.	M.	F.	T.	
113	126	239	17	26	43	130	154	284	181	198	379	30	47	77	211	245	456	ULSTER.
103	197	300	23	54	77	134	246	383	181	288	469	57	85	142	238	373	611	MUNSTER.
137	161	298	24	52	76	161	213	374	212	219	431	39	81	120	251	300	551	LEINSTER.
43	65	108	14	9	23	57	74	131	70	102	172	21	26	47	91	128	219	CONNAUGHT.
402	549	951	80	141	221	482	690	1172	644	807	1451	147	244	386	788	1051	1837	TOTAL, IRELAND.

No. 2.—RETURN showing the Number of Lunatics in Union Workhouses,

NAMES OF UNIONS.	Simple Lunatics.			Epileptic Lunatics.			Total of the Two preceding Classes.		
PROVINCE OF ULSTER.	M.	F.	T.	M.	F.	T.	M.	F.	T.
Co. ANTRIM:									
Antrim,	1	7	8	–	3	3	1	10	11
Ballycastle,	–	1	1	–	–	–	–	1	1
Ballymena,	44	45	[illegible]	6	3	9	50	48	[illegible]
Ballymoney,	–	3	3	–	–	–	–	3	3
Belfast,	79	151	230	14	17	31	93	168	261
Larne,	3	10	13	3	3	6	6	13	19
Lisburn,	4	6	10	–	–	–	4	6	10
Co. ARMAGH:									
Armagh,	3	8	11	–	2	2	3	10	13
Lurgan,	10	9	19	3	3	6	13	12	25
Co. CAVAN:									
Bailieborough,	1	1	2	–	–	–	1	1	2
Bawnboy,	2	3	5	–	1	1	2	4	6
Cavan,	2	2	4	–	–	–	2	2	4
Cootehill,	3	7	10	–	–	–	3	7	10
Co. DONEGAL:									
Ballyshannon,	1	–	1	–	–	–	1	–	1
Donegal,	1	3	4	–	–	–	1	3	4
Dunfanaghy,	–	–	–	–	–	–	–	–	–
Glenties,	3	3	6	–	–	–	3	3	6
Inishowen,	7	8	15	1	1	2	8	9	17
Letterkenny,	–	–	–	–	–	–	–	–	–
Milford,	1	2	3	1	–	1	2	2	4
Stranorlar,	–	1	1	–	–	–	–	1	1
Co. DOWN:									
Banbridge,	2	13	15	2	3	5	4	10	20
Downpatrick,	5	13	18	1	1	2	6	14	20
Kilkeel,	4	5	9	–	–	–	4	5	9
Newry,	5	16	21	2	4	6	7	20	27
Newtownards,	6	13	19	1	2	3	7	15	22
Co. FERMANAGH:									
Enniskillen,	8	3	11	1	5	6	9	6	17
Irvinestown,	–	–	–	–	–	–	–	–	–
Lisnaskea,	–	–	–	–	–	–	–	–	–
Co. LONDONDERRY:									
Coleraine,	1	4	5	–	–	–	1	4	5
Limavady,	–	14	14	–	–	–	–	14	14
Londonderry,	2	4	6	–	–	–	2	4	6
Magherafelt,	5	5	10	1	2	3	6	7	13
Co. MONAGHAN:									
Carrickmacross,	–	5	5	–	3	3	–	8	8
Castleblayney,	1	6	7	1	–	1	2	6	8
Clones,	–	2	2	–	–	–	–	2	2
Monaghan,	3	5	8	–	–	–	3	5	8
Co. TYRONE:									
Castlederg,	1	1	2	–	–	–	1	1	2
Clogher,	–	–	–	–	–	–	–	–	–
Cookstown,	4	1	5	1	–	1	5	1	6
Dungannon,	3	4	7	–	1	1	3	5	8
Gortin,	–	–	–	–	–	–	–	–	–
Omagh,	3	1	4	2	–	2	5	1	6
Strabane,	6	2	8	–	–	–	6	2	8
Total, Ulster,	231	387	611	40	54	94	264	441	[illegible]

Ireland, on 31st December, 1885, exclusive of Idiots and Epileptic Idiots.

Names of Unions.	Simple Lunatics.			Epileptic Lunatics.			Total of the two preceding Classes.		
PROVINCE OF MUNSTER.	M.	F.	T.	M.	F.	T.	M.	F.	T.
Co. Clare:									
Ballyvaghan,	1	1	2	–	–	–	1	1	2
Corrofin,	–	–	–	3	–	3	3	–	3
Ennis,	31	8	39	–	1	1	31	9	40
Ennistymon,	5	6	11	1	–	1	6	6	12
Killadysert,	3	4	7	1	–	1	4	4	8
Kilrush,	5	11	16	–	–	–	5	11	16
Scariff,	2	2	4	–	–	–	2	2	4
Tulla,	2	5	7	–	–	–	2	5	7
Co. Cork:									
Bandon,	3	6	9	–	–	–	3	6	9
Bantry,	–	–	–	–	–	–	–	–	–
Castletown,	–	2	2	–	–	–	–	2	2
Clonakilty,	2	2	4	1	–	1	3	2	5
Cork,	17	81	98	–	–	–	17	81	98
Dunmanway,	–	–	–	–	–	–	–	–	–
Fermoy,	2	5	7	–	1	1	2	6	8
Kanturk,	1	3	4	–	–	–	1	3	4
Kinsale,	–	2	2	–	2	2	–	4	4
Macroom,	3	–	3	–	–	–	3	–	3
Mallow,	1	–	1	–	–	–	1	–	1
Midleton,	1	2	3	–	–	–	1	2	3
Millstreet,	–	4	4	–	–	–	–	4	4
Mitchelstown,	–	–	–	–	–	–	–	–	–
Skibbereen,	–	–	–	–	–	–	–	–	–
Skull,	–	–	–	–	–	–	–	–	–
Youghal,	2	1	3	–	3	3	2	3	6
Co. Kerry:									
Cahirciveen,	–	–	–	–	–	–	–	–	–
Dingle,	–	2	2	–	–	–	–	2	2
Kenmare,	–	–	–	–	–	–	–	–	–
Killarney,	–	2	2	–	–	–	–	2	2
Listowel,	–	–	–	–	–	–	–	–	–
Tralee,	5	4	9	–	–	–	5	4	9
Co. Limerick:									
Croom,	5	7	12	1	1	2	6	8	14
Glin,	3	–	3	1	–	1	4	–	4
Kilmallock,	4	14	18	2	3	5	6	17	23
Limerick,	30	41	71	8	10	18	38	51	89
Newcastle,	–	–	–	–	–	–	–	–	–
Rathkeale,	3	4	7	1	–	1	4	4	8
Co. Tipperary:									
Borrisokane,	–	–	–	–	–	–	–	–	–
Carrick-on-Suir,	5	4	9	1	–	1	6	4	10
Cashel,	–	–	–	–	–	–	–	–	–
Clogheen,	2	1	3	–	–	–	2	1	3
Clonmel,	2	4	6	1	2	3	3	6	9
Nenagh,	1	3	4	–	1	1	1	4	5
Roscrea,	–	3	3	–	–	–	–	3	3
Thurles,	–	–	–	–	–	–	–	–	–
Tipperary,	5	8	13	2	3	5	7	11	18
Co. Waterford:									
Dungarvan,	2	2	4	–	–	–	2	2	4
Kilmacthomas,	–	5	5	1	3	4	1	8	9
Lismore,	4	9	13	–	–	–	4	9	13
Waterford,	–	–	–	–	–	–	–	–	–
Total, Munster,	180	227	407	24	29	53	174	256	460

No. 2.—Return of the Number of Lunatics in Union Workhouses, Ireland,

Names of Unions.	Simple Lunatics.			Epileptic Lunatics.			Total of the two preceding Classes.		
PROVINCE OF LEINSTER	M.	F.	T.	M.	F.	T.	M.	F.	T.
Co. Carlow:									
Carlow,	7	9	16	–	6	6	7	15	22
Co. Dublin:									
Balrothery,	3	2	5	–	–	–	3	2	5
Dublin, North,	44	64	108	13	2	15	57	66	123
Dublin, South,	42	73	115	14	50	64	56	123	179
Rathdown,	16	26	42	–	–	–	16	26	42
Co. Kildare:									
Athy,	–	–	–	–	–	–	–	–	–
Celbridge,	–	–	–	–	–	–	–	–	–
Naas,	1	4	5	–	–	–	1	4	5
Co. Kilkenny:									
Callan,	2	4	6	–	–	–	2	4	6
Castlecomer,	4	2	6	–	–	–	4	2	6
Kilkenny,	11	10	21	2	5	7	13	15	28
Thomastown,	1	–	1	–	–	–	1	–	1
Urlingford,	–	–	–	–	–	–	–	–	–
King's Co.:									
Edenderry,	–	2	2	–	–	–	–	2	2
Parsonstown,	1	4	5	–	1	1	1	5	6
Tullamore,	9	22	31	2	4	6	11	26	37
Co. Longford:									
Ballymahon,	–	–	–	–	–	–	–	–	–
Granard,	2	5	7	–	–	–	2	5	7
Longford,	–	2	2	–	–	–	–	2	2
Co. Louth:									
Ardee,	1	10	11	–	–	–	1	10	11
Drogheda,	10	6	16	6	5	11	16	11	27
Dundalk,	5	13	18	–	1	1	5	14	19
Co. Meath:									
Dunshaughlin,	2	–	2	–	–	–	2	–	2
Kells,	1	9	10	–	1	1	1	10	11
Navan,	8	6	14	1	–	1	9	6	15
Oldcastle,	4	5	9	–	1	1	4	6	10
Trim,	4	10	14	1	2	3	5	12	17
Queen's Co.:									
Abbeyleix,	3	–	3	–	–	–	3	–	3
Donaghmore,	–	–	–	–	–	–	–	–	–
Mountmellick,	3	3	6	1	3	4	4	6	10
Co. Westmeath:									
Athlone,	–	–	–	–	–	–	–	–	–
Delvin,	1	3	4	–	2	2	1	5	6
Mullingar,	2	8	10	–	–	–	2	8	10
Co. Wexford:									
Enniscorthy,	–	4	4	–	–	–	–	4	4
Gorey,	2	2	4	–	4	4	2	6	8
New Ross,	2	2	4	2	3	5	4	5	9
Wexford,	6	3	9	–	1	1	6	4	10
Co. Wicklow:									
Baltinglass,	1	–	1	1	–	1	2	–	2
Rathdrum,	3	15	18	–	–	–	3	15	18
Shillelagh,	–	–	–	–	–	–	–	–	–
Total, Leinster,	201	318	519	43	91	134	244	409	653

on 31st December, 1885, exclusive of Idiots and Epileptic Idiots—*con.*

Names of Unions.	Simple Lunatics.			Epileptic Lunatics.			Total of the two preceding Classes.		
PROVINCE OF CONNAUGHT.	M.	F.	T.	M.	F.	T.	M.	F.	T.
Co. Galway:									
Ballinasloe,	–	–	–	–	–	–	–	–	–
Clifden,	–	–	–	–	–	–	–	–	–
Galway,	3	6	9	4	1	5	7	7	14
Glennamaddy,	4	1	5	–	–	–	4	1	5
Gort,	–	–	–	–	–	–	–	–	–
Loughrea,	–	3	3	–	–	–	–	3	3
Mount Bellew,	–	–	–	–	–	–	–	–	–
Oughterard,	2	2	4	–	–	–	2	2	4
Portumna,	–	–	–	–		–	–	–	–
Tuam,	–	2	2	–	–	–	–	2	2
Co. Leitrim:									
Carrick-on-Shannon,	–	–	–	–	–	–	–	–	–
Manorhamilton,	1	2	3	–	–	–	1	2	3
Mohill,	–	–	–	–	–	–	–	–	–
Co. Mayo:									
Ballina,	–	–	–	–	–	–	–	–	–
Ballinrobe,	2	–	2	–	–	–	2	–	2
Belmullet,	1	1	2	–	–	–	1	1	2
Castlebar,	–	4	4	–	–	–	–	4	4
Claremorris,	1	2	3	–	–	–	1	2	3
Killala,	–	–	–	–	–	–	–	–	–
Newport,*	–	–	–	–	–	–	–	–	–
Swineford,	4	4	8	–	3	3	4	7	11
Westport,	–	–	–	–	–	–	–	–	–
Co. Roscommon:									
Boyle,	1	1	2			–	1	1	2
Castlerea,	–	–	–	–	–	–	–	–	–
Roscommon,	3	3	6	–	1	1	3	4	7
Strokestown,	4	5	9	–	–	–	4	5	9
Co. Sligo:									
Dromore West,	–	–	–	–	–	–	–	–	–
Sligo,	2	5	7	–	–	–	2	5	7
Tobercurry,	–	–	–	–	–	–	–	–	–
Total, Connaught,	28	41	69	4	5	9	32	46	78

* Now amalgamated with Westport Union.

SUMMARY OF PROVINCES.

	M.	F.	T.	M.	F.	T.	M.	F.	T.
Ulster,	224	387	611	40	54	94	264	441	705
Munster,	150	257	407	24	29	53	174	286	460
Leinster,	201	318	519	43	91	134	244	409	653
Connaught,	28	41	69	4	5	9	32	46	78
Total, Ireland,	603	1,003	1,606	111	179	290	714	1,182	1,896

APPENDIX B.

Central Asylum for Criminal Lunatics at Dundrum.

No. 1.—Return showing the Original and Present Asylum Accommodation.

				M.	F.	T.
Asylum,	Central.					
Year opened,	1850		Original Accommodation,	80	40	120
Year enlarged,	1864		Present Accommodation,*	122	42	164

	M.	F.	T.
Actual Number of Inmates on 31st December, 1885,	144	29	173

* The present accommodation as given above is calculated by allowing as nearly as possible about 800 cubic feet per bed. The accommodation as given for the male side includes the two hospital dormitories which were, until recently, wholly allocated to male patients. The actual numbers on the male side are a good deal in excess of the calculated accommodation.

No. 2.—Admissions, Discharges, and Deaths, &c., during the Year ended 31st December, 1885.

	Male.	Female.	Total.
In Asylum on 31st December, 1884,	144	27	171
Admitted to 31st December, 1885,	28	1	29
Total,	172	36	208
Discharged during the year 1885—Recovered,	7	3	10
Unimproved or incurable,	11	3	14
Total,	18	4	21
Deaths—From Natural Causes,	10	1	11
Escapes during 1885,	-	-	-
Total discharges, deaths, and escapes during the year,	28	7	35
Remaining in Asylum on 31st December, 1885,	144	29	173
Daily average number of patients in Asylum during 1885,	-	-	168
Per-cent. of deaths on admissions,	35·	33·	34·
Per-cent. of recoveries on admissions,	27·	75·	31·
Per-cent. of deaths on daily average number of Patients in the House,	7·	3·	6.5
Per-cent. of Deaths on total number in Asylum,	5·8	3·	5·

No. 3.—Physical Condition of those Admitted during the Year 1885.

—	Male.	Female.	Total.
In good bodily health and condition, ...	19	1	20
In indifferent health or reduced condition, . . .	5	3	8
In bad health or exhausted condition, ...	2	-	2
Total, ...	26	4	30

No. 4.—Previous History of the Admissions during the Year 1885.

—	Male.	Female.	Total.
Not Insane, ...	-	-	-
Re-admissions, ...	-		-
First admission, but stated not to be the first attack of Insanity,	4	-	4
First attack or no information on the subject, ...	22	4	26
Total, . . .	26	4	30
Known to have actually attempted suicide, . .	1	-	1
Regarded as being suicidal, ...	-	-	-
Stated not to have attempted suicide, or no information on the subject, ...	25	4	29
Total, ...	26	4	30
Affected with Epilepsy or Epileptiform Convulsions, .	1	-	1
Not so affected, ...	25	4	29
Total, ...	26	4	30

No. 5.—Classification of the Crimes and Sentences of Patients admitted into the Asylum during the Year 1885.

Crime.	Total Number admitted during the Year.			Period at which Insanity was recognized.								
				Found Insane by Jury on Arraignment.			Acquitted on the ground of Insanity.			Certified to be Insane while undergoing sentence of Penal Servitude.		
	M.	F.	T.	M.	F.	T.	M.	F.	T.	M.	F.	T.
Murder, ...	8	1	9	4	-	4	3	1	4	1	-	1
Violent Assault, ...	5	-	5	1	-	1	-	-	-	4	-	4
Common Assault, ...	2	-	2	-	-	-	-	-	-	2	-	2
Rape or Attempt, ...	-	-	-	-	-	-	-	-		-	-	
Arson, ...	-	-	-	-	-	-	-	-	-	-	-	
Theft, ...	2	3	5	-	-	-	-	-	-	2	3	5
Burglary, ...	2	-	2	-	-	-	-		-	2	-	2
Attempt at Suicide, . . .	1	-	1	-	-	-	1	-	1	-	-	-
Breach of the Articles of War, .	6	-	6	-	-	-	-	-	-	6	-	6
Other Offences, ...	-	-	-	-	-	-	-	-	-	-	-	-
Total, ...	26	4	30	5	-	5	4	1	5	17	3	20

No. 6.—Classification of the Crimes and Sentences of Patients remaining in the Asylum on 31st December, 1885.

Crimes.	Total Number at end of Year 1885.			Period at which Insanity was recognised.								
				Found Insane on Arraignment and incapable of pleading.			Acquitted on the ground of Insanity.			Certified to be Insane while undergoing sentences of Penal Servitude.		
	M.	F.	T.	M.	F.	T.	M.	F.	T.	M.	F.	T.
Murder,	65	11	76	17	5	22	40	4	44	8	–	8
Violent Assault,	25	3	28	6	2	8	20	–	18	1	1	4
Common Assault,	3	–	3	–	–		–			3	–	3
Rape or Attempt,	–	–	–	–	–	–	–		–	–	–	–
Arson,	3	1	4		–		–	1	1	3	–	3
Theft,	14	10	24	3	–	3		–	–	11	10	21
Burglary,	8	–	8	–	–	–	3	–	3	5	–	5
Attempt at Suicide,	–	1	1	–		–	–	1	1		–	–
Breach of the Articles of War,	5	–	5	–	–	–	–		–	5		5
Other Offences,	11	–	11	3	–	3	5	–	5	3	–	3
Total,	141	29	174	29	7	36	74	11	85	41	11	52

No. 7.—Ages with respect to the Admissions, Discharges, and Deaths, during the Year 1885.

Ages.	Admissions.			Discharges.						Deaths.		
				Recovered.			Transferred to other Asylums.					
	M.	F.	T.	M.	F.	T.	M.	F.	T.	M.	F.	T.
From 5 to 10 Years,	–	–	[illegible]	–	–	–	–	–	–	–	–	–
" 10 to 15 "	–	–	–	–	–	–	–	–	–	–	–	–
" 15 to 20 "	1	–	1	–	–	–	1	–	1	–	–	–
" 20 to 30 "	7	1	8	2	2	4	3	–	3	1	–	1
" 30 to 40 "	4	2	6	4	–	4	4	–	4	–	–	–
" 40 to 50 "	10	1	11	–	–	–	3	1	4	2	1	3
" 50 to 60 "	2	–	2	1	1	2	–	1	1	3	–	1
" 60 to 70 "	2	–	2	–	–	–	–	–	–	3		3
" 70 to 80 "	–	–	–	–	–	–	–	–	–	1	–	1
" 80 to 90 "	–	–	–	–	–	–	–	1	1	–	–	–
" 90 and upwards,	–		–	–	–	–	–	–	–	–	–	–
Total,	26	4	30	7	3	10	11	3	14	10	1	11

	Males.	Females.
Average age at death,	51 years	42 years.

No. 8.—Ages of Patients remaining in the Central Asylum on 31st December, 1885.

Ages.	Male.	Female.	Total.
Under 20 years,	–	–	–
From 20 to 30 years,	21	5	[illegible]
" 30 " 40 "	28	3	31
" 40 " 50 "	37	8	45
" 50 " 60 "	34	6	40
" 60 " 70 "	13	1	14
" 70 and upwards,	6	6	12
Unknown,	–	–	–
Total,	144	29	173

No. 9.—Form of Mental Disease of Patients admitted during the Year ending 31st December, 1885.

Form of Disease.	Male.	Female.	Total.
Mania,	8	3	11
Melancholia,	3	–	3
Dementia,	13	–	13
Monomania,	–	–	–
General Paralysis,	1	–	1
Idiocy,	–	–	–
Puerperal Insanity,	–	1	1
Mental affections complicated with Epilepsy,	1	–	1
Supposed not Insane,	–	–	–
Total,	26	4	30

No. 10.—Form of Mental Disease of Patients remaining in Asylum on 31st December, 1885.

Form of Disease.	Male.	Female.	Total.
Mania,	70	12	82
Melancholia,	6	1	7
Dementia,	55	5	60
Monomania,	1	–	1
General Paralysis,	1	–	1
Idiocy,	–	1	1
Puerperal Insanity,		1	1
Mental affections complicated with Epilepsy,	7	2	9
Supposed not Insane,	3	4	7
Total,	144	29	173

C

No. 11.—Educational Condition of Patients admitted during the Year 1885.

—	Male.	Female.	Total.
Well Educated, ...	–	–	–
Can Read and Write well, ...	2	–	2
" " indifferently, . .	14	3	17
Can Read only, ...	5	–	5
Cannot Read or Write, ...	5	1	6
Unascertained, ...	–	–	–
Total, ...	26	4	30

No. 12.—Educational Condition of Patients remaining in Asylum on 31st December, 1885.

—	Male.	Female.	Total.
Well Educated, ...	4	–	4
Can Read and Write well, ...	14	–	14
" " indifferently, . . .	50	9	59
Can Read only, ...	30	7	37
Cannot Read or Write, . .	46	13	59
Unascertained, . . .	–	–	–
Total, ...	144	29	173

No. 13.—Social Condition of Patients Admitted, Discharged, and Deceased, during the Year 1885.

—	Admissions.			Discharges. Recovered.			Discharges. Transferred to other Asylums.			Deaths.		
	M.	F.	T.	M.	F.	T.	M.	F.	T.	M.	F.	T.
Married, ...	3	1	4	1	–	1	–	–	–	2	1	3
Single, ...	15	3	18	6	3	9	9	3	12	8	–	8
Widowed, ...	7	–	7	–	–	–	–	–	–	–	–	–
Not ascertained, ...	1	–	1	–	–	–	2	–	2	–	–	–
Total, ...	26	4	30	7	3	10	11	3	14	10	1	11

No. 14.—Social Condition of Patients remaining in the Asylum on 31st December, 1885.

—	Male.	Female.	Total.
Married, ...	23	1	24
Single, ...	99	27	126
Widowed, ...	16	-	16
Unascertained, ...	6	–	6
Total, ...	144	29	173

No. 15.—Classification as to Conduct of Patients remaining in Asylum on 31st December, 1885.

—	Male.	Female.	Total.
Recovered, or supposed not Insane, . . .	2	5	7
Quiet and orderly, but Insane, ...	51	18	69
Moderately tranquil, ...	58	4	62
Noisy and refractory, ...	28	7	35
Total, ...	141	32	173
Of Suicidal tendencies, ...	1	1	2

No. 16.—Numbers affected with Epilepsy and Paralysis remaining in the Asylum on the 31st December, 1885.

—	Male.	Female.	Total.
Epilepsy, ...	7	2	9
Paralysis, General, ...	1	–	1
Epilepsy and Paralysis, ...	–	1	1
Total, ...	8	3	11

No. 17.—Previous Occupation of Patients remaining in Asylum on 31st December, 1885.

—	Male.	Female.	Total
Agriculturists,	77	–	77
Domestic Servants,	6	8	14
Clerks,	–	–	–
Shopkeepers,	1	–	1
Tailors and Seamstresses,	3	1	4
Painters and Glaziers,	2	–	2
Smiths and Workers in Metals,	5	–	5
Masons and Bricklayers,	–	–	–
Carpenters,	3	–	3
Weavers,	–	–	–
Shoemakers,	7	–	7
Hatters,	–	–	–
Factory Workers,	–	–	–
Victuallers,	1	–	1
Pedlars and Hucksters,	–	–	–
Lawyers,	–	–	–
Medical Men,	1	–	1
Members of Religious Communities,	1	–	1
Students and Teachers,	1	–	1
Soldiers and Pensioners,	15	–	15
Police,	2	–	2
Sailors,	2	–	2
Publicans,	–	–	–
Mendicants,	4	–	4
Various other employments,	14	3	17
No occupation, or unascertained,	4	18	22
Total,	146	29	175

No. 18.—Condition as regards Mental Recovery of those in Asylum on 31st December, 1885.

—	Male.	Female.	Total.
Sane Lunatics,	2	5	7
Lunatics probably Curable,	6	5	11
" " Incurable, but not Epileptic,	129	16	145
Idiots,	–	1	1
Epileptics,	7	2	9
Total,	144	29	173

No. 10.—Causes of Death during the Year ended 31st December, 1885.

Name (or Initials).	Age	Male.	Female.	Cause of Death.
W. C. . .	81	1	-	Nervous exhaustion.
H. D. . .	41	1	-	Epilepsy.
J. B. . .	41	1	-	Disease of Kidney and Purpura.
H. T. .	44	1	-	Exhaustion consequent on Brain Disease.
C. S.	48	–	1	Cancer of Rectum and Uterus.
P. F. . .	65	1	–	Inflammation of Lungs.
O. D. . .	60	1	–	Peritonitis.
P. F. . .	76	1	-	Exhaustion consequent on disease of Knee Joint.
D. O. . .	51	1	-	Phthisis.
P. M. . .	38	1	-	Phthisis.
W. McN. . .	43	1	-	Chronic Spinal Meningitis.
Total, .	–	10	1	

Total Deaths, 11.
Average Age at Death, males, [illegible] years; females, [illegible] years.

No. 20.—Daily Average Number of Patients employed during the Year ended 31st December, 1885.

Male Employment.	Number Employed.	Female Employment.	Number Employed.
Farm Labourers, ...	60	Laundry, ...	9
Tailors, ...	6	Needlework, ...	4
Shoemakers, ...	5	Scrubbing and Scouring, . .	7
Carpenters, ...	–	Miscellaneous, ...	2
Yard, Cows, Piggery, &c., .	10	Unemployed, on special exercise, or confined to bed.	5
Miscellaneous, (including pumping water).	10		
Unemployed, on special exercise, or confined to bed.	64		
Total, ...	111	Total. . . .	27

No. 21.—Summary of Expenditure in the Year ended 31st March, 1886.

Average Number Maintained,		Males.	Females.	Total.
	Attendants,	20	12	32
	Patients,	14[illegible]	40	1[illegible]

Head of Service.				Amount.			Yearly Average Cost per Patient Resident.		
	£	s.	d.	£	s.	d.	£	s.	d.
Salaries and Wages,				2,169	11	5	12	14	6
Victualling,				3,160	5	5	18	17	3
Tobacco,				64	16	6	0	7	8
Uniform for Attendants and Servants, Clothing for Patients,				610	18	1	3	13	6
Medicines, Surgical Instruments, &c.,				46	13	11	0	5	0
Allowance in lieu of Quarters, &c.,				7	8	5	—		
Escort and Conveyance of Patients,				61	0	11	0	8	7
Incidental Expenses,				101	19	10	0	12	1
				6,220	5	4	37	0	5
Less Receipts, viz.:—									
Sale of Old Stores,	9	2	2						
Farm Cash Sales,	2	10	0						
Deceased Patient's Cash,	13	13	7						
	25	5	9	25	5	9	0	3	0
Total,				6,201	2	7	36	17	5

No. 22.—Details of the foregoing.

	£	s.	d.
A. Salaries and Wages—			
Officers,	1,043	10	0
Attendants and Servants,	1,075	15	2
Total,	*2,118	5	2
B. Victualling, viz.—			
Meat,	1,190	0	10
Bread,	674	11	8
Butter,	172	19	7
Groceries, Tea, Sugar, Cocoa, &c.	333	1	2
Bacon, Eggs, Salt, &c.,	109	11	3
B. Victualling—*continued.*			
Oatmeal and Flour,	73	2	8
Potatoes and Vegetables,	15	5	8
Porter, Bass's Ale,	163	10	2
Wine and Spirits,	60	1	0
Farm Produce valued at cost price,	357	2	6
Sundries,	17	2	6
Total,	3,160	5	5
C. Tobacco,	64	16	6

* Includes £[illegible] to attendants, £3 11s. 6d., and £4 2s. 3d. house rent, Head Attendant.

No. 22.—Details of the foregoing—*continued.*

	£	s.	d.
D. Uniform for Attendants, estimated at,	137	6	0
Clothing for Patients,	481	17	1
Total,	618	19	1
E. Incidental Expenses, viz.—			
Advertising,	33	11	6
Books, Stationery,	4	16	7
Sweeping Chimneys,	12	0	0
E. Incidental Expenses—*con.*			
Postage, &c.,	0	15	0
Travelling Expenses,	7	5	0
Funeral Expenses,	8	10	0
Carriage of Goods,	4	0	0
Crockery, Ironmongery, Brushes, &c.,	7	15	3
Small Sundries,	13	12	0
Total,	101	19	10

No. 23.—Account of the Sum Expended, compared with the Sum Granted by Parliament for the Central Asylum in the Year ended 31st March, 1886, showing a Surplus or Deficit upon each sub-head of the Vote.

Service.	Parliamentary Grant			Expenditure.			Expenditure compared with Grant.					
							Less than granted.			More than granted.		
	£	s.	d.	£	s.	d.	£	s.	d.	£	s.	d.
Salaries and Wages,	2,150	0	0	2,139	11	3	10	8	9	–		
Victualling,	3,697	0	0	3,167	5	5	519	14	7	–		
Tobacco,	45	0	0	44	10	6	0	9	6	–		
Uniform for Attendants and Servants,	130	0	0	137	0	0				7	0	0
Clothing for Patients,	594	0	0	481	17	1	112	2	11	–		
Medicines and Surgical Instruments,	15	0	0	19	14	11	–			4	14	11
Allowance in lieu of Quarters, &c.,	95	0	0	7	2	6	87	17	7	–		
Escort and Conveyance of Patients,	50	0	0	91	0	11	–			41	0	11
Incidental Expenses,	90	0	0	101	19	10	–			11	19	10
Total,	6,817	0	0	6,776	6	4	664	17	5	64	0	9
Deduct Excess,	—			—			64	0	9	—		

Saving on total grant, . . . £640 11s. 8d.

N.B.—The allowance for Quarters is included under the sub-head of Salaries and Wages in the Estimates. This sub-head therefore, shows on the whole, a saving of £1 14s. 1d.

Uniform and Patient's Clothing also form but one sub-head, D. The excess of expenditure on the whole of this sub-head is therefore only [illegible]

No. 24.—Detailed Statement of Salaries and Wages, showing the Rates of Pay and Allowances as well as the actual Payments for the Year ended 31st March, 1886.

No. actually employed.	Description of Office.	Salary of Office. Minimum.	Annual Increase.	Maximum.	Amounts actually paid during the year.	Allowances.	Valued at.
		£ s. d.	£ s. d.	£ s. d.	£ s. d.		£ s. d.
1	Resident Physician and Governor,	300 0 0	30 0 0	450 0 0	450 0 0	Unfurnished apartments; fuel, light, bread, milk, vegetables, butter, and washing,	300 0 0
1	Visiting Physician,	—	—	174 0 0	173 0 0	None	—
1	Assistant Physician,	100 0 0	10 0 0	130 0 0	150 0 0	Furnished apartments; provisions, washing, and attendance.	172 0 0
1	Female Superintendent,	35 0 0	1 0 0	46 0 0	43 15 6	Do. do. do.	93 11 0
1	Storekeeper, with £60 commuted allowance,	50 0 0	5 0 0	60 0 0	170 0 0	Dinner,	11 0 0
1	Protestant Chaplain,	—	—	50 0 0	50 0 0	None.	—
1	Roman Catholic Chaplain,	—	—	40 0 0	40 0 0	None.	—
1	Head Male Attendant,	30 0 0	2 0 0	40 0 0	67 1 5	Rations and uniform, fuel and light, and a house; washing,	84 4 0
3	Male Attendants, 1st Class,	35 0 0	1 0 0	35 0 0	111 13 6	Room, rations, uniform, fuel, and light; washing,	46 14 8
11	Do. 2nd Class,	21 0 0	1 0 0	31 0 0	310 17 5		
1	Tailor,	—	—	33 0 0	33 0 0		
1	Shoemaker,	—	—	35 0 0	35 0 0		
1	Night Attendant,	31 0 0	1 0 0	41 0 0	34 10 1	Do. do. with extra rations,	48 14 9
1	Gatekeeper,	—	—	30 0 0	30 0 0	House, coal, milk, uniform,	38 5 5
1	Steward and Gardener,	30 0 0	1 0 0	40 0 0	35 11 5	House, coal, potatoes, partial clothing,	26 8 0
1	Farmyard-man,	—	—	31 0 0	31 0 0	Partial clothing,	—
1	Bandmaster,	—	—	16 0 0	15 17 0	None.	—
1	Assistant Storekeeper (Female) (temporary),	—	—	—	0 11 8	Rooms, rations, clothing, fuel, and light; washing,	—
1	Laundress,	27 0 0	1 0 0	27 0 0	24 0 0		
1	Cook,	22 0 0	1 0 0	27 0 0	27 0 0		
5	Female Attendants, 1st Class,	22 0 0	1 0 0	29 0 0	87 0 0	Room, rations, clothing, fuel, and light; washing,	47 5 0
8	Do. 2nd Class,	—	—	—	147 1 9		
1	Kitchenmaid,	—	—	18 0 0	17 0 0		
6	Married Male Attendants, 2s. 6d. per week extra,	—	—	—	39 0 0		—
2	Temporary Male Attendants,	—	—	—	23 0 2		—
		—	—	—	7,166 5 2		
	Less Fines on Attendants,	—	—	—	5 11 4		
			—	—	7,161 13 8		

No. 25.—Amusements, Games, Books, &c.

Description of Amusements and Games.	Class of Books and Periodicals supplied to Patients.	Numbers usually taking part in Games and Reading.
Bagatelle, Draughts, Handball.	Chambers's Journal. Good Words. Illustrated News. Graphic.	[illegible]

No. 26.—Number of Dormitories and Beds in each, also Number of Single Apartments, on 31st December, 1885.

Male Side.				Female Side.			
—	Dormitories.	Beds.	Single Rooms.	—	Dormitories.	Beds.	Single Rooms.
No. 1 Division, .	4	53	13	No. 4 Division, .	3	8	9
No. 2 " .	6	43	7	No. 5 " .	5	9	3
No. 3 " .	4	19	7	No. 6 " .	4	10	9
Hospital, .	not in use at present for patients.						
Total, .	14	117	27	Total, .	12	27	14
Total Male Accommodation,	144			Total Female Accommodation,	41		

No. 27.—Return of Contract Prices paid for the undermentioned Articles of Provisions, &c., for the Year 1st April, 1685, to 31st March, 1886.

Articles of Provisions.	Price.	Articles of Provisions.	Price.
	s. d.		s. d.
Beef, per lb. {rumps of beef without bone; rounds of beef and legs}	0 4½	Cocoa, shell, per cwt., .	16 0
		" nib, per lb., .	1 3
Mutton, per lb., . . .	0 4½	Butter, per lb., . . {Salt, . Fresh, .	1 0 1 4
Bread, white, per 4 lb. loaf, .	0 5	Eggs, per 120, ...	6 6
Oatmeal, per cwt., . . .	13 6	Wine, per doz., . . {Port, . Sherry, .	19 0 18 0½
Flour, per stone, .	—		
Rice, per cwt., . . .	11 5	Whiskey, per gallon, . . .	15 0
Tea, per lb., . . .	2 0	Milk, supplied from the Farm.	
Sugar, per lb., . . .	0 2	Coals, supplied by Board of Works.	

	M.	F.	T.	M.	F.	T.	M.	F.	T.	M.	F.	T.	M.	F.	T.
Armagh, . .	152	152	304	134	121	255	24	39	63	7	7	14	31	46	77
Galway, Roscommon, Town of Galway,	308	320	628	339	231	570	91	47	138	10	14	24	110	61	171
Antrim, Carrickfergus (Tn.)	314	[illegible]	34[illegible]	231	215	[illegible]	66	69	135	34	30	64	110	[illegible]	17[illegible]
Carlow and Kildare,	195	121	236	138	139	277	29	27	56	6	7	13	37	34	71
Mayo, . .	215	140	355	197	127	324	46	35	81	9	3	12	55	38	93
Tipperary (N. & S. R.)	243	225	470	235	227	462	13	39	52	14	8	22	57	47	104
Cork, City and County,	545	485	1030	415	457	902	109	118	227	17	21	38	126	138	264
Down, . .	270	150	420	228	157	385	40	41	81	9	17	26	49	58	107
Clare, . .	170	160	330	177	124	301	25	17	42	6	10	16	31	27	58
Wexford, . .	240	170	410	185	139	324	36	25	61	11	6	17	47	31	78
Kilkenny, City & County,	180	175	355	158	127	285	32	24	47	12	9	21	35	32	67
Kerry, . .	227	128	355	205	136	341	39	40	79	9	6	15	48	16	64
Donegal, . .	175	175	350	244	123	367	45	30	61	10	5	16	55	45	100
Limerick, City & County,	250	250	500	229	243	472	19	46	95	9	13	22	36	35	111
Derry, . .	178	143	320	177	159	336	37	32	69	17	14	31	[illegible]	41	77
King's & Queen's,	210	210	420	175	153	303	25	59	32	15	12	27	38	41	79
Cavan & Monaghan,	258	153	411	263	195	458	41	14	85	19	14	33	60	56	116
Meath, Westmeath, Longford,	215	215	430	222	207	429	60	55	115	14	6	20	74	51	125
Fermanagh, Tyrone,	256	234	510	296	233	529	72	47	119	20	15	35	97	65	155
Dublin, City & Co. Wicklow, Louth, Drogheda (Town),	508	592	1100	526	563	1089	160	186	346	57	43	100	217	231	[illegible]
Leitrim and Sligo,	257	220	470	224	167	391	46	49	95	17	7	24	63	36	116
Waterford, . .	150	150	300	153	142	295	25	41	66	9	10	19	34	48	82

M.	F.	T.	M.	F.	T.	M.	F.	T.	M.	F.	T.	M.	F.	T.	M.	F.	T.
[illegible]	167	332	[illegible]	12	34	4	1	3	1	1	2	27	14	41	[illegible]	10	1[illegible]
1[illegible]	[illegible]	781	46	[illegible]	75	5	–	5	–	–	–	31	[illegible]	[illegible]	34	[illegible]	6[illegible]
431	30[illegible]	73[illegible]	46	[illegible]	85	27	[illegible]	49	3	7	10	7[illegible]	6[illegible]	14[illegible]	19	[illegible]	21
175	173	348	18	13	33	5	7	12	1	–	1	24	22	46	9	[illegible]	17
25[illegible]	14[illegible]	417	14	15	29	3	2	7	1	–	1	[illegible]	17	37	17	1[illegible]	3[illegible]
[illegible]	25[illegible]	567	21	17	38	9	11	13	–	–	–	23	28	51	19	[illegible]	27
57[illegible]	[illegible]	1,16[illegible]	30	43	73	36	46	82	5	2	7	71	8[illegible]	16[illegible]	[illegible]	[illegible]	[illegible]
377	215	59[illegible]	42	45	87	9	5	7	2	4	6	46	54	10[illegible]	1[illegible]	7	1[illegible]
20[illegible]	151	35[illegible]	9	19	21	2	1	3	2	1	3	13	14	27	13	7	2[illegible]
23[illegible]	16[illegible]	40[illegible]	21	24	45	7	3	5	2	[illegible]	[illegible]	34	23	57	10	4	14
15[illegible]	16[illegible]	35[illegible]	21	23	44	2	1	3	1	–	1	24	24	48	21	6	27
253	18[illegible]	43[illegible]	14	16	30	4	4	[illegible]	–	–	–	19	22	41	16	16	[illegible]
29[illegible]	16[illegible]	467	26	17	43	6	4	10	2	–	2	34	21	55	27	2[illegible]	5[illegible]
2[illegible]	29[illegible]	5[illegible]	12	17	29	11	11	22	7	4	11	31	3[illegible]	6[illegible]	2[illegible]	2[illegible]	5[illegible]
22[illegible]	204	43[illegible]	31	24	55	1	9	10	3	2	5	43	3[illegible]	7[illegible]	11	11	2[illegible]
21[illegible]	170	384	14	16	30	9	5	14	–	1	1	22	22	45	14	16	4[illegible]
[illegible]	254	577	18	13	31	11	19	30	4	4	8	33	3[illegible]	6[illegible]	20	16	35
33[illegible]	[illegible]	62[illegible]	37	31	68	14	6	20	1	–	1	32	3[illegible]	[illegible]	15	17	32
34[illegible]	2[illegible]	6[illegible]	36	33	69	14	5	27	16	2	18	54	51	105	26	16	1[illegible]
74[illegible]	794	1,337	[illegible]	[illegible]	17[illegible]	54	89	143	6	–	6	150	16[illegible]	31[illegible]	8[illegible]	54	13[illegible]
2[illegible]	22[illegible]	510	7[illegible]	10	17	9	2	11	–	–	–	37	21	58	24	14	3[illegible]
1[illegible]	[illegible]	[illegible]	11	2[illegible]	3[illegible]	[illegible]	17	[illegible]	1	3	[illegible]	21	40	61	[illegible]	17	2[illegible]
[illegible]	[illegible]739	1263[illegible]	[illegible]	571	119[illegible]	243	273	51[illegible]	5[illegible]	33	[illegible]	[illegible]	[illegible]	[illegible]	[illegible]	[illegible]	[illegible]

SUMMARY of ADMISSIONS,

No. 1.—TABLE showing the Number of Patients who were in District Lunatic … Discharged, Died, or who …

Asylums.	Counties comprised in present Districts.	Total Number of Deaths which occurred during the year ending the 31st December, 1885.			Number of Escapes which occurred during the year ending the 31st December, 1885.			Total Number of Discharges, Deaths, and Escapes, which occurred during the year ending the 31st December, 1885.			Total Number Remaining in each Asylum on 31st December, 1885.			Daily Average Number Resident in each Asylum during the year 1885.		
		M.	F.	T.	M.	F.	T.	M.	F.	T.	M.	F.	T.	M.	F.	T.
Armagh, .	Armagh, . .	8	10	18	–	–	–	35	24	59	132	143	275	137	115	247
Ballinasloe,	Galway, Roscommon, Town of Galway,	34	29	63	–	–	–	88	55	143	354	274	628	337	217	554
Belfast, .	Antrim, Carrickfergus (Tn.)	12	9	21	–	–	–	88	77	165	343	227	570	312	215	527
Carlow, .	Carlow and Kildare,	9	8	17	–	–	–	33	30	63	146	140	286	152	137	289
Castlebar,	Mayo, . . .	17	18	35	–	–	–	37	35	72	214	134	348	196	121	317
Clonmel,	Tipperary (N. & S. R.)	19	8	27	–	–	–	42	36	78	241	248	489	232	229	[illegible]
Cork, .	Cork, City and County.	37	30	67	–	–	–	108	143	251	463	453	916	453	436	889
Down, .	Down, . . .	12	8	20	–	–	–	55	65	120	218	155	373	222	156	378
Ennis, .	Clare, . . .	13	7	20	–	1	1	32	29	61	176	127	303	181	132	313
Enniscorthy, .	Wexford, . .	10	4	14	–	–	–	40	31	71	199	132	331	189	130	319
Kilkenny,	Kilkenny, City & County.	21	6	27	–	–	–	45	30	75	140	138	278	158	123	281
Killarney, .	Kerry, . . .	18	18	36	–	1	1	37	41	78	216	141	357	200	134	334
Letterkenny, .	Donegal, . .	27	28	55	–	–	–	61	49	110	238	119	357	236	127	363
Limerick,	Limerick, City & County.	28	23	51	–	–	–	60	54	114	227	218	445	240	244	484
Londonderry,	Derry, . . .	11	11	22	–	–	–	48	46	94	180	155	335	174	148	322
Maryborough,	King's & Queen's,	14	18	32	–	–	–	37	40	77	173	134	307	174	146	320
Monaghan, .	Cavan & Monaghan,	20	15	35	–	–	–	53	51	104	270	203	473	257	195	452
Mullingar,	Meath, Westmeath, Longford,	15	17	32	–	–	–	67	55	122	289	218	507	277	212	489
Omagh, .	Fermanagh, Tyrone,	25	19	44	–	–	–	103	76	179	279	228	507	272	215	487
Richmond,	Dublin, City & Co. Wicklow, Louth, Drogheda (Town),	83	54	137	–	–	–	233	223	456	510	571	1081	500	565	1065
Sligo, .	Leitrim and Sligo,	24	14	38	–	–	–	61	35	96	226	188	414	230	170	400
Waterford, .	Waterford, . .	8	17	25	–	–	–	28	57	85	160	148	308	156	136	292

DISCHARGES, DEATHS, &c.—*continued.*

Asylums on 31st December, 1885; also the Number who were Admitted
Escaped during the year.

Daily Average Number Resident in each Asylum during the year 1885.			Persons under care during the year 1885.			Persons under care during the year [illegible].			Persons Admitted during the year 1885.			Persons Recovered during the year 1885.			Transferred from other Asylums during the year 1885.			Transferred to other Asylums during the year 1885.			Asylums.
M.	F.	T.	M.	F.	T.	M.	F.	T.	M.	F.	T.	M.	F.	T.	M.	F.	T.	M.	F.	T.	
127	135	260	165	115	[illegible]	162	166	[illegible]	[illegible]	46	76	22	12	34	-	-	-	-	-	-	Armagh.
346	230	579	401	272	677	[illegible]	262	650	91	47	138	34	23	61	1	1	[illegible]	-	-	-	Ballinasloe.
[illegible]	[illegible]	534	401	292	693	477	306	737	106	87	193	45	39	84	-	-	-	-	-	-	Belfast.
187	139	376	167	168	335	174	173	347	[illegible]	32	70	18	14	32	-	-	-	-	-	-	Carlow.
200	133	335	232	142	374	248	169	419	54	38	92	14	15	29	-	-	-	-	-	-	Castlebar.
228	248	476	276	272	548	290	262	552	54	45	99	21	17	38	-	-	-	-	-	-	Clonmel.
463	460	923	592	576	1168	569	592	1161	122	126	248	30	45	75	-	-	-	[illegible]	1	4	Cork.
216	153	369	275	202	477	276	207	483	16	50	[illegible]	41	43	84	-	-	-	-	-	-	Down.
174	131	305	219	162	381	207	150	357	30	26	56	9	12	21	-	-	-	-	-	-	Ennis.
191	135	326	217	170	387	233	167	390	45	31	76	21	24	45	-	-	-	-	-	-	Enniscorthy.
160	133	293	187	153	340	191	158	349	34	33	67	20	23	43	-	-	-	-	-	-	Kilkenny.
208	134	342	238	167	405	245	180	425	46	46	92	14	18	[illegible]	1	-	1	-	-	-	Killarney.
242	120	362	289	171	460	298	163	461	54	42	96	25	17	42	-	-	-	-	-	-	Letterkenny.
262	216	478	299	301	600	284	299	583	57	56	113	13	17	30	-	-	-	-	-	-	Limerick.
190	157	347	218	185	403	271	198	416	46	44	90	30	24	54	-	1	1	-	-	-	Londonderry.
173	136	309	214	176	390	208	178	376	63	46	73	14	16	30	-	1	1	-	-	-	Maryborough
276	160	436	312	237	549	321	254	575	57	56	114	17	13	30	-	-	-	-	-	-	Monaghan.
391	212	603	355	259	614	355	[illegible]	623	74	61	135	37	83	[illegible]	1	-	1	-	-	-	Mullingar.
285	227	512	375	280	651	383	293	676	91	64	155	30	38	[illegible]	-	-	-	-	-	-	Omagh.
801	668	1069	686	737	1423	686	751	1437	160	188	348	37	31	68	3	-	3	-	-	-	Richmond.
225	176	401	286	202	487	282	220	502	61	54	115	27	19	46	-	-	-	-	-	-	Sligo.
137	151	308	191	181	372	187	204	391	32	61	92	12	20	32	-	-	-	-	-	-	Waterford.

No. 2.—Table showing the length of Residence in Asylums of Patients

Asylums.	Months.														
	Under 1.			1 to 3.			3 to 6.			6 to 9.			9 to 12.		
	M.	F.	T.	M.	F.	T.	M.	F.	T.	M.	F.	T.	M.	F.	T.
Armagh, . .	–	–	–	3	1	4	5	5	10	7	3	10	1	3	4
Ballinasloe, . .	–	–	–	11	4	15	8	7	15	6	6	12	7	5	12
Belfast, . .	–	–	–	17	11	28	14	15	29	9	7	16	3	3	6
Carlow, .		–	–	5	3	8	4	4	8	3	2	5	3	3	6
Castlebar, . .	–	–	–	7	3	10	4	7	11	1	2	3	–	2	2
Clonmel, .	–	–	–	9	5	14	4	3	7	2	4	6	1	1	2
Cork, . . .	–	1	1	8	6	14	4	13	17	7	14	21	3	5	8
Down, . .	3	1	4	11	11	22	8	13	21	5	3	13	6	2	8
Ennis, . . .	–	–	–	1	5	6	4	3	7	1	–	1	1	1	2
Enniscorthy, .	6	2	8	5	5	10	4	5	9	2	3	5	1	2	3
Kilkenny, . .	–	1	1	7	1	8	3	8	11	2	3	5	2	1	3
Killarney, . .	–	–	–	2	2	4	6	9	15	2	–	2	2	2	4
Letterkenny, .	–	–	–	1	1	2	9	7	16	5	5	10	3	–	3
Limerick, . .	1	–	1	6	4	10	2	7	9	3	4	7	–	1	1
Londonderry, .	–	–	–	11	3	14	8	7	15	–	4	4	1	3	4
Maryborough, .	–	–	–	4	2	6	5	4	9	1	6	7	1	1	2
Monaghan, . .	–	–	–	6	3	9	8	6	14	–	1	1	1	1	2
Mullingar, . .	–	–	–	8	6	14	10	6	16	10	10	20	5	3	8
Omagh, . .	1	1	2	21	10	31	14	14	28	10	5	15	1	1	2
Richmond, . .	3	–	3	10	3	13	29	21	50	11	27	38	16	14	30
Sligo, . . .	–	–		8	5	13	11	7	18	3	4	7	2	1	3
Waterford, . .	1	–	1	5	6	11	5	6	11	1	5	6	–	1	1
Total, . .	17	6	23	104	100	204	169	177	346	91	122	213	60	59	119

Discharged Recovered during the Year ending 31st December, 1883.

Years.															Asylums.
1 to 2.			2 to 3.			3 to 5.			5 to 7.			7 to 10.			
M.	F.	T.	M.	F.	T.	M.	F.	T.	M.	F.	T.	M.	F.	T.	
6	–	6	–	–	–	–	–	–	–	–	–	–	–	–	Armagh.
6	4	10	3	1	4	2	2	4	1	–	1	1	–	1	Ballinasloe.
1	3	4	1	–	1	1	–	1	–	–	–	–	–	–	Belfast.
2	2	4	–	–	–	1	–	1	–	–	–	–	–	–	Carlow.
1	1	2	1	–	1	–	–	–	–	–	–	–	–	–	Castlebar.
4	2	6	1	1	2	–	–	–	–	1	1	–	–	–	Clonmel.
4	4	8	2	1	3	2	–	2	–	1	1	–	–	–	Cork.
5	6	11	3	1	4	1	1	2	–	2	2	–	1	1	Down.
1	1	2	1	–	1	–	2	2	–	–	–	–	–	–	Ennis.
2	–	2	1	1	2		1	1	–	2	2	–	–	–	Enniscorthy
5	2	7	1	1	2	1	–	1	–	2	2	–	2	2	Kilkenny.
1	3	4	1	2	3	–	–	–	–	–	–	–	–	–	Killarney.
6	3	9	1	1	2	1	–	1	–	–	–	–	–	–	Letterkenny.
1	1	2	–	–	–	–	–	–	–	–	–	–	–	–	Limerick.
7	5	12	2	1	3	1	–	1	1	–	1	–	1	1	Londonderry.
–	1	1	1	1	2	1	1	2	1	–	1	–	–	–	Maryborough.
2	1	3	1	1	2	–	–	–	–	–	–	–	–	–	Monaghan.
2	2	4	3	2	5	1	1	2	–	–	–	–	2	2	Mullingar.
2	3	5	–	1	1	1	–	1	–	–	–	–	1	1	Omagh.
12	9	21	6	4	10	–	1	1	3	–	3	–	1	1	Richmond.
2	2	4	–	–	–	1	–	1	1	–	1	–	–	–	Sligo.

No. 2.—Table showing the length of Residence in Asylums of Patients Discharged Recovered during the Year ended 31st December, 1885—*con.*

Asylums.	Years.									Total.		
	10 to 12.			12 to 15.			15 to 20.					
	M.	F.	T.	M.	F.	T.	M.	F.	T.	M.	F.	T.
Armagh,	–	–	–	–	–	–	–	–	–	23	11	34
Ballinasloe,	–	–	–	–	–	–	–	–	–	40	35	75
Belfast,	–	–	–	–	–	–	–	–	–	46	39	85
Carlow,	–	1	1	–	–	–	–	–	–	18	15	33
Castlebar,	–	–	–	–	–	–	–	–	–	14	15	29
Clonmel,	–	–	–	–	–	–	–	–	–	21	17	38
Cork,	–	–	–	–	–	–	–	–	–	30	45	75
Down,	–	–	–	–	–	–	–	–	–	42	45	87
Ennis,	–	–	–	–	–	–	–	–	–	9	12	21
Enniscorthy,	–	2	2	–	1	1	–	–	–	21	24	45
Kilkenny,	–	1	1	–	1	1	–	–	–	21	23	44
Killarney,	–	–	–	–	–	–	–	–	–	14	18	32
Letterkenny,	–	–	–	–	–	–	–	–	–	26	17	43
Limerick,	–	–	–	–	–	–	–	–	–	13	17	30
Londonderry,	–	–	–	–	–	–	–	–	–	31	24	55
Maryborough,	–	–	–	–	–	–	–	–	–	14	16	30
Monaghan,	–	–	–	–	–	–	–	–	–	18	13	31
Mullingar,	–	–	–	–	–	–	–	–	–	37	32	69
Omagh,	–	–	–	–	–	–	–	–	–	50	30	80
Richmond,	–	–	–	–	–	–	–	–	–	92	80	172
Sligo,	–	–	–	–	–	–	–	–	–	28	19	47
Waterford,	–	–	–	–	–	–	–	–	–	12	20	32
Total,	–	4	4	–	2	2	–	–	–	625	571	1,196

No. 8.—Table showing the length of Residence of Patients who Died in District Lunatic Asylums during the Year ended 31st December, 1865.

Asylums.	Months.															Years.		
	Under 1.			1 to 3.			3 to 6.			6 to 9.			9 to 12.			1 to 2.		
	M.	F.	T.	M.	F.	T.	M.	F.	T.	M.	F.	T.	M.	F.	T.	M.	F.	T.
Armagh,	1	–	1	1	–	1	–	–	–	–	1	1	–	2	2	2	3	5
Ballinasloe,	–	–	–	1	–	1	2	2	4	1	1	2	2	2	4	6	4	10
Belfast,	1	2	3	–	–	–	3	–	3	1	1	2	–	–	–	3	–	3
Carlow,	–	–	–	1	1	2	–	–	–	–	–	–	1	1	2	1	2	3
Castlebar,	–	–	–	2	2	4	–	1	1	–	1	1	–	2	2	6	3	9
Clonmel,	2	–	2	2	–	2	3	–	3	1	–	1	–	–	–	2	1	3
Cork,	2	2	4	1	1	2	4	2	6	2	1	3	2	2	4	3	8	11
Down,	–	1	1	–	–	–	–	2	2	–	–	–	1	1	2	3	1	4
Ennis,	2	–	2	–	–	–	1	1	2	–	–	–	–	–	–	–	1	1
Enniscorthy,	–	–	–	1	–	1	–	–	–	1	–	1	–	–	–	–	2	2
Kilkenny,	1	1	2	1	1	2	2	–	2	–	–	–	–	–	–	3	–	3
Killarney,	1	1	2	1	1	2	1	2	3	–	–	–	–	1	1	2	4	6
Letterkenny,	2	2	4	3	1	4	2	2	4	2	–	2	2	1	3	3	8	11
Limerick,	2	1	3	–	–	–	4	1	5	1	–	1	–	–	–	–	6	6
Londonderry,	–	2	2	1	–	1	2	2	4	–	1	1	–	–	–	1	–	1
Maryborough,	–	2	2	1	2	3	1	–	1	2	1	3	–	2	2	3	3	6
Monaghan,	–	1	1	2	–	2	1	1	2	1	–	1	1	1	2	3	1	4
Mullingar,	2	–	2	2	1	3	2	3	5	–	1	1	1	–	1	1	–	1
Omagh,	3	3	6	1	–	1	1	–	1	1	1	2	1	1	2	1	4	5
Richmond,	9	2	11	2	–	2	5	6	11	7	3	10	13	6	19	13	11	24
Sligo,	1	3	4	2	3	5	1	–	1	4	–	4	–	1	1	1	2	3
Waterford,	1	–	1	1	–	1	–	2	2	2	–	2	–	2	2	1	3	4
Total,	30	23	53	16	13	29	37	27	64	24	15	39	21	25	46	57	67	124

[continued.

No. 3.—TABLE showing the length of Residence of
Year ended 31st

ASYLUMS.	YEARS.																	
	2 to 3.			3 to 5.			5 to 7.			7 to 10.			10 to 12.			12 to 15.		
	M.	F.	T.	M.	F.	T.	M.	F.	T.	M.	F.	T.	M.	F.	T.	M.	F.	T.
Armagh,	–	1	1	3	2	5	–	–	–	1	–	1	–	–	–	–	–	–
Ballinasloe,	8	2	10	4	8	12	1	2	3	1	2	3	2	1	3	2	–	2
Belfast,	–	–	–	–	1	1	–	–	–	1	–	1	1	1	2	1	5	6
Carlow,	1	–	1	1	1	2	1	1	2	1	–	1	–	–	–	–	1	1
Castlebar,	4	–	4	–	1	1	–	1	1	2	1	3	–	2	2	1	1	2
Clonmel,	3	2	5	1	1	2	4	–	4	–	–	–	–	–	–	–	–	–
Cork,	10	1	11	6	9	15	5	9	14	1	2	3	–	2	2	–	1	1
Down,	2	1	3	–	–	–	–	1	1	1	–	1	1	–	1	1	–	1
Ennis,	2	–	2	2	1	3	1	1	2	1	1	2	2	–	2	–	1	1
Enniscorthy,	2	–	2	–	–	–	3		3	1	–	1	1	1	2	–	–	–
Kilkenny,	2	2	4	2	–	2	2	–	2	2	–	2	2	–	2	–	–	
Killarney,	–	2	2	5	2	7	2	1	3	2	2	4	–	–	–	1	–	1
Letterkenny,	4	2	6	3	8	11	1	3	4	3	–	3	2	–	2	–	–	–
Limerick,	3	3	6	6	3	9	2	1	3	2	–	2	1	1	2	1	2	3
Londonderry,	–	2	2	1	–	1	–	1	1	1	–	1	1	2	3	2	1	3
Maryborough,	1	1	2	–	–	–	–	1	1	2	1	3	–	–	–	2	2	4
Monaghan,	1	2	3	4	2	6	1	4	5	3	2	5	1	–	1	–	1	1
Mullingar,	1	3	4	2	3	5	–	–	–	1	2	3	2	–	2	–	1	1
Omagh,	1	2	3	3	1	4	1	1	2	1	3	4	3	–	3	–	1	1
Richmond,	9	7	16	9	8	17	2	3	5	2	2	4	2	–	2	3	1	4
Sligo,	4	4	8	4	–	4	–	–	–	1	–	1	1	–	1	1	–	1
Waterford,	–	3	3	1	1	2	–	–	–	2	1	3	2	2	4	–	–	–
Total,	58	45	103	58	52	110	26	30	56	37	12	51	25	12	37	15	15	30

Patients who Died in District Lunatic Asylums during the ... December, 1885—*continued.*

15 to 20.			20 to 25.			25 to 30.			30 to 35.			35 to 40.			Of doubtful ages or not ascertained.			Total			Asylums.
M.	F.	T.	M.	F.	T.	M.	F.	T.	M.	F.	T.	M.	F.	T.	M.	F.	T.	M.	F.	T.	
-	-	-	-	1	1	-	-	-	-	-	-	-	-	-	-	-	-	8	10	18	Armagh.
1	-	1	-	1	1	1	1	2	2	-	2	-	1	1	-	2	2	34	29	63	Ballinasloe.
-	-	-	1	-	1	-	-	-	-	-	-	1	2	3	-	-	-	12	9	21	Belfast.
1	-	1	-	-	-	1	-	1	-	1	1	-	-	-	-	-	-	9	8	17	Carlow.
2	3	5	-	-	-	-	-	-	-	-	-	-	-	-	-	-	-	17	18	35	Castlebar.
-	1	1	1	2	3	-	-	-	-	-	-	-	-	-	-	1	1	19	8	27	Clonmel.
-	4	4	-	1	1	1	1	2	-	1	1	-	-	-	-	-	-	37	30	67	Cork.
3	1	4	-	-	-	-	-	-	-	-	-	-	-	-	-	-	-	12	8	20	Down.
2	1	3	-	-	-	-	-	-	-	-	-	-	-	-	-	-	-	13	7	20	Ennis.
1	1	2	-	-	-	-	-	-	-	-	-	-	-	-	-	-	-	10	4	14	Enniscorthy.
-	-	-	1	-	1	-	1	1	2	1	3	-	-	-	-	-	-	21	6	27	Kilkenny.
-	1	1	1	-	1	1	-	1	1	1	2	-	-	-	-	-	-	18	18	36	Killarney.
-	1	1	-	-	-	-	-	-	-	-	-	-	-	-	-	-	-	27	28	55	Letterkenny.
2	4	6	1	-	1	3	-	3	-	-	-	-	-	-	-	-	-	23	28	51	Limerick.
1	-	1	1	-	1	-	-	-	-	-	-	-	-	-	-	-	-	11	11	22	Londonderry.
3	-	3	-	2	2	-	1	1	-	-	-	-	-	-	-	-	-	14	18	32	Maryborough.
2	-	2	-	-	-	-	-	-	-	-	-	-	-	-	-	-	-	20	15	35	Monaghan.
-	-	-	-	1	1	1	1	2	-	-	-	-	-	-	-	-	-	15	17	32	Mullingar.
6	-	6	1	-	1	1	1	2	-	1	1	-	-	-	-	-	-	25	19	44	Omagh.
3	2	5	-	-	-	3	-	3	-	-	-	-	-	-	-	1	1	83	54	137	Richmond.
2	-	2	-	-	-	2	1	3	-	-	-	-	-	-	-	-	-	24	14	38	Sligo.
-	-	-	-	1	1	-	-	-	-	-	-	-	-	-	-	-	-	8	17	25	Waterford.
27	19	46	7	9	16	14	7	21	5	5	10	1	3	4	-	4	4	466	390	856	Total.

No. 4.—Table showing in Quinquennial Periods the Ages of those Admitted

Asylums.	Years.																	
	5 to 10.			10 to 15.			15 to 20.			20 to 25.			25 to 30.			30 to 35.		
	M.	F.	T.	M.	F.	T.	M.	F.	T.	M.	F.	T.	M.	F.	T.	M.	F.	T.
Armagh, . .	–	–	–	–	–	–	6	2	8	3	6	9	2	4	6	5	10	15
Ballinasloe, .	1	–	1	1	1	2	8	2	10	5	4	9	22	16	38	20	10	30
Belfast, . .	–	–	–	–	–	–	7	6	13	21	9	30	12	19	31	20	11	31
Carlow, . .	–	–	–	–	–	–	2	2	4	7	5	12	5	4	9	6	4	10
Castlebar, .	–	–	–	1	–	1	–	5	5	10	4	14	7	9	16	7	4	11
Clonmel, . .	–	–	–	–	–	–	3	–	3	[illegible]	5	17	7	[illegible]	14	[illegible]	5	10
Cork, . .	–	–	–	2	–	2	8	6	14	30	17	47	26	5	31	16	27	33
Down, . .	1	–	1	–	–	–	6	4	10	8	8	16	5	7	12	10	5	15
Ennis, . .	–	–	–	–	–	–	2	3	5	3	5	8	6	2	8	6	3	9
Enniscorthy, .	–	–	–	–	–	–	4	2	6	3	5	8	8	4	12	4	1	5
Kilkenny, .	–	–	–	–	1	1	1	4	5	5	2	7	7	1	8	5	4	9
Killarney, .	–	–	–	–	–	–	4	5	9	6	11	17	6	3	9	3	3	6
Letterkenny, .	–	–	–	–	–	–	3	4	7	3	3	6	7	7	14	14	4	18
Limerick, .	–	–	–	1	1	2	2	2	4	12	6	18	9	8	17	6	10	16
Londonderry, .	–	–	–	–	1	1	4	6	10	6	6	12	4	4	8	3	4	7
Maryborough, .	–	–	–	1	–	1	2	4	6	4	3	7	6	8	14	5	5	10
Monaghan, .	–	–	–	1	–	1	4	3	7	9	10	19	8	8	16	10	7	17
Mullingar, .	–	–	–	–	–	–	4	2	6	10	8	18	12	13	25	7	6	13
Omagh, . .	–	–	–	1	–	1	8	2	10	13	11	24	10	13	23	7	4	11
Richmond, .	1	–	1	3	1	4	16	11	27	28	24	52	32	36	68	27	28	55
Sligo, . .	–	–	–	–	–	–	3	6	9	14	8	22	8	4	12	12	7	19
Waterford, .	–	–	–	–	–	–	4	5	9	5	6	11	5	12	17	6	4	10
Total, .	3	–	3	12	5	17	105	83	188	216	169	385	216	198	414	201	178	379

into District Lunatic Asylums during the year ending the 31st December, 1885.

Years. 35 to 40.			40 to 45.			45 to 50.			50 to 55.			55 to 60.			60 to 65.			Asylums.
M.	F.	T.	M.	F.	T.	M.	F.	T.	M.	F.	T.	M.	F.	T.	M.	F.	T.	
3	5	8	5	3	8	–	3	3	4	3	7	1	1	2	2	5	7	Armagh.
16	5	21	14	4	18	4	10	14	3	2	5	2	1	3	6	2	8	Ballinasloe.
7	12	19	5	9	14	6	10	16	11	3	14	6	1	7	1	4	5	Belfast.
1	4	5	3	4	7	2	2	4	2	3	5	4	–	4	3	2	5	Carlow.
2	5	7	5	4	9	8	2	10	2	1	3	2	1	3	4	2	6	Castlebar.
11	5	16	5	5	10	9	3	12	1	–	1	1	2	3	2	–	2	Clonmel.
10	16	26	7	24	31	8	13	21	7	14	21	2	4	6	4	6	10	Cork.
5	8	13	2	12	14	2	3	5	–	4	4	2	1	3	3	1	4	Down.
3	1	4	3	3	6	2	3	5	2	2	4	–	–	–	3	3	6	Ennis.
4	3	7	9	6	15	6	2	8	1	3	4	1	1	2	2	3	5	Enniscorthy.
3	2	5	6	7	13	6	2	8	3	4	7	–	2	2	–	5	5	Kilkenny.
6	3	9	5	5	10	7	2	9	4	6	10	4	1	5	1	–	1	Killarney.
6	5	11	4	6	10	7	2	9	1	5	6	–	1	1	4	2	6	Letterkenny.
9	2	11	7	5	12	9	8	17	2	6	8	–	1	1	2	4	6	Limerick.
6	5	11	4	7	11	6	3	9	4	4	8	5	1	6	3	3	6	Londonderry.
2	6	8	6	2	8	5	2	7	1	5	6	2	2	4	2	2	4	Maryborough.
7	9	16	4	8	12	5	8	13	5	–	5	2	2	4	–	1	1	Monaghan.
5	10	15	8	3	11	7	8	15	3	3	6	2	4	6	–	1	1	Mullingar.
10	6	16	9	5	14	8	6	14	6	7	13	6	6	12	8	3	11	Omagh.
19	29	48	24	27	51	11	18	29	17	21	38	8	9	17	5	7	12	Richmond.
8	4	12	4	8	12	5	3	8	2	4	6	–	4	4	4	5	9	Sligo.
4	7	11	2	6	8	4	9	13	1	2	3	2	5	7	–	2	2	Waterford.
147	146	293	135	169	304	127	122	249	87	108	195	51	50	101	59	63	122	Total.

[continued

No. 4.—Table showing in Quinquennial Periods the ages of those Admitted into District Lunatic Asylums during the Year ending the 31st December, 1885—*continued.*

Asylums.	Years.																		Total.		
	65 to 70			70 to 75.			75 to 80.			80 to 85.			85 to 90.			Unknown					
	M.	F.	T.	M.	F.	T.	M.	F.	T.	M.	F.	T.	M.	F.	T.	M.	F.	T.	M.	F.	T.
Armagh,	1	-	1	1	1	2	-	-	-	-	-	-	-	-	-	-	1	1	31	46	77
Ballinasloe,	1	-	1	1	1	2	-	-	-	-	-	-	-	-	-	-	-	-	110	61	171
Belfast,	1	3	4	2	-	2	-	-	-	-	-	-	-	-	-	8	1	9	110	89	199
Carlow,	2	1	3	2	1	3	-	-	-	-	-	-	-	-	-	-	-	-	37	34	71
Castlebar,	4	-	4	2	1	3	-	-	-	1	-	1	-	-	-	-	-	-	55	33	88
Clonmel,	2	2	4	1	2	3	2	1	3	-	-	-	-	-	-	-	1	1	57	47	104
Cork,	1	1	2	1	3	4	-	-	-	-	-	-	-	-	-	9	9	18	126	139	265
Down,	2	1	3	-	-	-	-	-	-	-	-	-	-	-	-	1	-	1	69	38	107
Ennis,	1	-	1	-	1	1	-	1	1	-	-	-	-	-	-	-	-	-	31	27	58
Enniscorthy,	3	-	3	1	1	2	1	-	1	-	-	-	-	-	-	-	-	-	47	31	78
Kilkenny,	1	1	2	-	-	-	1	-	1	-	-	-	-	-	-	-	-	-	35	33	68
Killarney,	-	-	-	-	1	1	-	-	-	-	1	1	-	-	-	2	1	3	48	46	94
Letterkenny,	3	-	3	-	1	1	-	-	-	-	-	-	-	-	-	3	4	7	54	[illegible]	108
Limerick,	-	-	-	1	2	3	-	-	-	-	-	-	-	-	-	-	-	-	58	59	117
Londonderry,	1	-	1	-	2	2	-	1	1	-	-	-	-	-	-	1	-	1	49	46	95
Maryborough,	3	3	6	1	2	3	-	-	-	-	-	-	-	1	1	-	-	-	38	41	79
Monaghan,	3	2	5	3	-	3	-	-	-	-	-	-	-	-	-	-	-	-	60	58	118
Mullingar,	3	1	4	-	1	1	-	1	1	-	-	-	-	-	-	8	-	8	71	64	135
Omagh,	2	1	3	1	1	2	-	-	-	-	-	-	-	-	-	1	-	1	92	65	157
Richmond,	4	1	5	3	2	5	-	1	1	-	-	-	-	-	-	19	16	35	217	236	453
Sligo,	-	2	2	-	2	2	-	-	-	-	-	-	-	-	-	-	-	-	83	36	119
Waterford,	-	3	3	1	2	3	-	-	-	-	-	-	-	-	-	-	-	-	34	[illegible]	97
Total,	38	22	60	31	16	47	4	5	9	1	1	2	-	1	1	33	34	67	1176	1137	[illegible]

No. 5.—Table showing in Quinquennial Periods the Ages of those who were Discharged Recovered during the Year ending 31st December, 1885.

Asylums.	Years.																	
	5 to 10.			10 to 15.			15 to 20.			20 to 25.			25 to 30.			30 to 35.		
	M.	F.	T.	M.	F.	T.	M.	F.	T.	M.	F.	T.	M.	F.	T.	M.	F.	T.
Armagh,	–	–	–	–	–	–	3	1	4	5	1	6	2	1	3	2	1	3
Ballinasloe,	–	–	–	–	–	–	4	3	7	7	5	12	11	3	14	5	5	10
Belfast,	–	–	–	–	–	–	3	3	6	4	6	10	7	9	16	8	3	11
Carlow,	–	–	–	–	–	–	–	1	1	3	3	6	3	2	5	2	2	4
Castlebar,	–	–	–	–	–	–	–	4	4	2	–	2	2	4	6	2	2	4
Clonmel,	–	–	–	–	–	–	1	–	1	3	4	7	5	5	10	–	–	–
Cork,	–	–	–	–	–	–	4	5	9	8	8	16	3	3	6	2	7	9
Down,	–	–	–	–	–	–	3	1	4	4	4	8	3	4	7	–	5	5
Ennis,	–	–	–	–	–	–	2	2	4	1	3	4	1	2	3	1	1	2
Enniscorthy,	–	–	–	–	–	–	1	–	1	3	2	5	4	2	6	4	4	8
Kilkenny,	–	–	–	–	–	–	–	1	1	3	–	3	2	2	4	5	2	7
Killarney,	–	–	–	–	–	–	1	2	3	1	3	4	–	2	2	4	3	7
Letterkenny,	–	–	–	–	–	–	1	4	5	3	–	3	5	2	7	3	2	5
Limerick,	–	–	–	–	–	–	1	5	6	5	3	8	–	2	2	–	4	4
Londonderry,	–	–	–	–	–	–	2	1	3	6	1	7	2	4	6	3	3	6
Maryborough,	–	–	–	–	–	–	–	–	–	4	3	7	1	2	3	1	4	5
Monaghan,	–	–	–	–	1	1	2	2	4	4	–	4	2	6	8	3	4	7
Mullingar,	–	–	–	1	1	2	–	2	2	7	6	13	7	6	13	5	2	7
Omagh,	–	–	–	–	–	–	2	3	5	10	4	14	6	4	10	4	6	10
Richmond,	–	–	–	–	1	1	4	8	12	14	15	29	11	5	16	15	12	27
Sligo,	–	–	–	–	–	–	5	2	7	4	4	8	7	2	9	6	2	8
Waterford,	–	–	–	–	–	–	1	–	1	1	1	2	4	2	6	4	3	7
Total,	–	–	–	1	5	6	39	50	89	101	75	176	87	73	160	81	75	156

[continued.

No. 5.—Table showing in Quinquennial Periods the Ages of those who were

Asylums.	Years.																	
	25 to 30.			30 to 35.			35 to 40.			40 to 45.			45 to 50.			50 to 55.		
	M.	F.	T.	M.	F.	T.	M.	F.	T.	M.	F.	T.	M.	F.	T.	M.	F.	T.
Armagh,	2	–	2	–	2	2	2	3	5	2	1	3	–	–	–	2	2	4
Ballinasloe,	3	6	9	4	2	6	3	2	5	4	2	6	2	1	3	2	–	2
Belfast,	4	7	11	3	4	7	4	3	7	5	1	6	1	–	1	–	2	2
Carlow,	4	2	6	1	1	2	1	1	2	–	–	–	1	2	3	–	–	–
Castlebar,	2	1	3	2	1	3	1	–	1	1	1	2	–	1	1	2	–	2
Clonmel,	5	2	7	3	1	4	5	2	7	1	–	1	–	–	–	–	–	–
Cork,	3	5	8	1	5	6	–	4	4	3	3	6	–	–	–	1	1	2
Down,	11	5	16	5	11	16	2	5	7	4	2	6	4	4	8	3	1	4
Ennis,	–	1	1	2	–	2	–	–	–	–	2	2	–	–	–	–	–	–
Enniscorthy,	3	4	7	4	2	6	–	2	2	1	1	2	1	–	1	1	3	4
Kilkenny,	2	1	3	4	4	8	1	3	4	2	4	6	1	4	5	–	2	2
Killarney,	2	1	3	2	4	6	3	3	6	–	–	–	1	–	1	–	–	–
Letterkenny,	5	2	7	3	4	7	2	–	2	–	1	1	–	–	–	2	1	3
Limerick,	2	–	2	2	–	2	3	5	8	1	–	1	–	–	–	1	–	1
Londonderry,	5	3	8	3	3	6	2	3	5	5	5	10	4	–	4	–	–	–
Maryborough,	2	–	2	2	2	4	3	1	4	–	–	–	–	–	–	–	–	–
Monaghan,	2	1	3	–	1	1	–	1	1	2	1	3	1	1	2	–	–	–
Mullingar,	6	8	14	3	1	4	2	2	4	3	3	6	–	1	1	1	–	1
Omagh,	3	5	8	4	7	11	4	–	4	6	3	9	5	3	8	4	3	6
Richmond,	10	11	21	14	10	24	4	6	10	4	3	7	2	4	6	2	–	2
Sligo,	1	2	3	2	3	5	1	1	2	–	–	–	1	1	2	1	–	1
Waterford,	1	6	7	–	4	4	1	3	4	–	–	–	–	–	–	–	–	–
Total,	65	69	134	67	73	140	41	50	91	40	33	73	25	23	48	21	15	36

Discharged Recovered during the Year ending 31st December,

Years.																		Total.		
65 to 70.			70 to 75.			75 to 80.			80 to 85.			85 to 90.			Unknown.					
M.	F.	T.	M.	F.	T.	M.	F.	T.	M.	F.	T.	M.	F.	T.	M.	F.	T.	M.	F.	T.
1	-	1	1	-	1	-	-	-	-	-	-	-	-	-	-	-	-	22	17	
-	-	-	1	-	1	-	-	-	-	-	-	-	-	-	-	-	-	46	29	
-	-	-	-	1	1	-	-	-	-	-	-	-	-	-	5	-	5	46	39	
-	1	1	-	-	-	-	-	-	-	-	-	-	-	-	-	-	-	18	15	
-	-	-	-	1	1	-	-	-	-	-	-	-	-	-	-	-	-	14	15	
-	1	1	-	-	-	-	-	-	-	-	-	-	-	-	-	-	-	21	17	
-	-	-	-	-	-	-	1	1	-	-	-	-	-	-	-	5	5	30	45	
-	1	1	1	2	3	-	-	-	-	-	-	-	-	-	1	-	1	42	45	
-	-	-	-	1	1	-	-	-	-	-	-	-	-	-	2	-	2	9	12	
-	2	2	-	-	-	1	-	1	-	-	-	-	-	-	-	-	-	21	24	
1	-	1	-	-	-	-	-	-	-	-	-	-	-	-	-	-	-	21	23	
-	-	-	-	-	-	-	-	-	-	-	-	-	-	-	-	-		14	16	
1	-	1	-	1	1	-	-	-	-	-	-	-	-	-	1	-	1	25	17	
1	-	1	-	-	-	-	-	-	-	-	-	-	-	-	-	-	-	13	17	
2	-	2	-	-	-	-	-	-	-	-	-	-	-	-	-	-	-	31	24	
1	2	3	-	1	1	-	-	-	-	-	-	-	1	1	-	-	-	14	16	
-	-	-	-	-	-	-	-	-	-	-	-	-	-	-	1	-	1	18	13	
-	-	-	-	-	-	-	-	-	-	-	-	-	-	-	-	1	1	37	32	
-	1	1	-	-	-	-	-	-	-	-	-	-	-	-	1	-	1	30	39	
-	1	1	-	-	-	-	-	-	-	-	-	-	-	-	12	4	16	92	80	
-	1	1	-	1	1	-	-	-	-	-	-	-	-	-	-	-	-	28	19	
-	1	1	-	-	-	-	-	-	-	-	-	-	-	-	-	-	-	12	20	

No. 6.—Table showing in Quinquennial Periods the Ages
Year ending the 31st

Asylums.	Years.																	
	5 to 10.			10 to 15.			15 to 20.			20 to 25.			25 to 30.			30 to 35.		
	M.	F.	T.	M.	F.	T.	M.	F.	T.	M.	F.	T.	M.	F.	T.	M.	F.	T.
Armagh, . .	–	–	–	–	–	–	1	–	1	1	–	1	–	1	1	1	–	1
Ballinasloe, .	–	–	–	1	–	1	1	–	1	3	3	6	4	3	7	3	3	[illegible]
Belfast, . .	–	–	–	–	–	–	–	–	–	2	–	2	–	–	–	1	–	1
Carlow, . .	–	–	–	–	–	–	–	–	–	–	–	–	1	–	1	1	1	2
Castlebar, .	–	–	–	–	–	–	1	1	2	3	3	6	2	1	3	1	1	2
Clonmel, . .	–	–	–	–	–	–	1	–	1	3	–	3	3	1	4	–	–	–
Cork, . .	–	–	–	–	–	–	–	1	1	1	2	3	7	6	13	6	6	12
Down, . .	–	–	–	–	–	–	–	–	–	–	–	–	1	1	2	–	1	1
Ennis, . .	–	–	–	–	–	–	–	–	–	–	–	–	1	2	3	3	–	3
Enniscorthy, .	–	–	–	–	–	–	–	–	–	–	–	–	–	–	–	2	1	3
Kilkenny, .	–	–	–	–	–	–	–	–	–	2	–	2	1	1	2	2	–	2
Killarney, .	–	–	–	–	–	–	–	–	–	–	2	2	3	4	7	2	1	3
Letterkenny, .	–	–	–	–	–	–	1	–	1	5	5	10	3	5	8	4	[illegible]	4
Limerick, .	–	–	–	–	–	–	–	–	–	3	–	3	2	5	7	1	[illegible]	1
Londonderry, .	–	–	–	–	–	–	–	–	–	[illegible]	1	2	1	1	2	–	1	1
Maryborough, .	–	–	–	–	–	–	–	1	1	–	3	3	–	–	–	3	1	4
Monaghan, .	–	–	–	–	–	–	1	–	1	1	2	3	3	2	5	–	1	1
Mullingar, .	–	–	–	–	–	–	2	–	2	1	1	2	3	–	3	–	–	–
Omagh, . .	–	–	–	–	–	–	–	–	–	–	2	2	2	1	3	2	1	3
Richmond, .	–	–	–	2	1	3	1	1	2	7	6	13	13	10	23	10	5	15
Sligo, . .	–	–	–	1	–	1	1	1	2	1	3	4	4	–	4	1	–	
Waterford, .	–	–	–	–	–	–	2	–	2	–	–	–	–	1	1	1	2	3
Total,	–	–	–	4	1	5	12	5	17	34	33	67	52	43	95	41	[illegible]	71

of those who Died in District Lunatic Asylums during the
December, 1885.

Years.																	
35 to 40.			40 to 45.			45 to 50.			50 to 55.			55 to 60.			60 to 65.		
M.	F.	T.	M.	F.	T.	M.	F.	T.	M.	F.	T.	M.	F.	T.	M.	F.	T.
1	–	1	1	2	3	–	2	2	–	1	1	–	–	–	–	4	4
1	2	3	2	2	4	2	3	5	2	4	6	1	2	3	3	–	3
3	–	3	–	1	1	3	1	4	–	1	1	2	1	3	–	1	1
–	1	1	1	–	1	5	3	8	3	–	3	–	–	–	2	1	3
–	4	4	1	–	1	–	3	3		–	–	3	2	5	3	1	4
1		1	2	–	2	2	3	5	1	–	1	1	–	1	2	2	4
5	6	11	3	5	8	4	8	12	4	3	7	–	4	4	2	1	3
1	–	1	4	2	6	1	1	2	3	1	4	–	–	–	1	2	3
1	3	4	–	–	–	–	–	–	2	–	2	2	1	3	2	1	3
1	2	3	1	–	1	2	–	2	–	–	–	1	–	1	–	–	–
1	–	1	3	–	3	1	–	1	3	–	3	2	1	3	1	2	3
5	3	8	3	1	4	1	3	4	3	3	6	–	–	–	1	–	1
2	5	7	3	6	9	1	1	2	1	3	4	1	–	1	2	3	5
1	3	4	2	3	5	8	3	11	2	–	2	–	1	1	3	1	4
1	1	2	1	1	2	1	2	3	1	3	4	1	–	1	3	–	3
2	3	5	2	1	3	–	1	1	–	3	3	3	3	6	2	2	4
3	1	4	–	–	–	3	–	3	3	–	3	2	2	4	4	2	6
2	2	4	2	2	4	–	3	3	1	1	2	1	1	2	–	–	–
1	1	2	4	3	7	3	2	5	4	3	7	1	2	3	2	1	3
11	3	14	9	6	15	4	4	8	8	4	12	4	2	6	4	2	6
2	1	3	3	3	6	3	–	3	1	2	3	1	1	2	1	2	3
1	–	1	1	3	4	1	1	2	1	2	3	–	1	1	–	1	1
26	41	67	49	39	[illegible]	42	42	84	43	35	78	20	34	54	40	33	73

No. 6.—Table Showing in Quinquennial Periods the Ages of those who Died in District Lunatic Asylums during the Year ending the 31st December, 1883—*continued.*

Asylums	Years																		Total		
	65 to 70.			70 to 75.			75 to 80.			80 to 85.			85 to 90.			Unknown.					
	M.	F.	T.	M.	F.	T.	M.	F.	T.	M.	F.	T.	M.	F.	T.	M.	F.	T.	M.	F.	T.
Armagh,	2	-	2	1	-	1	-	-	-	-	-	-	-	-	-	-	-	-	[illegible]	10	18
Ballinasloe,	5	1	6	4	1	5	1	1	2	1	1	2	-	-	-	-	-	-	34	29	63
Belfast,	-	2	2	-	1	1	-	1	1	-	-	-	-	-	-	1	-	1	12	9	21
Carlow,	-	1	1	-	1	1	-	1	1	-	-	-	-	-	-	-	-	-	9	8	17
Castlebar,	-	1	1	2	1	3	-	-	-	1	-	1	-	-	-	-	-	-	17	18	35
Clonmel,	1	-	1	2	-	2	-	1	1	-	-	-	-	-	-	-	-	-	19	8	27
Cork,	1	1	2	-	1	1	2	1	3	-	-	-	-	-	-	2	-	2	37	50	87
Down,	1	-	1	2	-	2	1	-	1	-	-	-	-	-	-	-	-	-	12	8	[illegible]
Ennis,	1	-	1	1	2	3	-	-	-	-	-	-	-	-	-	-	-	-	18	7	[illegible]
Enniscorthy,	2	1	3	-	-	-	-	-	-	1	-	1	-	-	-	-	-	-	16	8	[illegible]
Kilkenny,	1	1	2	1	2	3	1	-	1	-	-	-	-	-	-	-	-	-	21	6	27
Killarney,	1	-	1	1	1	2	-	-	-	-	1	1	-	-	-	-	-	-	18	18	36
Letterkenny,	2	-	2	-	-	-	-	-	-	-	1	1	-	-	-	-	-	-	27	28	55
Limerick,	1	-	1	3	2	5	2	1	3	-	1	1	1	-	1	-	-	-	28	23	51
Londonderry,	1	-	1	-	1	1	-	-	-	-	-	-	-	-	-	-	-	-	12	11	23
Maryborough,	2	-	2	-	-	-	-	-	-	-	-	-	-	-	-	-	-	-	14	18	32
Monaghan,	-	3	3	-	2	2	1	-	1	-	-	-	-	-	-	-	-	-	20	15	35
Mullingar,	1	2	3	2	3	5	-	1	1	-	-	-	-	-	-	-	2	2	15	12	27
Omagh,	4	1	5	-	-	-	-	1	1	-	-	-	-	1	1	-	-	-	25	19	44
Richmond,	6	5	11	1	1	2	-	-	-	-	-	-	-	-	-	6	3	9	82	74	156
Sligo,	3	-	3	-	-	-	-	1	1	-	-	-	-	-	-	-	-	-	20	14	33
Waterford,	1	-	1	-	2	2	-	-	-	-	4	4	-	-	-	-	-	-	8	17	25
Total,	33	19	52	20	20	40	8	9	17	5	6	11	1	1	2	7	7	14	460	360	820

No. 7.—Table showing in Quinquennial Periods the Ages of those remaining in District Lunatic Asylums on 31st December, 1885.

Asylums	Years.																	
	5 to 10.			10 to 15.			15 to 20.			20 to 25.			25 to 30.			30 to 35.		
	M.	F.	T.	M.	F.	T.	M.	F.	T.	M.	F.	T.	M.	F.	T.	M.	F.	T.
Armagh, . .	–	–	–	–	–	–	6	4	10	9	[illegible]	18	13	10	23	13	26	39
Ballinasloe, .	2	–	2	–	2	2	14	3	17	36	16	52	32	[illegible]	83	58	42	100
Belfast, . .	–	–	–	–	–	–	4	6	10	25	16	41	46	[illegible]	73	55	26	81
Carlow, . .	–	–	–	–	–	–	1	–	1	5	[illegible]	13	16	10	26	21	27	48
Castlebar, .	–	–	–	1	–	1	1	2	3	14	10	24	29	20	49	27	20	47
Clonmel, .	–	–	–	–	–	–	2	2	4	5	11	16	14	20	34	33	30	63
Cork, . .	–	–	–	6	–	6	13	7	20	59	51	110	87	58	145	120	121	241
Down, . .	–	–	–	–	1	1	6	4	10	13	9	22	19	11	30	32	12	44
Ennis, . .	–	–	–	–	–	–	3	2	5	11	8	19	15	8	23	21	17	38
Enniscorthy, .	–	–	–	–	1	1	4	2	6	7	4	11	17	4	21	23	9	32
Kilkenny, .	–	–	–	–	1	1	3	3	6	4	8	12	17	7	24	22	16	38
Killarney, .	–	–	–	–	–	–	4	3	7	18	17	35	24	15	39	23	16	39
Letterkenny, .	–	–	–	1	–	1	6	2	8	17	6	23	14	14	28	34	13	47
Limerick, .	–	–	–	2	2	4	2	3	5	10	1	11	10	15	25	30	29	59
Londonderry, .	–	–	–	–	1	1	1	3	3	13	10	23	17	16	33	26	13	39
Maryborough, .	–	–	–	1	–	1	5	2	7	6	3	9	25	11	36	22	14	36
Monaghan, .	–	–	–	2	–	2	5	4	9	24	17	41	36	20	56	13	26	69
Mullingar, .	–	–	–	–	–	–	6	1	7	22	13	35	26	17	43	35	31	66
Omagh, . .	–	–	–	–	–	–	7	2	9	23	11	34	31	22	53	21	20	41
Richmond, .	3	–	3	4	1	5	35	27	62	59	48	107	77	58	135	60	67	127
Sligo, . .					1	1		6		15	7	22	24	20	44	31	17	48
Waterford, .	–	–	–	–	–	–	1	6	7	14	7	21	28	15	43	17	13	30
Total, .	6	–	6	17	10	27	130	94	224	406	308	714	623	440	1,063	762	605	1,367

[continued.

No. 7.—Table showing in Quinquennial Periods the Ages of those

Asylums.	Years.																	
	35 to 40.			40 to 45.			45 to 50.			50 to 55.			55 to 60.			60 to 65.		
	M.	F.	T.	M.	F.	T.	M.	F.	T.	M.	F.	T.	M.	F.	T.	M.	F.	T.
Armagh, .	20	16	36	15	27	42	12	10	22	18	9	27	8	10	18	5	7	[illegible]
Ballinasloe, .	49	46	95	46	25	71	34	20	54	21	14	35	18	10	28	24	11	[illegible]
Belfast, . .	50	35	85	46	31	77	37	26	63	30	27	57	12	13	25	15	9	24
Carlow, . .	16	16	32	27	22	33	27	20	47	17	16	33	11	10	21	2	3	5
Castlebar, .	28	17	45	30	22	52	35	10	45	12	7	23	10	4	14	7	3	10
Clonmel, .	47	46	93	27	47	74	34	23	57	30	31	61	15	8	23	11	7	18
Cork, . .	60	55	115	35	37	72	20	16	36	20	20	40	11	15	26	1	-	1
Down, . .	23	23	46	29	27	56	29	16	45	30	24	54	11	4	15	11	8	19
Ennis, . .	25	18	43	26	22	48	34	19	53	16	11	27	8	6	14	8	9	17
Enniscorthy, .	29	20	49	35	26	61	30	10	40	17	19	36	9	10	19	9	11	20
Kilkenny, .	23	15	38	27	16	43	18	12	30	12	17	29	5	11	16	7	13	20
Killarney, .	28	18	46	29	16	45	16	12	28	18	18	37	16	6	22	12	6	18
Letterkenny, .	38	19	57	34	13	47	29	12	41	18	10	28	12	7	19	13	8	21
Limerick, .	31	36	67	26	35	61	30	20	50	30	35	65	19	21	40	13	10	23
Londonderry, .	14	19	33	29	18	47	19	21	40	27	26	53	14	8	22	13	9	22
Maryborough, .	17	20	37	27	21	48	25	17	42	19	15	34	15	7	22	8	7	15
Monaghan, .	29	27	56	35	29	64	31	27	58	16	13	29	12	10	22	5	8	13
Mullingar, .	38	26	64	30	33	63	25	22	47	42	23	65	19	17	36	6	23	29
Omagh, . .	33	30	63	42	46	88	41	29	70	31	22	53	27	13	40	14	15	29
Richmond, .	62	53	115	61	73	134	34	63	97	37	51	88	25	21	32	6	17	23
Sligo, . .	32	24	56	29	25	54	33	29	62	17	20	37	13	17	30	10	13	23
Waterford, .	16	21	37	16	11	27	24	28	52	14	5	19	11	16	27	10	6	16
Total, .	731	633	1364	707	624	1331	612	478	1090	499	432	931	300	264	564	215	212	[illegible]

remaining in District Lunatic Asylums on 31st December, 1895—*con.*

Years.																		Total			Asylum
65 to 70.			70 to 75.			75 to 80.			80 to 85.			85 to 90.			Unknown.						
M.	F.	T.	M.	F.	T.	M.	F.	T.	M.	F.	T.	M.	F.	T.	M.	F.	T.	M.	F.	T.	
6	5	11	2	1	3	–	1	1	–	–	–	–	–	–	–	6	6	130	142	272	Armagh.
6	–	6	1	–	1	5	–	5	–	–	–	–	–	–	–	–	–	364	224	588	Ballinasloe
12	7	19	2	1	3	2	–	2	3	–	3	–	–	–	3	3	6	343	227	570	Belfast.
2	1	3	1	1	2	–	–	–	–	–	–	–	–	–	–	–	–	147	142	289	Carlow.
9	1	10	1	1	2	–	1	1	–	–	–	–	–	–	–	–	–	215	130	345	Castlebar.
12	4	16	5	8	13	3	2	5	1	2	3	–	–	–	–	–	–	241	246	487	Clonmel.
–	–	–	1	2	3	–	–	–	1	–	1	–	–	–	29	40	69	463	453	916	Cork.
8	4	12	2	1	3	2	–	2	1	–	1	1	1	2	2	5	7	219	153	372	Down.
5	2	7	3	3	6	1	2	3	–	–	–	–	–	–	3	–	3	176	129	305	Ennis.
5	6	11	6	5	11	3	–	3	–	1	1	–	–	–	–	–	–	194	137	331	Enniscorthy.
5	7	12	3	1	4	–	–	–	1	1	2	1	–	1	–	–	–	118	152	270	Kilkenny.
12	6	18	4	3	7	3	1	4	3	–	3	–	–	–	–	–	–	216	141	357	Killarney.
10	4	14	2	1	3	2	–	2	2	–	2	–	–	–	14	6	20	238	119	357	Letterkenny.
10	8	18	3	13	16	–	2	2	–	–	–	–	–	–	–	–	–	237	238	475	Limerick.
4	[illegible]	6	4	8	12	–	4	4	–	–	–	–	–	–	–	–	–	180	138	318	Londonderry.
1	5	6	7	3	10	2	2	4	–	1	1	–	–	–	–	–	–	173	134	307	Maryborough
4	4	8	6	1	7	–	–	–	1	–	1	–	–	–	20	13	33	270	302	572	Monaghan.
9	7	16	2	–	2	1	2	3	–	–	–	–	–	–	18	7	25	293	215	508	Mullingar.
4	14	18	2	6	8	3	–	3	–	–	–	1	–	1	–	6	6	272	275	547	Omagh.
3	1	4	1	4	5	–	2	2	–	–	–	1	1	2	13	13	26	510	571	1081	Richmond.
10	7	17	2	3	5	3	1	4	1	–	1	–	–	–	–	–	–	226	188	414	Sligo.
4	11	15	3	5	8	1	5	6	–	1	1	–	–	–	–	–	–	160	149	309	Waterford.

No. 8.—Table showing the Authority for Admission of Patients, and Number Admitted, during the Year ending 31st December, 1885.

Asylums	Ordinary cases admitted by Order of the Board.			Ordinary cases as urgent by the Physician.			Ordinary cases admitted under the Army Act, 1881 sec. 91.			Soldiers admitted temporarily under the Privy Council Rule, passed 20th April, 1868.			Dangerous Lunatics admitted by Warrant of the Lord Lieutenant.			Admitted from Central Asylum and other District Asylums.			Lunatics charged with Offences, admitted by Warrant of the Lord Lieutenant.			Lunatics detained in default of Recognizance to keep the Peace, by Warrant of the Lord Lieutenant.			Dangerous Lunatics committed by Justices, under the Act 30 & 31 Vic., c. 118.			Paying Patients admitted during the year, under P.C. Rule, upon transmission of form to the Inspectors' Office.			Total admitted during the year ending 31st December, 1885.		
	M.	F.	T.	M.	F.	T.	M.	F.	T.	M.	F.	T.	M.	F.	T.	M.	F.	T.	M.	F.	T.	M.	F.	T.	M.	F.	T.	M.	F.	T.	M.	F.	T.
Armagh,	–	–	–	9	26	35	–	–	–	1	–	1	–	–	–	–	–	–	1	–	1	–	–	–	18	19	37	2	1	3	31	46	77
Ballinasloe,	–	–	–	22	14	36	–	–	–	–	–	–	–	–	–	1	1	2	8	1	9	–	–	–	82	42	124	–	–	–	110	61	171
Belfast,	–	1	1	37	31	68	–	–	–	3	–	3	–	–	–	–	–	–	3	2	5	–	–	–	63	34	97	1	3	4	110	89	199
Carlow,	–	–	–	11	14	25	–	–	–	4	–	4	–	–	–	–	–	–	–	–	–	–	–	–	21	20	41	1	–	1	37	34	71
Castlebar,	10	14	24	–	–	–	–	–	–	–	–	–	–	–	–	1	1	2	1	–	1	–	–	–	40	26	66	–	–	–	55	38	93
Clonmel,	–	–	–	16	20	36	–	–	–	1	–	1	1	–	1	–	–	–	–	–	–	–	–	–	39	27	66	–	–	–	57	47	104
Cork,	7	18	25	37	67	104	2	–	2	4	–	4	2	4	6	–	–	–	–	–	–	–	–	–	71	50	121	–	–	–	138	125	263
Down,	1	1	2	18	40	58	–	–	–	–	–	–	1	–	1	–	–	–	1	–	1	–	–	–	28	17	45	–	–	–	49	58	107
Ennis,	–	1	1	5	6	11	–	–	–	–	–	–	–	1	1	–	–	–	–	–	–	–	–	–	26	17	43	–	–	–	31	27	58
Enniscorthy,	–	–	–	14	11	25	1	–	1	–	–	–	–	2	2	–	–	–	2	–	2	–	–	–	30	18	48	–	–	–	47	31	78
Kilkenny,	–	–	–	10	17	27	–	–	–	1	–	1	–	–	–	–	–	–	–	–	–	–	–	–	24	16	40	–	–	–	35	33	68
Killarney,	–	2	2	10	7	17	–	–	–	1	–	1	–	–	–	1	–	1	–	–	–	–	–	–	36	37	73	–	–	–	45	46	91
Letterkenny,	–	–	–	8	10	18	–	–	–	–	–	–	1	–	1	–	–	–	–	–	–	–	–	–	48	33	81	–	–	–	55	45	100
Limerick,	–	–	–	21	30	51	–	–	–	1	–	1	5	1	6	–	–	–	–	–	–	–	–	–	27	27	54	4	1	5	58	59	117
Londonderry,	1	–	1	16	30	46	–	–	–	1	–	1	–	–	–	–	–	–	–	–	–	–	–	–	30	11	41	1	2	3	49	46	95
Maryborough,	4	5	9	13	17	30	–	–	–	–	–	–	–	–	–	–	1	1	–	–	–	–	–	–	18	17	35	3	1	4	38	41	79
Monaghan,	–	1	1	–	1	1	–	–	–	–	–	–	–	–	–	–	–	–	–	–	–	–	–	–	60	56	116	–	–	–	60	58	118
Mullingar,	1	3	4	8	7	15	–	–	–	–	–	–	3	–	3	1	–	1	–	–	–	–	–	–	59	51	110	–	–	–	74	61	135
Omagh,	–	–	–	16	17	33	–	–	–	–	–	–	–	–	–	–	–	–	3	1	4	1	1	2	72	46	118	–	–	–	92	65	157
Richmond,	7	18	25	6	15	21	–	–	–	3	–	3	–	–	–	5	–	5	14	11	25	–	–	–	181	182	363	1	5	6	217	231	448
Sligo,	–	–	–	8	17	25	–	–	–	–	–	–	–	–	–	–	–	–	2	2	4	–	–	–	53	37	90	–	–	–	63	56	119
Waterford,	–	2	2	19	43	62	–	–	–	–	–	–	3	1	4	–	–	–	–	–	–	–	–	–	12	17	29	–	–	–	34	63	97
Total,	31	63	97	304	460	764	3	–	3	20	–	20	18	8	27	9	3	12	32	20	52	1	1	2	1041	805	1846	13	13	26	1476	1374	2,850

No. 9.—Table showing the Cause of Death of Patients in Irish District Asylums during the Year ending 31st December, 1885.

Asylums.	Abdominal Affections.			Cerebral and Cerebro Spinal Affections.			Thoracic Affections.			Disease of Heart and Arteries.			Debility and Old Age.			Fever and other Diseases.			Accidents, Violence, or Suicide.			Total Deaths.		
	M.	F.	T.	M.	F.	T.	M.	F.	T.	M.	F.	T.	M.	F.	T.	M.	F.	T.	M.	F.	T.	M.	F.	T.
Armagh,	1	1	2	1	3	4	5	3	8	–	–	–	2	3	5	2	–	2	–	–	–	8	10	18
Ballinasloe,	9	1	10	16	11	27	4	9	13	2	1	3	3	7	10	–	–	–	–	–	–	34	29	63
Belfast,	–	–	–	6	5	10	1	3	4	3	2	5	–	2	2	–	–	–	–	–	–	12	9	21
Carlow,	1	–	1	1	3	4	5	–	5	–	3	3	2	2	4	–	–	–	–	–	–	9	8	17
Castlebar,	–	–	–	6	4	10	4	11	15	–	–	–	1	5	6	3	1	4	–	–	–	17	18	35
Clonmel,	1	–	1	9	3	12	3	–	3	1	1	2	1	3	4	4	1	5	–	–	–	19	18	37
Cork,	1	3	4	8	2	10	16	12	28	–	1	1	9	31	40	2	1	3	1	–	1	37	50	87
Down,	1	–	1	10	6	16	–	1	1	1	–	1	–	–	–	–	–	–	–	1	1	12	8	20
Ennis,	3	–	3	1	1	2	3	2	5	–	–	–	6	3	9	1	1	2	–	–	–	13	7	20
Enniscorthy,	1	3	4	1	1	2	4	1	5	1	–	1	2	–	2	–	–	–	–	–	–	10	4	14
Kilkenny,	7	3	10	3	–	3	9	3	12	–	–	–	1	–	1	1	–	1	–	–	–	21	6	27
Killarney,	–	–	–	9	6	15	6	7	13	1	–	1	5	5	10	–	–	–	–	–	–	18	16	34
Letterkenny,	2	–	2	14	17	31	10	9	19	1	–	1	–	3	3	–	–	–	–	–	–	27	26	53
Limerick,	1	2	3	7	3	10	13	14	27	4	1	5	3	2	5	–	–	–	1	–	1	29	22	51
Londonderry,	2	1	3	3	7	10	5	1	6	–	–	–	2	2	4	1	–	1	–	–	–	11	11	22
Maryborough,	2	1	3	5	11	16	6	5	11	–	–	–	1	1	2	–	–	–	–	–	–	14	[illegible]	[illegible]
Monaghan,	–	3	3	7	4	11	10	4	14	1	2	3	2	2	4	–	–	–	–	–	–	20	15	35
Mullingar,	4	5	9	3	2	5	5	3	8	–	3	3	3	3	6	1	1	2	–	–	–	15	17	32
Omagh,	1	1	2	1	–	1	16	7	23	1	–	1	3	7	10	3	3	6	–	1	1	25	19	44
Richmond,	16	7	23	16	12	28	29	20	49	8	3	11	12	14	[illegible]	8	–	8	–	–	–	83	54	137
Sligo,	4	1	5	3	3	6	11	7	18	–	1	1	3	1	4	1	1	2	–	–	–	24	14	38
Waterford,	–	1	1	3	2	5	3	3	6	1	1	2	2	9	11	–	1	1	–	–	–	9	17	26
Total,	57	12	69	133	103	236	162	125	287	23	19	42	61	99	163	25	11	36	2	2	4	465	350	[illegible]

No. 10.—Table showing the Educational Condition of Patients in District Asylums on 31st December, 1885.

Asylums.	Well Educated.			Can Read and Write well.			Can Read and Write indifferently.			Can Read only.			Cannot Read or Write.			Unknown.			Total.		
	M.	F.	T.	M.	F.	T.	M.	F.	T.	M.	F.	T.	M.	F.	T.	M.	F.	T.	M.	F.	T.
Armagh,	24	15	39	12	3	15	41	25	66	16	33	49	27	47	74	10	31	41	130	148	278
Ballinasloe,	40	34	74	158	72	230	90	40	130	20	30	50	60	40	100	–	8	8	354	234	588
Belfast,	25	22	47	46	10	56	110	100	210	15	29	44	44	24	68	64	43	107	323	247	570
Carlow,	18	17	35	40	25	65	26	30	56	17	25	42	23	26	49	18	20	38	140	113	253
Castlebar,	18	11	29	36	19	55	40	28	68	36	21	57	66	48	114	18	4	22	215	130	345
Clonmel,	11	17	28	44	50	94	56	53	109	58	43	101	51	66	117	21	16	37	231	258	489
Cork,	33	10	43	63	58	121	268	240	508	20	35	55	42	52	94	42	55	97	463	453	916
Down,	5	2	7	152	82	234	–	1	1	15	21	36	14	26	40	38	20	58	219	157	376
Ennis,	8	11	19	28	23	51	84	40	124	19	9	28	35	41	76	7	5	12	176	129	305
Enniscorthy,	7	1	8	28	18	46	50	14	64	34	27	61	65	67	132	9	13	22	196	185	381
Kilkenny,	13	7	20	30	20	50	41	47	88	12	26	38	41	35	76	–	–	–	148	130	278
Killarney,	24	13	37	63	27	90	61	29	90	8	10	18	49	43	92	14	19	33	216	141	357
Letterkenny,	4	–	4	11	8	19	68	21	89	14	16	30	62	42	104	82	33	115	238	119	357
Limerick,	15	30	45	56	75	131	67	16	83	52	59	111	33	66	99	4	–	4	226	249	475
Londonderry,	1	4	5	13	10	23	143	18	161	1	62	63	13	50	63	13	2	15	180	158	338
Maryborough,	11	9	20	38	21	59	67	41	108	10	34	44	41	36	77	1	–	1	173	134	307
Monaghan,	10	4	14	41	23	64	107	78	185	42	21	63	63	67	130	5	8	13	270	208	478
Mullingar,	9	10	19	60	30	90	71	70	141	47	43	90	66	22	88	34	38	72	289	213	502
Omagh,	5	8	13	12	7	19	134	72	206	48	59	107	49	45	94	28	37	65	279	228	507
Richmond,	64	104	168	101	130	231	205	120	325	42	141	183	42	98	140	33	9	42	510	571	1,081
Sligo,	4	3	7	10	13	23	101	79	180	38	38	76	67	71	138	–	–	–	226	188	414
Waterford,	11	10	21	31	23	54	41	40	81	39	39	78	15	20	35	23	17	40	160	149	309
Total,	351	350	701	1,093	740	1,833	1,692	1,413	3,105	644	774	1,418	955	1,016	1,971	439	373	812	5,104	4,470	9,574

No. 11.—Table showing the Social Condition as to Marriage of Patients who were admitted into District Lunatic Asylums during the Year ending the 31st of December, 1885.

Asylums	Married.			Single.			Widowers and Widows.			Unknown.			Total.		
	M.	F.	T.	M.	F.	T.	M.	F.	T.	M.	F.	T.	M.	F.	T.
Armagh, . .	16	11	27	14	28	42	–	3	3	–	5	5	31	46	77
Ballinasloe, . .	39	21	60	68	38	106	3	2	5	–	–	–	110	61	171
Belfast, . . .	42	27	62	33	31	104	1	9	10	12	2	14	110	82	192
Carlow, . . .	9	11	20	26	20	46	4	3	7	–	–	–	37	34	71
Castlebar, . .	19	14	33	31	22	53	2	2	4	–	–	–	52	38	93
Clonmel, . .	18	17	35	37	28	65	3	2	4	–	–	–	57	47	104
Cork, . . .	27	53	63	83	64	147	4	7	11	11	13	24	126	138	265
Down, . . .	15	22	35	34	26	60	1	8	9	1	2	3	49	58	107
Ennis, . . .	6	14	20	23	10	33	-	3	3	–	–	–	31	27	58
Enniscorthy, . .	17	9	26	29	19	48	1	3	4	–	–	–	47	31	78
Kilkenny, . .	7	3	10	27	20	47	1	4	5	–	–	–	35	33	68
Killarney, . .	24	20	44	22	23	45	–	2	2	1	–	1	46	48	94
Letterkenny, . .	18	15	33	31	26	60	2	3	5	1	1	2	55	45	100
Limerick, . .	20	22	42	30	28	58	2	8	10	–	–	–	58	59	117
Londonderry, . .	17	12	29	31	30	61	–	4	4	1	–	1	49	46	95
Maryborough, . .	9	12	21	25	21	51	–	8	8	–	–	–	34	41	79
Monaghan, . .	21	12	40	34	36	72	3	3	6	–	–	–	60	58	118
Mullingar, . .	16	26	36	43	31	74	1	6	7	10	1	11	74	61	135
Omagh, . . .	28	24	34	30	30	60	3	6	9	5	1	6	69	63	137
Richmond, . .	69	76	145	109	104	213	7	3	10	12	43	55	217	231	448
Sligo, . . .	21	16	37	41	26	67	1	14	15	–	–	–	63	56	119
Waterford, . .	10	22	32	24	33	57	–	8	8	–	–	–	34	63	97
Total, . .	455	476	931	898	714	1,612	38	118	156	82	52	134	1,476	1,374	2,850

No. 12.—Table showing the State as to Probability of Recovery of Patients in District Asylums on 31st December, 1885.

Asylums.	Lunatics probably Curable.			Lunatics probably Incurable.			Idiots.			Epileptics.			Total.		
	M.	F.	T.	M.	F.	T.	M.	F.	T.	M.	F.	T.	M.	F.	T.
Armagh, . . .	15	40	55	66	94	160	1	1	2	18	8	26	130	147	277
Ballinasloe, . . .	130	90	220	200	116	316	18	11	29	16	7	23	364	224	588
Belfast, . . .	58	43	101	244	170	414	12	1	13	29	13	42	343	227	570
Carlow, . . .	65	60	125	69	74	143	—	—	—	8	9	17	142	143	285
Castlebar, . . .	78	43	121	107	76	183	14	4	18	16	7	23	215	130	345
Clonmel, . . .	36	44	80	183	184	367	2	5	7	21	14	35	241	268	509
Cork, . . .	147	144	291	281	300	581	13	17	30	22	10	32	463	453	916
Down, . . .	26	20	46	180	121	301	2	3	5	11	9	20	219	153	372
Ennis, . . .	19	18	37	146	107	253	—	—	—	11	4	15	176	129	305
Enniscorthy, . . .	30	29	59	151	101	252	3	3	6	9	5	14	193	138	331
Kilkenny, . . .	45	14	59	93	82	175	1	2	3	9	2	11	148	130	278
Killarney, . . .	22	25	47	180	114	294	2	1	3	12	1	13	216	141	357
Letterkenny, . . .	16	6	22	212	110	322	3	2	5	7	1	8	238	119	357
Limerick, . . .	62	17	79	187	191	378	—	—	—	8	7	15	237	246	476
Londonderry, . . .	41	33	74	125	115	240	4	2	6	10	8	18	180	158	338
Maryborough, . . .	56	37	93	91	91	182	11	—	11	15	6	21	173	134	307
Monaghan, . . .	10	11	21	230	172	402	7	5	12	23	15	38	270	203	473
Mullingar, . . .	30	32	62	236	166	402	6	3	9	17	12	29	289	213	502
Omagh, . . .	64	75	139	160	170	330	8	8	16	27	12	39	279	288	567
Richmond, . . .	246	315	561	207	208	415	2	10	12	55	38	93	510	571	1,081
Sligo, . . .	50	48	98	161	129	290	2	1	3	10	10	20	228	186	414
Waterford, . . .	7	5	12	143	137	280	—	2	2	10	5	15	160	149	309
Total, .	1,243	1,174	2,417	3,684	3,012	6,696	111	81	192	364	203	567	5,402	4,470	9,872

No. 13.—TABLE showing the Social Condition as to Marriage of Patients in District Asylums discharged Recovered during the Year ending the 31st December, 1885.

Asylum.	Married.			Single.			Widowers and Widows.			Unknown.			Total.		
	M.	F.	T.	M.	F.	T.	M.	F.	T.	M.	F.	T.	M.	F.	T.
Armagh,	8	8	16	14	3	17	–	–	–	–	1	1	22	12	34
Ballinasloe,	25	19	44	21	10	31	–	–	–	–	–	–	46	29	75
Belfast,	17	17	34	26	18	44	–	4	4	6	–	6	49	39	88
Carlow,	6	4	10	10	9	19	2	2	4	–	–	–	18	15	33
Castlebar,	6	3	9	8	12	20	–	–	–	–	–	–	14	15	29
Clonmel,	9	4	13	12	12	24	–	1	1	–	–	–	21	17	38
Cork,	10	24	34	18	18	36	1	2	3	1	1	2	30	45	75
Down,	17	20	37	24	18	42	–	7	7	1	–	1	42	45	87
Ennis,	–	5	5	8	7	15	–	–	–	1	–	1	9	12	21
Enniscorthy,	4	3	7	16	20	36	1	1	2	–	–	–	21	24	45
Kilkenny,	3	9	12	18	11	29	–	3	3	–	–	–	21	23	44
Killarney,	10	8	18	4	10	14	–	–	–	–	–	–	14	18	32
Letterkenny,	6	7	13	18	8	26	2	1	3	–	1	1	26	17	43
Limerick,	7	6	13	5	9	14	1	2	3	–	–	–	13	17	30
Londonderry,	11	4	15	19	16	35	1	3	4	–	1	1	31	24	55
Maryborough,	4	6	10	10	7	17	–	3	3	–	–	–	14	16	30
Monaghan,	6	5	11	10	7	17	2	1	3	–	–	–	18	13	31
Mullingar,	5	8	13	30	21	51	1	2	3	1	1	2	37	32	69
Omagh,	21	21	42	22	16	38	3	3	6	2	1	3	48	41	89
Richmond,	30	24	54	46	37	83	1	5	6	16	13	29	93	80	173
Sligo,	7	8	15	19	7	26	2	3	5	–	1	1	28	19	47
Waterford,	2	8	10	10	10	20	–	2	2	–	–	–	12	20	32
Total,	212	222	434	364	290	654	19	43	62	25	20	45	620	575	1,195

No. 14.—Table showing the Social Condition as to Marriage of Patients who Died in District Lunatic Asylums during the Year ending the 31st of December, 1885.

Asylums.	Married.			Single.			Widowers and Widows.			Unknown.			Total.		
	M.	F.	T.	M.	F.	T.	M.	F.	T.	M.	F.	T.	M.	F.	T.
Armagh,	3	7	10	4	3	7	1	–	1	–	–	–	8	10	18
Ballinasloe,	15	13	28	19	14	33	–	–	–	–	2	2	34	29	63
Belfast,	2	3	5	8	4	12	–	2	2	–	1	1	12	9	21
Carlow,	2	1	3	7	4	11	–	3	3	–	–	–	9	8	17
Castlebar,	4	3	7	10	13	23	3	2	5	–	–	–	17	18	35
Clonmel,	11	1	12	8	6	14	–	1	1	–	–	–	19	8	27
Cork,	8	16	24	26	31	57	2	5	7	1	8	9	37	50	87
Down,	4	3	7	7	2	9	1	3	4	–	1	1	12	8	20
Ennis,	4	3	7	6	3	12	–	–	–	–	1	1	15	7	20
Enniscorthy,	5	1	6	5	3	8	–	–	–	–	–	–	10	4	14
Kilkenny,	6	1	7	11	3	17	1	2	3	–	–	–	21	6	27
Killarney,	1	5	6	13	11	24	1	1	2	–	1	1	16	18	36
Letterkenny,	12	11	23	16	10	30	1	–	1	–	1	1	27	28	55
Limerick,	6	3	9	19	13	34	2	4	5	3	–	3	29	22	51
Londonderry,	5	4	9	3	8	10	1	2	3	–	–	–	11	11	22
Maryborough,	7	8	15	6	12	18	1	–	1	–	–	–	16	18	37
Monaghan,	9	5	14	10	7	17	1	3	4	–	–	–	20	15	35
Mullingar,	3	3	6	10	7	17	1	3	4	1	2	3	15	17	32
Omagh,	5	6	16	12	8	20	2	4	6	3	1	4	22	18	11
Richmond,	17	14	38	53	32	85	3	1	7	8	4	12	83	54	137
Sligo,	6	5	11	15	7	22	1	4	5	–	–	–	21	16	38
Waterford,	3	1	4	4	7	11	–	6	6	1	3	4	8	17	25
Total,	119	172	261	270	203	462	21	48	68	17	27	41	460	396	856

No. 15.—TABLE showing the Relationship to each other of Patients who were in District Asylums during the Year ending 31st December, 1885.

ASYLUMS.	Husbands and Wives			Parents and Children			Brothers and Sisters			Uncles and Aunts, Nephews and Nieces			DEGREE OF RELATIONSHIP: First Cousins			Second Cousins			More distant degrees of Relationship			Patients who had Relatives in Asylums previous to the period of these Returns		
	M.	F.	T.	M.	F.	T.	M.	F.	T.	M.	F.	T.	M.	F.	T.	M.	F.	T.	M.	F.	T.	M.	F.	T.
Armagh,	–	–	–	2	2	4	2	4	5	1	1	2	–	2	2	3	1	4	–	–	–	2	–	2
Ballinasloe,	–	–	–	1	9	10	6	8	14	7	8	15	8	9	17	7	8	15	–	–	–	21	18	39
Belfast,	–	–	–	5	4	9	12	7	19	3	1	4	7	3	10	4	–	4	–	–	–	15	11	26
Carlow,	–	–	–	–	–	–	2	2	4	1	–	1	2	1	3	1	2	3	–	–	–	6	5	11
Castlebar,	–	–	–	–	–	–	7	3	10	–	–	–	6	–	6	–	–	–	–	–	–	3	–	3
Clonmel,	2	2	4	–	2	2	10	8	18	2	–	2	4	6	10	3	6	9	5	4	9	27	31	58
Cork,	–	–	–	2	2	4	4	2	6	1	3	4	1	1	2	2	2	4	–	–	–	6	1	7
Down,	–	–	–	–	–	–	12	2	14	2	2	4	–	–	–	4	–	4	–	–	–	4	1	5
Ennis,	–	–	–	1	1	2	7	5	12	–	2	2	3	3	6	7	14	21	9	8	17	22	19	41
Enniscorthy,	–	–	–	–	6	6	5	2	7	2	–	2	5	1	6	13	1	14	2	–	2	–	–	–
Kilkenny,	–	–	–	–	–	–	2	2	4	–	–	–	7	3	10	2	2	4	1	1	2	32	23	55
Killarney,	–	–	–	–	–	–	9	3	12	7	1	8	4	4	8	–	–	–	23	11	34	27	16	43
Letterkenny,	–	–	–	2	–	2	2	2	4	1	1	2	1	1	2	–	–	–	–	–	–	–	–	–
Limerick,	1	1	2	2	2	4	7	5	12	1	5	6	4	1	5	2	3	5	–	–	–	–	–	–
Londonderry,	–	–	–	3	4	7	9	9	18	3	2	5	5	9	14	4	2	6	–	–	–	12	10	22
Maryborough,	–	–	–	3	3	6	5	6	11	1	1	2	3	1	4	8	4	12	–	–	–	11	12	23
Monaghan,	–	–	–	1	4	5	7	15	22	1	1	2	3	2	5	1	2	3	6	5	11	5	6	11
Mullingar,	–	–	–	–	2	2	5	1	6	–	–	–	–	–	–	–	1	1	–	–	–	–	–	–
Omagh,	–	–	–	1	3	4	6	5	11	2	2	4	5	6	11	8	8	16	–	–	–	24	20	44
Richmond,	1	1	2	2	3	5	6	10	16	1	1	2	–	2	2	2	–	2	–	–	–	–	–	–
Sligo,	–	–	–	1	1	2	9	11	20	6	6	12	4	4	8	–	–	–	–	–	–	17	13	30
Waterford,	–	–	–	2	2	4	1	3	4	–	–	–	3	3	6	–	2	2	–	–	–	6	8	14
Total,	4	4	8	28	50	78	134	116	250	47	34	81	75	59	134	71	61	132	46	29	75	240	198	438

No. 16.—TABLE showing Paying Patients in District Lunatic Asylums, admitted from 1st of January to 31st of December, 1885, and Patients in Asylums who are known or supposed to have Means, but who do not contribute to their Support.

ASYLUMS.	Paying Patients			Amount received from Paying Patients.	Yearly Payment (average).	Was minimum maintained at Inspector's Office under Privy Council Rule?	Return of Patients known or supposed to have Means.		
	M.	F.	T.	£ s. d.	£ s. d.		M.	F.	T.
Armagh, . .	2	1	3	42 15 0	20 16 8	Yes.	1		1
Ballinasloe, . .	-	-	-	—	—	—	-	-	-
Belfast, .	2	4	6	76 0 0	16 3 4	Yes.	-	-	-
Carlow, .	1	-	1	11 10 0	23 0 0	Yes.	-	-	-
Castlebar, . .	-	-	-	—	—	—	-	-	-
Clonmel, . .	2	-	2	13 10 0	19 10 0	Yes.	1	-	1
Cork, . .	12	7	19	71 15 0	13 9 1	Yes.	7	3	10
Down, . . .	-	-	-	—	—	—	-	-	-
Ennis, . . .	2	1	3	33 9 6	13 6 8	Yes.	3	-	3
Enniscorthy, .	3	-	3	7 10 0	17 6 8	Yes.	-	-	-
Kilkenny, . .	1	1	2	40 0 0	20 0 0	Yes.	1	-	1
Killarney, . .	-	-	-	—	—	—	1	1	2
Letterkenny, .	-	-	-	—	—	—	-	-	-
Limerick, .	4	1	5	23 1 0	18 0 0	Yes.	1	-	1
Londonderry, .	1	2	3	25 13 4	17 13 4	Yes.	1	-	1
Maryborough, .	3	1	4	51 1 0	14 3 6	Yes.	1	-	1
Monaghan, . .	-	-	-	—	—	—	-	1	1
Mullingar, . .	-	-	-	—	—	—	-	1	1
Omagh . .	-	-	-	—	—	—	1	-	1
Richmond, . .	1	5	6	61 6 8	13 17 8	—	6	2	8
Sligo, . . .	-	-	-	—		—	-	-	-
Waterford, . .	-	-	-	—	—	—	-	-	-
Total, . .	34	23	57	461 14 0	—	—	24	8	32

No. 17.—TABLE showing the Number of BOARD MEETINGS held, and Attendance of GOVERNORS thereat, during the year ending 31st December, 1883.

ASYLUMS.	January.		February.		March.		April.		May.		June.		July.		August.		September.		October.		November.		December.		Total Number of Meetings held during the year.	Average Number of Governors at each Meeting.
	No. of Meetings.	No. of Governors in attendance.	No. of Meetings.	No. of Governors in attendance.	No. of Meetings.	No. of Governors in attendance.	No. of Meetings.	No. of Governors in attendance.	No. of Meetings.	No. of Governors in attendance.	No. of Meetings.	No. of Governors in attendance.	No. of Meetings.	No. of Governors in attendance.	No. of Meetings.	No. of Governors in attendance.	No. of Meetings.	No. of Governors in attendance.	No. of Meetings.	No. of Governors in attendance.	No. of Meetings.	No. of Governors in attendance.	No. of Meetings.	No. of Governors in attendance.		
Armagh,	1	4	1	7	1	5	1	3	1	3	1	3	1	3	1	4	1	4	1	3	1	5	1	5	12	4
Ballinasloe,	1	4	1	5	2	10	1	8	1	13	1	6	1	12	1	3	1	5	1	5	1	5	1	4	13	6
Belfast,	1	4	1	7	1	8	1	4	1	9	1	3	1	4	2	8	1	7	1	4	1	4	1	7	13	6
Carlow,	1	4	1	1	1	9	1	3	1	3	1	3	1	6	1	4	1	3	1	6	1	5	1	3	12	4
Castlebar,	1	4	1	4	1	4	1	3	1	6	1	6	1	4	1	8	1	3	1	1	1	4	1	3	12	4
Clonmel,	1	11	1	30	1	8	1	9	1	10	1	12	1	9	1	17	1	9	1	4	1	7	2	18	13	10
Cork,	1	16	1	5	2	25	2	15	1	16	2	23	1	10	1	11	1	7	1	13	2	18	1	10	17	10
Down,	1	6	1	8	2	14	3	27	1	4	1	4	1	3	1	3	1	5	1	9	3	21	1	11	17	6
Ennis,	1	5	1	7	1	7	1	4	1	4	1	7	1	5	1	5	1	5	2	9	1	8	1	3	13	5
Enniscorthy,	1	3	1	2	1	4	1	4	1	8	1	8	1	11	1	5	1		1	5	2	10	1	4	13	5
Kilkenny,	1	5	1	4	1	7	1	3	1	6	1	7	1	8	1	8	1	3	1	5	1	5	1	3	13	5
Killarney,	1	10	1	4	1	6	1	3	2	10	1	5	2	8	2	9	1	4	1	5	1	3	1	5	15	5
Letterkenny,	2	10	2	12	1	7	1	7	1	4	1	4	1	5	1	4	1	7	1	4	1	10	2	9	15	5
Limerick,	1	9	1	11	1	8	1	9	1	4	1	4	1	6	1	3	1	6	1	7	1	7	1	8	12	7
Londonderry,	1	13	1	8	1	10	1	6	1	4	1	5	1	11	1	11	1	7	1	12	2	14	1	11	13	9
Maryborough,	1	4	1	4	1	7	1	4	1	5	1	6	1	9	1	8	1	7	1	5	1	6	1	6	12	6
Monaghan,	1	3	1	15	2	12	1	6	1	10	1	6	1	8	2	16	1	16	1	6	1	3	2	18	15	8
Mullingar,	1	6	1	6	1	9	1	29	1	8	1	3	1	3	1	4	1	6	1	6	1	6	1	7	12	7
Omagh,	1	8	1	7	1	7	1	8	1	11	1	10	1	13	1	6	1	5	1	7	1	7	1	12	12	8
Richmond,	1	7	1	4	2	13	2	7	2	13	2	16	1	7	1	5	3	21	2	13	2	5	2	13	22	8
Sligo,	1	5	1	4	1	4	1	5	1	3	1	3	1	8	1	6	1	4	1	7	1	3	3	8	13	4
Waterford,	1	7	1	9	1	11	1	5	1	11	2	15	1	8	1	9	1	8	2	21	2	8	1	4	15	8

No. 18.—Table, showing Return in accordance with the Act 31 & 32 District Lunatic Asylums in Ireland which have been Disallowed, Year 1884—together with the amount of any Disallowances, Reductions, Governors, and of any steps which have been taken at Law for the

Asylums.	Date of Commencement of Audit.	Date of Conclusion of Audit.	Particulars of all Charges and Payments which have been Disallowed, Reduced, or Inserted by the Auditors.
Armagh, . . .	4 May, 1885,	6 May, 1885,	None,
Ballinasloe, . .	17 May, 1885,	19 May, 1885,	None,
Belfast, . . .	18 May, 1885,	21 May, 1885,	None,
Carlow, . . .	5 May, 1885,	7 May, 1885,	None.
Castlebar, . .	7 July, 1885,	8 July, 1885,	None,
Clonmel, . . .	24 March, 1885,	27 March, 1885,	None.
Cork, . .	6 May, 1885,	16 May, 1885,	Moneys received by the late clerk for paying patients.
Down, . .	7 May, 1885,	20 May, 1885,	None,
Ennis, . . .	23 May, 1885,	23 May, 1885,	Amount paid to Guardians for seven patients in Ennis Workhouse.
Enniscorthy, . .	3 Aug., 1885,	4 Aug., 1885,	None,
Kilkenny, . . .	28 April, 1885,	30 April, 1885,	None,
Killarney, . . .	26 April, 1885,	30 April, 1885,	None,
Letterkenny, . .	28 Sept., 1885,	30 Sept., 1885,	None
Limerick, . . .	23 April, 1885,	29 April, 1885,	None,
Londonderry, . .	21 Sept., 1885,	23 Sept., 1885,	None,
Maryborough, . .	11 May, 1885,	13 May, 1885,	None,
Monaghan, . .	14 May, 1885,	16 May, 1885,	None,
Mullingar, . .	4 May, 1885,	7 May, 1885,	None,
Omagh, . . .	11 Sept., 1885,	14 Sept., 1885,	None,
Richmond, . .	14 April, 1885,	17 April, 1885,	None,
Sligo, . . .	18 May, 1885,	22 May, 1885,	None,
Waterford, . .	13 April, 1885,	15 April, 1885,	None,

d.		£	s.	d.	£	s.	d.	
	None,	6,118	10	2	29	1	0	Col. R. Massy Stoddert.
	None	10,196	4	10	21	10	0	Colonel James O'Hara.
	None,	12,740	0	6	—			Col. R. Massy Stoddert.
	None,	6,187	6	6	—			C. Croker, esq.
	None,	7,259	4	0	—			Colonel James O'Hara.
	None,	12,863	6	11	31	10	0	C. Pelly, esq.
5	Refunded,	19,931	11	1	33	0	0	A. M'Hugh, esq.
	None,	9,168	10	2	24	10	0	Col. R. Massy Stoddert.
0	This disallowance has since been remitted by the auditor.	7,259	5	3	24	10	0	Colonel James O'Hara.
	None,	7,620	1	3	—			George W. Finlay, esq.
	None,	5,438	2	2	24	10	0	C. Croker, esq.
	None,	8,853	10	7	24	10	0	A. M'Hugh, esq.
	None,	7,636	17	11	—			Loftus Bushe Fox, esq.
	None,	13,328	13	0	—			C. Pelly, esq.
	None,	7,213	5	10	—			Loftus Bushe Fox, esq.
	None,	7,276	3	3	—			Captain Gibson.

No. 19.—Table showing the previous Occupation of those admitted into District Asylums during the year ending 31st December, 1885.

Asylums.	Labouring Class.			Farming.			Domestic Servants.			Clerks.			Shopkeepers.			Tailors and Dressmakers.			Artizans.			Painters and Glaziers.			Smiths and Workers in Metals.		
	M.	F.	T.	M.	F.	T.	M.	F.	T.	M.	F.	T.	M.	F.	T.	M.	F.	T.	M.	F.	T.	M.	F.	T.	M.	F.	T.
Armagh,	9	6	15	6	1	7	–	6	6	–	–	–	–	–	–	–	2	2	–	–	–	1	–	1	–	–	–
Ballinasloe,	58	34	92	19	18	37	6	7	13	1	–	1	2	–	2	–	1	1	1	–	1	–	–	–	–	–	–
Belfast,	29	1	30	9	–	9	–	10	10	2	–	2	3	–	2	1	8	9	5	–	5	–	–	–	7	–	7
Carlow,	16	19	35	4	5	9	1	6	7	–	–	–	1	–	1	–	1	1	–	–	–	–	–	–	2	–	2
Castlebar,	24	4	28	19	3	22	–	7	7	–	–	–	–	1	1	–	1	1	–	–	–	–	–	–	–	–	–
Clonmel,	11	8	22	16	15	31	2	9	11	–	–	–	–	–	–	1	1	2	–	–	–	–	–	–	–	–	–
Cork,	36	9	45	30	16	46	–	17	17	8	–	8	4	2	6	1	9	10	–	–	–	–	–	–	1	–	1
Down,	13	3	16	10	–	10	1	10	11	2	–	2	–	–	–	–	–	–	3	–	3	–	–	–	–	–	–
Ennis,	9	5	14	16	10	26	–	1	1	–	–	–	–	1	1	–	–	–	–	–	–	–	–	–	–	–	–
Enniscorthy,	14	6	20	16	7	22	2	12	14	–	–	–	–	–	–	–	–	–	3	–	3	–	–	–	2	–	2
Kilkenny,	10	10	20	8	7	15	–	1	1	1	–	1	1	1	2	–	3	3	–	–	–	–	–	–	–	–	–
Killarney,	21	11	32	12	13	25	–	9	9	–	–	–	1	4	5	–	–	–	1	1	2	–	–	–	1	–	1
Letterkenny,	28	2	30	21	11	32	–	8	8	–	–	–	–	1	1	–	3	3	–	–	–	–	–	–	–	–	–
Limerick,	30	12	42	6	12	18	2	8	10	4	–	4	4	1	5	1	3	4	4	–	4	–	–	–	1	–	1
Londonderry,	21	8	29	12	2	11	–	3	3	–	–	–	4	–	4	–	2	2	2	–	2	1	–	1	–	–	–
Maryborough,	23	11	33	6	7	13	–	7	7	–	–	–	–	1	1	1	1	2	–	–	–	–	–	–	–	–	–
Monaghan,	25	25	50	19	3	22	1	10	11	–	–	–	3	–	3	1	3	4	–	–	–	–	–	–	–	–	–
Mullingar,	30	3	33	9	2	11	–	11	11	1	–	1	1	–	1	1	5	6	–	–	–	1	–	1	1	–	1
Omagh,	34	3	37	29	11	40	–	17	17	–	–	–	4	2	6	1	7	8	4	–	1	1	–	1	–	–	–
Richmond,	46	6	52	14	2	16	1	43	44	9	–	9	4	3	7	6	17	23	1	–	1	7	–	7	3	–	3
Sligo,	23	12	35	30	32	62	–	7	7	1	–	1	1	–	4	1	1	2	1	–	1	–	–	–	1	–	1
Waterford,	20	15	35	4	1	5	–	6	6	–	–	–	–	3	3	–	2	2	–	–	–	–	–	–	–	–	–
Total,	533	213	743	312	179	491	16	216	232	29	–	29	35	22	57	15	70	85	25	1	26	11	–	11	19	–	19

No. 19.—TABLE showing the previous Occupation of those admitted into District Asylums during the year ending 31st December, 1885—*continued.*

Asylums.	Masons and Bricklayers.			Carpenters.			Weavers.			Shoemakers.			Hatters.			Factory Workers.			Victuallers.			Pedlars and Hawkers.			Lawyers.			Medical Men.		
	M.	F.	T.	M.	F.	T.	M.	F.	T.	M.	F.	T.	M.	F.	T.	M.	F.	T.	M.	F.	T.	M.	F.	T.	M.	F.	T.	M.	F.	T.
Armagh,	1	–	1	2	–	2	1	6	7	1	–	1	–	–	–	1	1	2	–	–	–	–	1	1	–	–	–	1	–	1
Ballinasloe,	–	–	–	–	–	–	–	–	–	1	–	1	–	–	–	–	–	–	–	–	–	–	–	–	–	–	–	–	–	–
Belfast,	–	–	–	4	–	4	2	11	13	2	–	2	–	–	–	1	6	7	–	–	–	4	–	4	–	–	–	–	–	–
Carlow,	1	–	1	2	–	2	–	–	–	2	–	2	–	–	–	–	–	–	1	–	1	–	1	1	–	–	–	–	–	–
Castlebar,	1	–	1	1	–	1	1	–	1	1	–	1	–	–	–	–	–	–	–	–	–	–	–	–	–	–	–	–	–	–
Clonmel,	2	–	2	–	–	–	–	–	–	1	–	1	–	–	–	–	–	–	1	–	1	–	1	1	–	–	–	–	–	–
Cork,	2	–	2	3	–	3	1	–	1	–	–	–	–	–	–	–	2	2	1	–	1	–	3	3	–	–	–	–	–	–
Down,	–	–	–	4	–	4	2	–	2	1	–	1	–	–	–	1	2	3	–	–	–	–	–	–	–	–	–	–	–	–
Ennis,	–	–	–	–	–	–	–	–	–	–	–	–	–	–	–	–	–	–	–	–	–	–	–	–	–	–	–	–	–	–
Enniscorthy,	–	–	–	1	–	1	–	–	–	1	–	1	–	–	–	–	–	–	–	–	–	1	2	3	–	–	–	–	–	–
Kilkenny,	–	–	–	3	–	3	–	–	–	1	–	1	–	–	–	–	–	–	–	–	–	1	–	1	–	–	–	–	–	–
Killarney,	–	–	–	2	–	2	–	–	–	2	–	2	1	–	1	–	–	–	1	–	1	–	–	–	–	–	–	–	–	–
Letterkenny,	–	–	–	–	–	–	–	–	–	1	–	1	–	–	–	–	–	–	–	–	–	–	–	–	–	–	–	–	–	–
Limerick,	–	–	–	–	–	–	–	–	–	1	–	1	–	–	–	–	–	–	1	–	1	–	1	1	–	–	–	–	–	–
Londonderry,	–	–	–	–	–	–	–	1	1	–	–	–	–	–	–	–	3	3	–	–	–	–	2	2	–	–	–	–	–	–
Maryborough,	–	–	–	1	–	1	–	–	–	–	–	–	–	–	–	–	1	1	–	–	–	–	–	–	–	–	–	–	–	–
Monaghan,	–	–	–	–	–	–	–	–	–	–	–	–	–	–	–	1	–	1	1	–	1	–	–	–	–	–	–	–	–	–
Mullingar,	2	–	2	1	–	1	–	–	–	3	–	3	–	–	–	–	–	–	–	–	–	–	–	–	–	–	–	–	–	–
Omagh,	2	–	2	–	–	–	–	–	–	2	1	3	–	–	–	1	–	1	2	–	2	1	–	1	–	–	–	–	–	–
Richmond,	4	–	4	3	–	3	–	–	–	8	2	10	–	–	–	1	1	2	–	–	–	4	3	7	1	–	1	2	–	2
Sligo,	1	–	1	–	–	–	–	–	–	–	–	–	–	–	–	–	–	–	1	–	1	–	–	–	–	–	–	–	–	–
Waterford,	–	–	–	2	–	2	–	–	–	1	–	1	–	–	–	–	–	–	–	–	–	–	2	2	–	–	–	–	–	–
Total,	16	–	16	29	–	29	7	18	25	29	3	32	1	–	1	6	18	21	9	–	9	11	16	27	1	–	1	3	–	3

No. 10.—TABLE showing the previous Occupation of those admitted into District Asylums during the year ending 31st December, 1885—*continued.*

Asylums.	Members of Religious Communities			Students and Teachers			Soldiers and Pensioners, and Wives of do.			Police.			Sailors.			Publicans.			Mendicants.			Various Employments.			No Occupation, or Unknown.			Total.		
	M.	F.	T.	M.	F.	T.	M.	F.	T.	M.	F.	T.	M.	F.	T.	M.	F.	T.	M.	F.	T.	M.	F.	T.	M.	F.	T.	M.	F.	T.
Armagh,	–	–	–	1	–	1	1	–	1	–	–	–	–	–	–	–	–	–	–	–	–	3	–	3	3	23	26	31	46	77
Ballinasloe,	1	–	1	3	1	4	4	–	4	2	–	2	–	–	–	–	–	–	–	–	–	12	–	12	–	–	–	110	61	171
Belfast,	–	–	–	1	–	1	5	–	5	–	–	–	3	–	3	–	–	–	1	–	1	15	16	31	14	37	51	110	89	199
Carlow,	–	–	–	–	1	1	4	–	4	1	–	1	–	–	–	–	–	–	–	–	–	–	–	–	–	1	1	37	34	71
Castlebar,	–	–	–	–	–	–	1	–	1	1	–	1	–	–	–	–	–	–	–	4	4	1	1	2	5	17	22	55	38	93
Clonmel,	–	–	–	–	–	–	6	–	6	–	–	–	–	–	–	2	–	2	–	–	–	6	1	7	6	12	18	57	47	104
Cork,	–	1	1	1	2	3	8	–	8	–	–	–	2	–	2	–	2	2	–	–	–	8	28	36	20	48	68	126	139	265
Down,	–	–	–	1	–	1	1	–	1	–	–	–	1	–	1	–	2	2	–	–	–	5	21	26	3	20	23	49	58	107
Ennis,	–	–	–	–	–	–	1	–	1	–	–	–	–	–	–	–	–	–	–	1	1	5	–	5	1	9	10	31	27	58
Enniscorthy,	1	–	1	1	–	1	1	–	1	1	–	1	–	–	–	1	–	1	–	–	–	1	1	2	2	3	5	47	31	78
Kilkenny,	2	–	2	–	–	–	1	–	1	1	–	1	–	–	–	–	–	–	–	1	1	4	–	4	3	10	13	65	33	98
Killarney,	–	–	–	–	–	–	3	–	3	1	–	1	–	–	–	–	–	–	1	6	7	–	–	–	1	2	3	48	46	94
Letterkenny,	–	–	–	–	–	–	–	–	–	1	–	1	–	–	–	–	–	–	–	1	1	1	5	6	3	13	16	55	45	100
Limerick,	1	–	1	1	–	1	2	–	2	–	–	–	–	–	–	–	–	–	–	–	–	–	11	11	–	11	11	80	37	117
Londonderry,	–	–	–	1	1	2	–	–	–	–	–	–	–	–	–	1	–	1	–	–	–	–	–	–	4	22	26	49	46	95
Maryborough,	–	–	–	–	–	–	–	–	–	–	–	–	–	–	–	1	–	1	–	–	–	2	–	2	5	13	18	38	41	79
Monaghan,	–	–	–	–	–	–	2	–	2	1	–	1	–	–	–	–	–	–	–	3	3	5	5	10	1	9	10	60	58	118
Mullingar,	–	–	–	–	3	3	4	–	4	1	–	1	–	–	–	–	–	–	–	1	1	5	11	16	14	23	37	71	64	135
Omagh,	–	–	–	2	–	2	1	–	1	1	–	1	–	–	–	3	1	4	–	–	–	–	1	1	7	22	29	72	65	137
Richmond,	–	1	1	6	3	9	11	–	11	2	–	2	5	–	5	–	–	–	8	11	19	42	21	63	30	117	147	217	231	448
Sligo,	–	–	–	–	–	–	–	–	–	–	–	–	–	–	–	–	1	1	–	3	3	–	–	–	–	–	–	73	46	119
Waterford,	–	–	–	1	–	1	1	–	1	–	–	–	1	–	1	–	–	–	–	–	–	4	6	10	–	26	26	34	63	97
Total,	5	2	7	19	11	30	59	–	59	13	–	13	12	–	12	11	6	17	10	31	41	119	128	247	122	240	362	1,476	1,374	2,850

No. 20.—Table showing the quantity of Land connected with each Asylum, and how it is utilized.

Asylums.	Quantity of Land connected with each Asylum.																	
	Quantity of Land Cultivated.												Buildings, Courts, Wood, &c.			Total Quantity of Land.		
	By Spade.			By Plough.			In Grass.			In Garden.								
	A.	R.	P.	A.	R.	P.	A.	R.	P.	A.	R.	P.	A.	R.	P.	A.	R.	P.
Armagh, . .	5	3	0	15	0	0	6	2	0	1	0	15	7	0	33	33	2	8
Ballinasloe, . .	18	0	0		—		13	0	0	0	3	0	13	1	0	45	0	0
Belfast, . .	6	1	0	26	3	0	13	0	0	2	0	0	10	3	0	55	2	0
Carlow, . .	5	2	24	11	2	0	7	1	0	2	0	0	2	0	0	28	1	24
Castlebar, . .	10	0	0		—		21	0	0	1	0	0	6	0	0	38	0	0
Clonmel, . .	3	0	0	5	1	20	10	2	0	1	0	0	7	0	20	27	0	0
Cork, . . .	6	0	0	16	0	0	7	0	0	3	0	0	25	1	30	57	1	30
Down, . . .		—		27	2	3	49	0	7	6	1	0	27	2	15	110	1	25
Ennis, . . .	2	0	0	9	1	0	22	2	26		—		8	0	0	41	3	26
Enniscorthy, .	2	0	0	14	3	0	8	2	0	0	1	0	14	2	0	40	0	0
Kilkenny, . .	3	3	0		—		5	0	0	1	1	0	15	0	0	25	0	0
Killarney, . .	8	3	0	6	0	0	3	0	0	0	1	0	12	0	0	30	0	0
Letterkenny, .		—		25	0	0	1	0	0	2	0	0	12	0	0	40	0	0
Limerick, . .	5	2	27½	11	1	14	1	2	19	1	0	24½	15	1	28	35	0	33
Londonderry, .	10	0	0		—		9	0	0	1	0	0	5	0	0	25	0	0
Maryborough, .	2	0	0	10	0	0	22	0	0	2	0	28	7	1	31	43	2	19
Monaghan, . .	4	0	0	2	0	0	12	0	0	4	0	0	28	0	0	50	0	0
Mullingar, . .	14	0	0		—		18	0	0	1	0	0	11	2	0	44	2	0
Omagh, . .	16	1	0		—		21	3	9	0	3	0	13	2	26	52	1	35
Richmond, . .	5	2	0	15	2	0	17	1	3	2	0	0	14	0	0	54	1	3
Sligo, . .	19	0	0	9	0	0	34	0	0	1	0	0	14	3	0	77	3	0
Waterford, . .	10	0	0	1	0	0	4	0	0	0	3	0	9	1	0	25	0	0
Total, . .	153	2	11½	201	2	37	398	0	16	33	2	37	280	3	30	978	0	2

No. 21.—Table showing Outlay on and Produce of Farms connected with

Asylums.	Value of Produce in hands on 1st January, 1885.			Outlay.			Total Value.			Value of Produce Consumed.			Value of Produce Sold.		
	£	s.	d.	£	s.	d.	£	s.	d.	£	s.	d.	£	s.	d.
Armagh, . .	109	10	0	142	8	7	251	18	7	241	8	6	75	11	0
Ballinasloe, . . .	116	0	0	70	13	10	186	13	10	118	7	0	121	5	10
Belfast, . . .	53	8	2	110	8	9	163	16	11	140	12	7	111	11	0
Carlow, ...	66	1	0	173	1	10	239	2	10	294	6	7	51	15	6
Castlebar, . . .	131	0	0	139	16	8	271	16	8	137	17	5	149	13	10
Clonmel, . .	397	5	10	289	12	2	686	18	0	555	12	4	—		
Cork, . . .	285	0	0	202	15	11	487	15	11	483	10	3	—		
Down, . . .	1,214	11	2	846	18	1	2,061	11	3	463	2	7	164	16	5
Ennis, . . .	850	7	7	528	15	4	1,379	3	11	717	6	2	63	2	4
Enniscorthy, . . .	124	5	0	171	12	11	295	17	11	271	14	4	141	18	7
Kilkenny, . . .	101	10	10	28	3	10	129	14	8	134	13	6	23	6	6
Killarney, . .	250	7	4	117	0	3	367	7	7	313	17	9	91	10	3
Letterkenny, . . .	356	13	2	131	4	9	487	17	11	397	1	10	96	15	0
Limerick, . . .	139	6	8	176	0	8	315	7	4	350	12	8	—		
Londonderry, . .	149	10	0	221	5	9	370	15	9	209	9	10	254	11	0
Maryborough, . .	87	7	6	128	10	6	215	18	0	217	15	0	62	1	4
Monaghan, . . .	391	0	0	300	18	10	691	18	10	337	18	0	254	16	4
Mullingar, . . .	222	6	9	170	12	0	392	18	9	111	7	8	176	12	0
Omagh, . . .	345	10	0	183	6	3	528	16	3	319	14	9	709	18	10
Richmond, . . .	422	0	0	249	17	4	671	17	4	681	14	3½	87	16	11
Sligo, ...	753	10	0	232	6	0	985	16	0	720	15	6	56	9	0
Waterford, . . .	126	0	0	197	17	4	323	17	4	162	17	2	230	10	6
Total, . .	6,764	13	0	4,823	7	7	11,587	0	7	8,311	6	7½	2,425	15	0

District Lunatic Asylums, during the Year ending the 31st December, 1883.

Value of Produce on Hands on 31st December, 1883.	Total.	Net Profit.	Profit per Acre, approximated, on the Quantity of Land under Crops and Cultivation.	Profit per Acre, approximated, on the Total Quantity of Land.	Asylums.
£ s. d.	£ s. d.	£ s. d.	£ s. d.	£ s. d.	
153 7 0	414 8 0	167 9 11	6 12 2	5 2 10	Armagh.
121 0 0	363 15 10	167 7 0	9 5 4	4 14 5	Ballinasloe.
49 4 2	591 10 9	130 13 10	9 17 5	7 19 2	Belfast.
257 11 0	604 13 1	264 10 9	7 4 3	6 15 1	Carlow.
179 0 0	456 11 3	184 11 7	5 16 5	4 17 2	Castlebar.
408 13 4	1,?91 6 8	335 7 8	10 0 10	12 8 6	Clonmel
402 10 0	686 0 3	391 4 4	12 16 3	6 16 3	Cork.
1,348 3 4	2,144 4 3	492 12 11	5 3 1	5 16 10	Down.
774 18 8	1,570 5 3	171 0 1	5 1 8	4 1 8	Ennis
145 0 0	592 10 11	303 13 0	11 18 2	7 11 9	Enniscorthy.
90 16 7	250 16 7	131 1 11	12 2 2	4 16 10	Kilkenny.
244 10 4	652 16 3	185 10 8	15 9 2	7 14 7	Killarney.
328 5 0	692 1 10	331 3 11	11 18 8	8 7 1	Letterkenny.
159 11 8	480 15 4	265 6 0	9 3 0	4 14 0	Limerick.
103 0 0	558 0 10	187 5 1	9 7 3	7 9 9	Londonderry.
16 10 6	324 6 10	120 8 10	3 16 4	2 4 7	Maryborough
326 10 0	919 1 4	297 5 6	10 16 7	4 10 9	Monaghan.
230 5 0	578 4 6	103 3 11	3 6 4	3 [illegible] 4	Mullingar.
273 10 0	871 9 7	274 13 4	7 2 2	5 4 9	Omagh.
206 0 0	1,0?? 11 2½	382 15 0½	9 10 1	7 1 9	Richmond.
748 0 10	1,525 10 4	339 14 5	8 11 4	6 16 10	Sligo.
90 10 0	494 3 8	170 6 1	13 11 0	7 18 3	Waterford.
6,739 6 6	17,716 5 0½	5,84? 4 3½	8 7 0	5 19 7	Total.

AUDITE

No. 22.—TABLE showing the RECEIPTS and EXPENDITUR

ASYLUMS	RECEIPTS.							
	Balance in hands on the 31st December, 1883.	Total Amounts received levied off Counties, &c., in Districts.	Grant from Treasury at 4s. per Head per Week.	CASUAL RECEIPTS.				
				For Paying Patients.	For Farm and Garden Produce.	For Offal and Old Stores.	Fines on Servants.	Miscellaneous
	£ s. d.	£ s. d.	£ s. d.	£ s. d.	£ s. d.	£ s. d.	£ s. d.	£ s. d.
Armagh, .	3,640 11 7	8,948 16 11	2,303 14 0	131 11 4	64 15 6	9 5 0	—	20 11
Ballinasloe, .	4,571 1 8	6,401 8 0	3,041 10 0	217 12 4	110 0 0	71 5 4	8 3 0	1 15
Belfast, .	213 1 6	9,487 16 9	4,171 14 0	157 17 0	70 14 2	50 7 4	3 17 0	11 17
Carlow, .	2,943 19 0	4,044 6 8	2,446 6 0	756 19 4	11 16 6	1 12 0	—	41 11
Castlebar, .	164 10 6	6,477 19 8	4,019 19 0	81 16 4	160 7 4	1 4 3	—	4 1
Clonmel, .	2,426 16 5	7,169 1 8	4,119 0 0	716 8 8	48 0 8	8 7 0	0 12 6	55
Cork, .	7,016 13 10	9,243 14 10	9,797 4 0	920 17 1	75 0 0	0 7 8	—	114 1
Down, .	440 0 5	4,977 6 0	2,178 4 0	310 6 0	297 19 6	4 4 0	—	40 11
Ennis, .	472 16 5	2,440 13 1	3,977 8 0	347 14 8	195 1 4	7 11 8	1 1 4	1 4
Enniscorthy, .	—	4,093 16 10	2,231 0 0	144 7 10	125 14 7	20 19 0	0 14	7
Kilkenny, .	705 17 8	3,318 18 6	2,736 1 0	160 3 0	36 2 10	9 11 4	—	—
Killarney, .	1,940 17 0	3,476 18 7	3,741 8 0	257 5 6	107 3 1	1 0 9	7 16	36 11
Letterkenny, .	—	6,001 3 4	3,016 14 0	81 7 5	—	4 19 6	—	1 3
Limerick, .	2,184 14 5	4,650 7 9	4,370 14 0	330 13 6	77 15 1	8 15 0	—	14 19
Londonderry, .	704 17 7	3,602 6 10	1,036 8 0	137 14 2	748 15 7	30 3 3	—	1 2
Maryborough, .	716 17 3	3,448 6 11	4,107 0 0	217 13 7	109 11 6	11 1 8	0 17 6	14 1
Monaghan, .	2,447 19 1	4,920 0 0	4,231 10 0	161 15 8	749 0 11	10 16 0	1 0 0	23 17
Mullingar, .	2,123 17 4	[illegible] 17	1,413 1 8	712 0 0	201 5 4	11 0 0	—	108 13
Omagh, .	1,276 19 6	6,113 11 4	1,109 12 0	403 10 9	107 7 1	4 1 4	—	24 0
Richmond, .	4,874 11 0	10,513 19 4	10,470 14 0	449 4 11	30 4 4	84 2 8	3 0 0	10 19
Sligo, .	2,777 8 6	2,477 0 0	3,044 0 0	141 13 8	14 8	10 7 8	0 10 0	71 11
Waterford, .	3,107 11 10	2,915 17 0	2,901 4 0	249 14 4	230 0 7	11 0 3	—	14 14
Total, .	49,753 11 0	131,771 10 10	84,430 0 0	6,477 0 6	2,404 1 11	324 3 11	21 10 5	1,470 7

ASYLUMS.	EXPENDITURE—(continued).							
	Furniture.	Fuel and Light.	Soap and Candles.	Printing, Stationery, and Advertising.	Medicines, including Wines, Spirits, &c.	Repairs and Alterations.	Farm and Garden Expenses.	Incidental
	£ s. d.	£ s. d.	£ s. d.	£ s. d.	£ s. d.	£ s. d.	£ s. d.	£ s.
Armagh, .	124 5 0	245 13 10	15 19 4	43 10 0	241 9 7	731 9 5	144 19	94
Ballinasloe, .	276 17 3	748 10 6	111 19 6	68 11 8	320 13 10	646 6 11	48 1 3	22
Belfast, .	116 9 2	333 1	143 3 6	48 11 4	215 10 0	717 12 10	119 11	74
Carlow, .	91 6 9	193 13 7	77 7 10	92 7 1	191 19 5	384 17 4	131 8	21 11
Castlebar, .	41 8 5	170 1 10	52 11 1	40 3 4	779 16 5	479 1 10	175 14 11	79
Clonmel, .	379 1 10	779 4 3	117 18 1	174 6 11	118 11 10	249 13 9	106 19 4	47
Cork, .	775 13 11	1,084 6 6	181 6 0	274 17 2	410 10 1	1,450 4 4	144 4 1	54 11
Down, .	134 16 10	494 8 7	74 10 8	116 12 10	204 17 6	464 17 8	145 15 4	49
Ennis, .	50 7 0	441 1 11	84 11 1	34 17 2	91 4 9	347 7 3	314 1 1	43 14
Enniscorthy, .	85 18 0	317 10 0	78 4 11	47 7 3	875 1 7	343 14 11	217 1 8	71
Kilkenny, .	70 11 1	745 3 1	17 18 0	61 4 0	117 3 5	145 0 0	14 16	71 11
Killarney, .	874 8 7	134 14 10	140 1 4	43 16 0	343 14 0	231 11 2	170 0 11	40 11
Letterkenny, .	103 18 10	380 3 10	93 18 3	94 4 3	147 13 11	348 16 11	95 10 11	17
Limerick, .	107 2 10	464 4 4	471 18 7	177 5 11	730 18 8	1131 18 3	130 0	14
Londonderry, .	164 11 7	301 0 11	40 7 7	41 16 3	99 14 4	117 17 8	171 3 0	21
Maryborough, .	155 17 8	511 7 4	97 19 1	14 17 4	114 15 10	208 10 8	107 6 7	13
Monaghan, .	101 7 8	745 14 10	70 18 0	78 1 11	349 4 7	379 0 11	170 9 4	41
Mullingar, .	114 6 10	440 1 7	111 7 10	40 16 4	300 0 0	342 5 4	71 17 1	31
Omagh, .	43 1 8	474 14 11	94 14 6	61 13 0	712 18 8	214 19 11	101 19 1	17
Richmond, .	480 17 3	1,070 3 4	791 19 5	314 17 4	730 17 10	1,575 18 8	764 19 9	73
Sligo, .	14 10 4	479 17 11	71 10 3	80 7 4	173 6 10	464 11 6	167 1 7	94
Waterford, .	170 2 9	411 8 3	45 0 9	10 8 7	116 10 5	307 10 8	100 11 1	45
Total	4,377 0 7	11,372 0 6	3,545 10 8	1,909 3 11	3,006 8 5	13,154 11 0	1,019	907

	£ s. d.	£ s. d.	£ s. d.	£ s. d.	£ s. d.
—	5,[illegible] [illegible] 9	—	2,0[illegible] [illegible] 6	1,566 19 1	[illegible] 12 [illegible]
—	9,194 14 11	817 13 11	1,[illegible] 4 1	1,020 19 [illegible]	[illegible] 16 [illegible]
—	14,[illegible] 16 9	—	2,[illegible] 1 10	[illegible],712 11 0	[illegible] 8 1
—	5,[illegible] 8 9	—	1,[illegible] 3 0	3,[illegible] 16 11	[illegible] 4 [illegible]
—	7,340 1[illegible] 5	—	1,[illegible] 15 4	8,114 0 11	[illegible] 1[illegible] 7
—	11,[illegible] 3 4	—	7,718 10 0	[illegible] 8 5	140 12 4
—	16,[illegible] 19 11	—	1,[illegible] 15 [illegible]	4,[illegible] 11 11	[illegible] 1 16
—	10,[illegible] 8 1	—	2,304 6 1	[illegible] 0 4	[illegible] 10 11
—	20,[illegible] 17 1	—	[illegible] 5 5	17,[illegible] 12 [illegible]	[illegible] 8 8
—	10,107 9 5	—	1,[illegible] 10 4	[illegible] 5 2	[illegible] [illegible] 0
—	8,[illegible] 11 6	—	1,[illegible] 7 11	[illegible] 7 7	470 13 1
[illegible]	276,[illegible] 0 3	[illegible] 0 11	34,[illegible] 1[illegible] 1	[illegible] 11 10	[illegible] 14 [illegible]

EXPENDITURE—(*continued*).

Postage	Incidental Expenses	Superannuation	Total Expenditure	Balance due by Guardians on the 31st Dec., 1881	Daily Average Number of Paupers maintained from Public Funds
£ s. d.	£ s. d.	£ s. d.	£ s. d.	£ s. d.	Number
4 15 [illegible]	111 [illegible] [illegible]	[illegible] [illegible] 6	6,[illegible] 10 2	1,[illegible] 4 [illegible]	[illegible]
1 11 [illegible]	57 16 1	900 [illegible] 1	10,[illegible] 6 10	[illegible] 11 11	[illegible]
6 [illegible] 11	[illegible] 18 [illegible]	[illegible] 1 4	17,[illegible] 9 5	—	[illegible]
5 1[illegible] 10	[illegible] 10 [illegible]	116 5 3	[illegible] [illegible] [illegible]	1,[illegible] 1 2	[illegible]
3 3 [illegible]	1[illegible] 1 10	[illegible] 1 [illegible]	7,[illegible] [illegible] [illegible]	1,[illegible] 0 [illegible]	[illegible]
[illegible] 16 1	157 1[illegible] [illegible]	[illegible] 14 0	17,[illegible] [illegible] 11	[illegible] 1 3	[illegible]
15 [illegible] [illegible]	[illegible] 3 11	172 3 [illegible]	10,[illegible] 11 [illegible]	2,[illegible] 16 10	[illegible]
[illegible] 11 2	[illegible] [illegible] 4	—	[illegible] 16 2	[illegible] 0 10	[illegible]
[illegible] [illegible] 10	[illegible] 3 11	61 12 9	7,[illegible] [illegible] [illegible]	[illegible] 4 11	[illegible]
[illegible] 19 [illegible]	[illegible] 1 10	—	7,[illegible] 1 3	[illegible] 1 3	[illegible]
3 [illegible] [illegible]	91 [illegible] 3	150 16 0	[illegible] [illegible] 2	1,[illegible] 17 4	[illegible]
11 3 3	60 [illegible] [illegible]	[illegible] 11 [illegible]	[illegible] 1[illegible] [illegible]	[illegible] [illegible] 9	[illegible]

Balance in hands on the 31st December, 1864	Total Amounts received from Counties, &c., in Districts	Grant from Treasury at 4s. per Head per week	Casual Receipts. For Paying Patients	For Farm and Garden Produce	For Offal and Old Stores	Fines on Servants	Miscellaneous [illegible]
£ s. d.	£ s. d.	£ s. d.	£ s. d.	£ s. d.	£ s. d.	£ s. d.	£ s. d.
2,499 1 2	4,817 17 7	2,426 17 0	175 7 6	25 13 0	3 1 0	1 0 0	61 1 7
6,250 14 11	4,460 0 0	2,418 16 0	254 15 10	60 16 10	13 14 5	0 5 0	45 16 1
—	5,297 0 0	2,371 0 0	243 17 4	111 14 0	23 13 2	—	20 14 1
1,715 1 2	8,930 13 11	7,414 5 0	197 11 6	51 15 6	1 0 6	—	97 19 6
1,931 0 4	3,270 10 10	4,744 17 0	165 0 0	149 13 10	—	7 0 0	41 14 1
2,045 1 8	7,153 7 3	4,101 1 0	100 5 1	—	0 2 10	0 2 6	60 11 7
7,2[illegible] 18 10	6,703 10 0	9,782 12 0	840 0 1	—	91 10 8	1 17 0	103 4 1
316 0 10	5,119 0 0	3,316 5 0	172 11 10	164 10 8	3 17 0	—	31 0 0
237 4 11	3,087 15 3	2,045 17 0	246 17 8	68 7 1	9 4 6	2 10 0	16 1 1
887 1 3	4,611 10 4	4,249 6 0	112 17 0	103 18 7	1 5 5	0 7 0	77 9 1
1,320 12 5	8,410 0 6	8,197 0 0	101 10 0	25 0 6	4 17 0	—	1 3 0
656 8 2	3,178 7 10	3,376 17 0	130 0 0	74 10 2	8 2 6	3 17 0	11 1 11
1,219 4 1	4,181 10 0	5,713 10 0	76 7 3	116 11 3	—	—	—
917 6 0	9,702 15 4	4,911 0 0	403 18 1	—	70 19 6	0 15 0	73 15 1
79 16 11	8,760 16 7	3,399 5 0	138 7 9	252 11 0	21 0 2	—	534 7 7
70 15 6	4,086 17 7	2,347 1 0	701 4 11	67 1 4	11 6 7	0 7 0	—
1,610 11 11	3,600 0 0	1,730 0 0	113 5 10	244 16 4	4 19 7	3 0 0	47 1 0
4,[illegible] 2 6	692 17 7	4,241 16 0	219 0 0	176 17 0	—	—	41 11 6
[illegible] 4 8	3,402 0 0	6,149 6 0	871 0 8	729 10 10	6 4 2	1 0 0	[illegible] 11 6
12,283 8 0	11,447 5 4	10,330 0 0	600 4 11	87 14 11	145 1 7	1 0 4	701 15 0
2,993 0 3	1,780 5 0	1,694 0 0	118 11 0	36 0 0	6 0 6	1 10 0	16 4 4
2,[illegible] 5 6	3,031 11 0	2,779 5 0	201 11 10	220 14 6	11 15 11	2 18 0	40 11 5
43,116 2 4	111,028 5 1	[illegible] 0 0	5,137 5 1	2,388 19 3	[illegible] 13 8	[illegible] 13 7	[illegible]

EXPENDITURE—(continued).

Furniture.	Fuel and Light.	Soap and Candles.	Printing, Stationery, and Advertising.	Medicines, including Wines, Spirits, &c.	Repairs and Alterations.	Farm and Garden Expenses.	In[illegible]
£ s. d.	£ s. d.	£ s. d.	£ s. d.	£ s. d.	£ s. d.	£ s. d.	£ s. d.
118 6 7	741 10 2	13 4 6	55 15 6	165 5 6	823 0 10	143 6 7	50 7
183 6 6	347 17 7	110 11 7	81 19 0	218 0 8	331 18 1	70 13 10	66 0
68 6 7	410 19 11	195 11 0	46 15 0	194 10 5	712 2 1	110 0 9	80 1
616 5 6	118 14 0	80 16 1	90 10 9	136 10 11	474 11 9	183 1 10	71 11
48 2 7	473 0 11	47 7 1	84 19 1	193 7 0	419 1 5	259 18 8	79 11
672 13 0	201 8 11	117 4 11	130 8 6	815 14 7	656 13 6	709 17 2	61 0
985 1 10	1,300 1 0	138 14 0	111 9 0	483 8 5	693 3 0	700 6 11	61 11
274 7 10	546 10 4	40 5 0	701 10 9	753 0 10	439 4 0	476 10 1	55 4
736 5 7	873 3 10	86 15 10	98 11 7	104 13 8	720 13 0	640 15 4	55 5
77 16 0	673 10 2	111 7 10	64 7 6	119 9 1	461 13 11	124 18 11	55 4
73 3 1	724 6 1	60 1 0	41 1 8	701 18 1	131 11 0	76 3 10	30 1
403 8 1	912 8 0	106 10 6	90 12 11	184 18 6	700 13 0	171 11 10	47 13
100 18 2	421 4 7	37 6 7½	90 8 7	147 6 1	670 10 11	170 1 9½	17 1
701 10 8	760 10 3	164 13 1	77 7 11	708 10 8	1140 10 [illegible]	134 3 6	55 1
161 0 1	194 11 1	86 8 2	60 17 4	119 10 0	133 11 7	163 8 9	27 6
140 1 4	456 3 10	78 17 11	40 5 3	101 13 10	300 15 7	179 10 0	15 11
163 19 8	489 11 3	105 0 4	73 6 1	385 13 2	519 18 0	701 10 10	19 11
191 8 11	489 10 1	141 8 0	86 0 7	866 17 0	857 10 10	114 17 0	25 11
111 1 5	474 7 3	77 8 0	63 8 0	250 15 6½	191 2 10½	86 1 8	15 17
1019 7 2	1741 0 11	186 10 11	756 16 7	733 11 1	1671 6 7	740 17 1	73 10
8 19 0	298 2 0	89 16 1	26 16 10	86 19 9	684 10 11	812 4 0	24 1
45 1 1	230 6 7	90 16 8	39 8 0	163 0 11	696 0 1	187 17 4	75 0
1,804 6 4	14,810 15 7	2,420 4 9½	1,080 4 1	[illegible] 5 4½	20,[illegible] 4 0	2,[illegible] 10 0½	600 7

g 31st December, 1885.

EXPENDITURE.														
By Balance on the 31st December 1884.			Salaries and Wages.			Provisions and Groceries.			Clothing.			Bedding.		
£	s.	d.	£	s.	d.	£	s.	d.	£	s.	d.	£	s.	d.
—			1,283	11	6	1,087	8	9	463	19	1	208	17	
—			2,072	7	1	1,808	17	0	1,064	15	11	293	18	
256	5	9	2,703	14	8	3,711	9	8	1,446	11	3	198	17	
—			1,996	1	2	6,127	3	11	310	18	9	167	19	
—			1,679	9	3	2,768	19	2	418	1	8	209	16	
—			6,819	13	4	1,170	8	8	1,674	3	1	135	9	
—			4,083	9	8	8,577	11	1	1,417	13	10	432	15	
—			2,789	10	6	3,874	0	3	1,049	15	6	830	8	
—			1,362	14	11	7,106	15	0	357	1	8	167	11	
—			1,242	1	6	9,488	17	7	690	14	6	81	19	
—			1,706	14	6	1,164	4	7	971	11	2	118	1	
—			2,371	10	10	2,326	8	1	378	16	1	111	11	
—			1,804	18	3	7,897	11	8½	743	1	4	121	4	
—			2,607	14	11	3,176	6	7	789	17	7	167	0	
—			1,743	13	1	2,980	9	9	179	16	1	216	14	
—			1,673	1	4	2,910	10	7	620	9	9	168	3	
—			2,160	1	1	1,388	17	8	413	1	6	203	5	
—			1,287	1	9	6,642	19	2	840	5	1	671	10	
—			3,408	16	8	4,794	10	6	859	6	1½	79	3	
—			4,620	17	0	10,973	16	4	2,361	3	10	482	10	
—			1,917	8	11	3,489	18	11	637	4	4	276	3	
—			1,634	6	7	2,879	1	6	587	11	9	160	17	
256	5	7	47,289	16	5	88,180	13	0½	20,317	17	3½	3,851	17	

URE—(*continued*).												
Superannuation.			Total Expenditure.			Balance due by Governors, on the 31st Dec., 1885.			Daily Average No. of Patients maintained from the Public Funds during the year 1885.	Average Cost of Maintenance per head per annum.		
£	s.	d.	£	s.	d.	£	s.	d.	Number.	£	s.	d.
91	18	8	8,118	1	9	7,390	12	6	300	27	10	7
182	14	8	10,846	14	6	7,078	3	1	579	13	7	1
161	19	1	14,883	15	6	616	10	9	541	27	10	
157	16	8	6,887	4	9	3,092	1	8	294	21	10	1
78	7	4	7,847	7	4	1,800	1	1	336	20	12	5
879	3	11	11,447	4	11	4,063	10	4	478	23	18	4½
806	17	8	10,393	1	3	4,176	1	10	721	27	10	6
6	2	8	9,643	18	1	102	18	1	469	20	13	9
170	14	0	7,101	4	10	347	8	10	388	22	11	8
14	13	7	7,408	17	11	1,187	17	1	376	23	14	6
160	7	8	4,326	18	11	1,191	13	0	782	19	17	1
107	10	11	6,361	8	0	948	11	7	241	24	18	1
—			7,662	1	3	7,973	2	0	361	20	18	4
127	17	8	11,968	4	3	1,283	8	4	474	23	0	9
73	18	0	7,151	4	8	336	18	6	336	21	18	10
61	3	9	6,911	1	11	479	10	7	880	21	9	0
274	6	8	10,186	12	8	7,830	1	6	308	20	16	6
140	0	9	10,001	17	4	694	11	1	309	18	17	10
48	11	0	6,847	7	10	2,967	19	11	311	17	4	4½
667	18	3	26,767	1	11	6,302	9	10	1,069	21	11	0
67	7	0	7,724	10	7	489	13	7	161	19	0	10
31	5	0	6,777	7	7	1,459	14	1	405	21	19	1
3,841	10	0	216,799	17	4	52,830	11	8	7,984	21	19	4

No. 24.—Names of Governors and Dates of Appointment, with Number of Meetings attended during the Year ended 31st December, 1885.

Name	Date of Appointment	Number of Meetings attended.
Armagh.		
Hugh Boyle, Esq. J.P.	Oct. 11, 1861	6
*His Grace the Lord Primate	Nov 29, 1869	–
*Sir J. M. Stronge, Bart. J.P.	Dec 15, 1864	–
John Hancock, Esq. J.P.	Jan. 21, 1865	–
Dean Chaloner Brady, Esq. J.P., M.D.	Jan. 31, 1870	–
Joseph Atkinson, Esq. J.P. D.L.	do	–
Maxwell C. Close, Esq. J.P. D.L.	do.	–
John Hughes, Esq.	do	5
St. John Blacker Douglas, Esq. J.P. D.L.	do	–
Robt. B. Templer, Esq. J.P.	do.	1
The Most Rev. Archbishop D. M'Gettigan	Nov. 22, 1870	–
The Rt. Hon. the Earl of Charlemont, K.P.	Jan 13, 1873	–
The Rev. John Elliott	May 2, 1876	10
George D. Beresford, Esq. J.P. D.L.	Dec. 11, 1878	2
J. G. Winder, Esq. J.P.	do.	1
Rev. Jackson Smyth, D.D.	March 15, 1881	7
J. G. Richardson, Esq.	do	–
C. Reynolds, Esq.	March 1, 1867	–
R. Gillespie, Esq. J.P.	do.	1
T. Shillington, Esq.	do	[illegible]
The Rt. Hon. Lord Lurgan	[illegible]	–
W. Simpson, Esq.	[illegible]	3
Sir J. C. Stronge, Bart.	May 30, 1883	–
H. B. Armstrong, Esq. D.L. J.P.	Dec 21, 1883	–
W. J. Best, Esq.	do.	–
Rev. G. Chadwick, D.D.	do.	–
Colonel Geo. Dobbin, J.P.	do	–
F. Lavery, Esq. M.D. J.P.	do.	–
James Lonsdale, Esq. J.P.	do.	–
Joseph Murphy, Esq. J.P.	do.	–
The Very Rev. W. Reeves, D.D.	do.	–
*James Wynne, Esq.	do.	–
Ballinasloe.		
The Right Hon. Earl of Clancarty, J.P.	Nov. 19, 1860	1
Right Hon. Lord Clonbrock, J.P.	Aug 15, 1835	–
Major John D'Arcy, J.P.	July 15, 1865	1
Harry T. Potts, Esq. J.P.	do	–
Charles Filgate, Esq. J.P.	Sept. 13, 1861	–
Major H. J. Gascoyne, J.P.	do.	–
Cornelius O'Kelly, Esq. J.P.	do.	1
Andrew N. Comyn, Esq. J.P.	Mar. 29, 1861	1
John J. O'Shaughnessy, Esq. J.P.	Jan. 10, 1867	4
Captain S. J. Cowan, J.P.	Mar. 29, 1867	–
Rev. J. W. Whiteside	do	5
Thomas E. Mahon, Esq.	June 20, 1861	7
Capt. John Eyre, J.P.	do	7
M. J. Cheevers, Esq. D.L. J.P.	April 25, 1870	1
Most Rev. Bishop Duggan	Feb. 10, 1874	–
Ballinasloe—*continued*		
Jas. MacDermott, Esq. J.P.	Feb 10, 1874	2
Walter S. Taylor, Esq. J.P.	do.	–
Rt. Rev. Bishop of Tuam	Oct. 16, 1874	–
John Gairdner, Esq. J.P.	do.	6
Col. King Harman, D.L. M.P.	March 9, 1879	–
R. W. Fowler, Esq. J.P.	do.	10
John Ward, Esq.	Jan. 31, 1867	13
R. J. Kinkead, Esq. M.D.	do	2
E. C. Villiers, Esq. J.P.	do	8
J. Ross Mahon, Esq. J.P.	do.	9
Wm. T. Potts, Esq. J.P.	June 30, 1883	9
John W. Hynes, Esq.	July 6, 1883	4
Belfast.		
The Lord Bishop of Down, Connor, and Dromore	April, 1850	2
Earl Dufferin, K.P., K.C.B.	Dec. 1855	–
Sir Thomas M'Clure, Bart. V.L. J.P.	January, 1856	1
Colonel W. B. Forde, J.P. D.L.	March, 1857	–
The Right Rev. P. Dorrian, D.D.	Sept. 1866	1
Sir Edward Coey, J.P. D.L.	October, 1866	–
John Young, Esq. J.P. D.L.	do.	1
H. H. M'Neile, Esq. J.P. D.L.	do.	4
J. B. Houston, Esq. J.P. D.L.	do.	3
Viscount Templetown, K.C.B. D.L.	do	–
Lord Waveney, J.P. D.L.	do	–
Lord Dunleath, D.L.	March, 1867	–
Sir David Taylor, J.P.	Feb. 1868	10
William Ewart, Esq. J.P. M.P.	March, 1868	1
James Cuming, Esq. M.D.	March, 1869	4
M. R. Dalway, Esq. J.P. D.L.	do.	–
Sir Edward P. Cowan, J.P. D.L.	April, 1871	–
Sir Charles Lanyon, J.P.	October, 1876	3
Rev. Robt. Hanna, D.D.	April, 1880	1
Finlay M'Cance, Esq. J.P.	Nov. 1880	–
John P. Browne, Esq. J.P.	Nov. 1881	–
Henry Matier, Esq. J.P.	do	3
James Musgrave, Esq. J.P.	do.	5
Rev. Wm. Johnston, D.D.	October, 1881	9
Arthur Hamill, Esq. J.P.	do.	5
Right Hon. Earl of Shaftesbury	do	–
Sir E. J. Harland, Bart. J.P. (Mayor of Belfast)	January, 1885	9
Carlow.		
H. Rochfort, Esq. J.P. D.L.	May 5, 1855	1
R. C. Browne, Esq. J.P. D.L.	Feb. 18, 1857	10
W. F. Burton, Esq. J.P.	do.	–
H. Blackney, Esq. J.P.	do.	–
Rt. Hon. H. Bruen, P.C. J.P. D.L.	Dec. 21, 1858	5
Right Rev. Bishop Walshe	do	7
P. J. Newton, Esq. J.P. D.L.	do	–
T. Fitzgerald, Esq. J.P.	Jan. 29, 1866	–
Sir Thomas P. Butler, Bart. J.P. D.L.	May 6, 1865	4

* Died.

No. 24.—NAMES of GOVERNORS and Dates of Appointment, with Number of Meetings attended during the Year ended 31st December, 1883—*con.*

Name.	Date of Appointment.	Number of Meetings attended.
CARLOW—*continued.*		
A. M. Kavanagh, Esq. L.C.	June 1, 1867	-
W. B. Bulwer, Esq. J.P.	do.	-
Sir Charles W. C. Burton, Bart. J.P., D.L.	do.	3
J. Alexander, Esq. J.P.	do.	-
Very Rev. J. Kavanagh, D.D. P.P.	June 9, 1869	7
Right Hon. W. H. F. Cogan, P.C., D.L.	Jan. 21, 1870	-
Captain P. Butler,	do.	-
James Cassidy, Esq. J.P.	do.	1
Patrick Nolan, Esq.	do.	-
J. Middleton, Esq. J.P.	do.	-
P. M. Carroll, Esq. J.P.	do.	4
Michael Walshe, Esq.	do.	3
Baron de Robeck, J.P., D.L.	Jan. 8, 1875	1
Stewart Duckett, Esq. J.P.	do.	-
Hardy Eustace, Esq. J.P.	do.	7
Major Burrowes, J.P., D.L.	Sept. 13, 1878	5
Marquess of Kildare,	do.	7
CASTLEBAR.		
The Earl of Lucan, G.C.B., Lieut. of the County,	Mar. 28, 1866	-
Sir R. L. Blosse, Bart. J.P.	do.	-
J. Nolan Ferrall, Esq. D.L. J.P.	do.	
Chas. Strickland, Esq. J.P.	do.	-
John C. Walsh, Esq. D.L. J.P.	do.	-
Charles L. FitzGerald, Esq. D.L. J.P.	do.	1
Lord Oranmore, D.L., J.P.	June 11, 1869	-
A. C. Lambert, Esq. D.L.	Nov. 19, 1868	1
Sir George C. O'Donnell, Bart. D.L.	Nov. 26, 1866	-
M. H. Jordan, Esq. J.P.	Nov. 4, 1870	-
Thomas Tighe, Esq. J.P.	Dec. 10, 1874	8
D. A. Browne, Esq. D.L., J.P.	do.	4
O. O'Malley, Esq. J.P.	do.	6
Capt. Chas. Howe Knox, J.P., D.L.	Nov. 15, 1876	
Standish O'Grady M'Dermott, Esq. J.P.	Mar. 15, 1877	-
Ulred A. Knox, Esq. D.L. J.P.	Aug. 30, 1879	-
Col. M. J. Blake, J.P., D.L.	do.	1
Robt. Vesey Stoney, Esq. D.L. J.P.	do.	2
Wm. Livingstone, Esq.	do.	7
R. H. Percy, Esq. J.P.	Jan. 21, 1881	-
Chas. O'Malley, Esq. D.L.	do.	6
J. H. Peyton, Esq.	do.	5
A. C. Larminie, Esq.	do.	13
Most Rev. Dr. M'Evilly, D.D. Archbishop of Tuam,	June 11, 1881	-
Most Rev. Dr. M'Cormack, D.D. Bishop of Achonry,	do.	-
Most Rev. Dr. Conway, D.D. Bishop of Killala,	do.	-
Right Rev. Dr. Bernard, D.D. Bishop of Tuam,	do.	-
CLONMEL.		
Thomas Lalor, Esq. V.L.	Oct. 19, 1819	1
Nichd. U. Bayly, Esq. J.P.	Sept. 22, 1835	-
Percy Gough, Esq. J.P.	Oct. 1, 1845	4
CLONMEL—*continued.*		
Samuel Perry, Esq. D.L.	Sept. 16, 1867	1
William Davis, Esq.	do.	12
Thomas Butler Stoney, Esq. J.P.	Aug. 20, 1868	
Lieut.-Colonel William Knox, J.P.	do.	-
Edward M. Armstrong, Esq. J.P.	do.	1
Anthony Parker, Esq. J.P.	do.	1
Right Rev. Dr. Power	do.	-
Rev. Thos. English, P.P.	do.	-
William Ryan, Esq. J.P.	April 16, 1870	4
Jerome J. Geary, Esq. J.P.	April 11, 1872	-
Right Hon. the Earl of Donoughmore, D.L.	Oct. 16, 1874	-
Stephen Moore, Esq. D.L.	do.	8
T. Albert Quin, Esq. J.P.	do.	6
Capt. Villiers S. Morton, J.P.	Jan. 25, 1876	12
Francis W. Low, Esq. D.L.	May 2, 1877	5
Hugh F. Massy, Esq. J.P.	do.	-
Wm. A. Riall, Esq. D.L.	do.	6
The Mayor of Clonmel, *ex-officio*, J.P.	July 6, 1878	11
Benjamin Fayle, Esq. J.P.	Dec. 28, 1879	11
Darby J. Scully, Esq. J.P.	do.	5
Richard Bagwell, Esq. D.L.	do.	8
Edmund Woods, Esq. J.P.	do.	11
James J. Shee, Esq. J.P.	do.	11
Rev. C. J. Flavin, P.P.	July 28, 1881	4
Sir John C. Carden, Bart. J.P.	Mar. 8, 1853	-
Fitzgibbon Trant, Esq. J.P.	do.	2
Alderman E. Cantwell, J.P.	May 21, 1855	9
Geo. Edward Ryan, Esq. J.P., D.L.	do.	-
Thos. Butler, Esq. J.P., D.L.	do.	-
Wm. Murphy, Esq. J.P.	do.	-
G. K. B. Massy-Dawson, Esq. D.L.	do.	2
Bark Phillips, Esq. J.P., D.L.	do.	4
CORK.		
Sir C. D. O. J. Norreys, Bart. D.L.	Oct. 4, 1844	-
Lord Visct. Doneraile, D.L.	do.	-
R. T. Eyre, Esq. D.L.	do.	2
Right Rev. Dr. Delaney, D.D.	Mar. 12, 1846	-
D. Leahy Arthur, Esq. J.P.	do.	-
D. W. J. Norreys, Esq. J.P.	June 17, 1850	-
William Lumley Perrier, Esq. J.P.	Feb. 18, 1859	3
The O'Donovan, Esq. J.P.	do.	-
W. R. Meade, Esq. J.P.	do.	-
William Johnson, Esq. D.L.	Oct. 7, 1864	7
Henry L. Young, Esq. J.P.	Oct. 20, 1863	10
Isaac Morgan, Esq. J.P.	do.	10
John W. Carey, Esq. J.P.	do.	9
Robert Hall, Esq. J.P.	do.	-
Maurice Murray, Esq. D.L.	June 7, 1869	7
Martin Hayes, Esq.	Sept. 24, 1869	-
W. H. Lyons, Esq. J.P.	Jan. 19, 1872	10
D. F. Leahy, Esq. D.L.	do.	-
John Waters, Esq. J.P.	April 11, 1872	6
J. K. Pim, Esq. J.P.	May 30, 1871	17

No. 24.—Names of Governors and Dates of Appointment, with Number of Meetings attended during the Year ended 31st December, 1885—*con.*

Name.	Date of Appointment.	Number of Meetings attended.
Cork—*continued.*		
G. A. Wood, Esq. J.P.	Jan. 16, 1876	1
J. M'D. Webb, Esq. J.P.	Oct. 4, 1876	10
The Rt. Rev. Dr Gregg, D.D. Bishop of Cork, Cloyne, and Ross	Sep. 8, 1876	-
Sir Geo. St. J. Colthurst, Bart. D.L.	Dec. 25, 1879	4
D. R. Sarsfield, Esq. D.L.	do.	9
W. A. Fagan, Esq. J.P.	do.	10
Savage French, Esq. J.P.	do.	-
Ludlow Beamish, Esq. J.P.	do.	3
Colonel Colthurst	Aug. 31, 1880	7
Wm. Shaw, Esq. J.P.	do.	-
Geo. E. Roche, J.P.	Dec. 13, 1880	-
N. D. Murphy, Esq. D.L.	do.	-
*Sir G. Penrose, Ald. J.P.	March 29, 1881	5
*H. Dale, Esq. Ald.	do.	7
Rt. Rev. Dr. FitzGerald, D.D. Bishop of Ross	Mar. 30, 1883	-
The Earl of Bandon	Mar. 6, 1884	-
Col. R. A. Shuldham, D.L.	do.	4
P. Kennedy, Esq. J.P.	do.	8
B. J. Sheehan, Esq. J.P.	July 28, 1884	10
*P. J. Madden, Esq. Mayor	Jan. 5, 1885	3
Downpatrick.		
The Right Hon. Earl Dufferin, K.P.	Dec. 2, 1846	-
The Right Rev. the Lord Bishop of Down	do.	-
Lord Duramore, D.L.	do.	-
Colonel W. B. Forde, D.L.	do.	14
Major Robert P. Maxwell, D.L.	do.	11
John B. Houston, Esq. D.L.	do.	-
Maj. Andw. Nugent, D.L.	do.	1
John J. Whyte, Esq. D.L.	do.	-
Fitzherbert Filgate, Esq. J.P.	do.	-
Robert Gordon, Esq. J.P.	do.	12
Wm. Johnston, Esq. M.P.	March 23, 1859	8
Sir Thomas M'Clure, Bart. V.L.	do.	-
Colonel John Craig, J.P.	do.	6
George H. Gartlan, Esq. J.P.	do.	1
Alex. J. R. Stewart, Esq. D.L.	Oct. 21, 1863	-
Charles Russell, Esq. J.P.	Aug. 10, 1870	-
William N. Wallace, Esq. D.L.	Nov. 3, 1870	13
Lieut.-Gen. The Rt. Hon. Lord de Ros, D.L.	Oct. 16, 1874	4
John Mulholland, Esq.	Oct. 27, 1875	-
Col. G. R. Hamilton, D.L.	Aug. 7, 1880	5
Lord Arthur W. Hill, M.P.	Oct. 30, 1880	-
John Cleland, Esq. J.P.	do.	13
Earl of Roden, D.L.	July 28, 1881	-
Rev. William Clarke	Nov. 1, 1881	5
Francis Heron, Esq.	do.	9
Robt. S. Corbett, Esq. J.P.	Nov. 1, 1881	5
Viscount Bangor, D.L.	Jan. 31, 1882	2
Hon. H. Ward, J.P.	July 3, 1882	7
William Gordon, Esq. M.D. J.P.	do.	2
Downpatrick—*con.*		
George Murphy, Esq. J.P.	June 14, 1884	-
G. H. Gernian, Esq. D.L.	do.	1
T. D'Arcy Hoey, Esq. J.P.	do.	-
Major Alexander Gracey	Dec. 1, 1884	1
Ennis.		
Capt. C. G. O'Callaghan, D.L.	Nov. 30, 1867	-
Richard Stacpoole, Esq. D.L.	do.	-
J. F. V. Fitzgerald, Esq. D.L.	do.	-
James O'Brien, Esq. D.L.	do.	-
T. R. Henn, Esq. Q.C. D.L.	do.	-
Robt. W. C. Reeves, Esq. D.L.	do.	-
Maj. Chas. F. Studdert, J.P.	do.	1
Major G. N. Studdert, J.P.	do.	-
Thomas Greene, Esq. J.P.	do.	7
Col. Marcus Paterson, J.P.	Dec. 12, 1861	-
Major Wm. Mills Molony, D.L.	March 5, 1862	-
James Frost, Esq. J.P.	Aug. 29, 1869	-
John M'Donnell, Esq. J.P.	Jan. 21, 1870	
The Most Rev. Dr. Ryan, R.C. Bishop of Killaloe	April 11, 1872	-
Capt. C. M. Parkinson, J.P.	do.	-
Pierce O'Brien, Esq. J.P.	do.	9
Rt. Hon. Lord Inchiquin, Lord Lieut., Co. Clare	Oct. 26, 1872	3
Matthew Kelly, Esq. J.P.	Aug. 1, 1873	4
J. W. Scott, Esq. J.P.	Oct. 6, 1876	11
Col. G. C. Synge, J.P.	Oct. 16, 1878	5
Col. H. M. Studdert, J.P.	do.	-
Thomas Crowe, Esq. D.L.	do.	9
M. H. Crowe, Esq. J.P.	June 26, 1883	1
V. J. Sherrard, Esq. J.P.	do.	-
Most Rev. The Bishop of Killaloe	June 16, 1884	-
Francis W. Hickman, Esq. J.P.	do.	-
Michael Roche Kelly, Esq. J.P.	do.	1
Thomas O'Gorman, Esq. J.P.	do.	
Enniscorthy.		
Right Hon. the Earl of Courtown, D.L.	Nov. 11, 1861	-
Lt.-Col. Harry Alcock, D.L.	do.	10
George Le Hunte, Esq. J.P.	do.	8
Francis Augustine Leigh, Esq. J.P.	do.	-
Stephen Ram, Esq. D.L.	do.	-
Henry Lambert, Esq. D.L.	do.	-
Walter M. Westropp-Dawson, Esq. D.L.	do.	1
Edward Tottenham Irvine, Esq. D.L.	do.	1
Arthur M. Kavanagh, Esq. L. & C. R.	do.	-
Geo. C. Roberts, Esq. J.P.	do.	10
Right Hon. Henry Bruen, D.L.	do.	-
Lorenzo Dundas, Esq. J.P.	do.	4
Charles Tottenham, Esq. J.P.	Nov. 29, 1867	-

* Thus marked are ex-officio—so long as they hold their respective offices.

No. 24.—NAMES of GOVERNORS and Dates of Appointment, with Number of Meetings attended during the Year ended 31st December, 1885—*con.*

Name.	Date of Appointment.	Number of Meetings attended
ENNISCORTHY—*con.*		
Right Hon. the Earl of Courtown, K.P.	Dec. 20, 1861	–
Anthony Cliffe, Esq., D.L.	Jan. 17, 1863	–
Right Hon. the Lord Templemore, D.L.	May 5, 1864	–
Nathaniel N. Cochrane, Esq. J.P.	do.	12
Matthew A. Maher, Esq. D.L.	do.	–
Sir John Talbot Power, Bart. D.L.	Dec. 9, 1869	8
*James P. Devereux, Esq. jun.	Jan. 19, 1872	–
Patrick Breen, Esq. J.P.	do.	–
Edward Thos. Solly Flood, Esq. D.L.	do.	1
Capt. Thomas Walker, J.P.	do.	7
Capt. Percy L. Harvey, D.L.	do.	1
*John Thomas Devereux, Esq. D.L.	June 3, 1877	–
William Cookman, Esq. J.P.	May 16, 1874	11
C. M. Doyne, Esq. J.P., D.L.	Jan. 26, 1876	–
Richd. Donovan, esq. D.L.	Mar. 13, 1877	–
The Mayor of Wexford	July 9, 1878	1
Lord Maurice Fitzgerald, L. and C.B.	Jan. 24, 1881	–
Sir G. H. Porter, Knt. M.D. J.P.	do.	–
Lieut.-General Solomon Richards, J.P.	March 7, 1882	4
Rev. Robert S. Carew Blacker, J.P.	do.	–
KILKENNY		
Sir John Blunden, Bart. D.L.	April 26, 1852	9
John B. Jones, Esq. D.L.	do.	–
Thomas Lalor, Esq. D.L.	do.	–
W. H. Flood, Esq. D.L.	do.	4
Lord James Butler, J.P.	May 16, 1853	–
Col. Sir J. Langrishe, Bart. D.L.	May 8, 1865	
The Right Hon. the Earl of Carrick	Sept. 16, 1865	–
The Most Noble the Marquess of Ormonde, Lord Lieutenant of the County	Oct. 20, 1865	–
The Right Hon. the Earl of Desart	June 6, 1867	–
Michael Dan Keating, Esq. D.L.	Feb. 18, 1861	–
R. Warren, Esq. D.L.	Jan. 13, 1872	2
M. Langrishe, Esq.	Feb. 10, 1875	–
H. M. De Montmorency, Esq. J.P.	do.	–
M. M. Wild, Esq. J.P.	April 23, 1876	–
W. F. Blunden, Esq. J.P.	do.	2
F. B. M. Beatie, Esq. J.P.	Mar. 20, 1878	–

Name.	Date of Appointment.	Number of Meetings attended
KILKENNY—*con.*		
Sir R. Power, Bart. D.L.	Mar. 31, 1879	–
James Poe, Esq.	do.	4
R. Colles, Esq.	do.	4
Right Rev. Dr. Walshe	do.	4
Lord Arthur Butler, D.L.	do.	1
Captain M. J. Kane, J.P.	do.	1
James Sullivan, Esq. J.P.	do.	7
E. Smithwick, Esq. J.P.	do.	4
Col. H. V. Stuart, D.L.	Jan. 26, 1881	–
Rev. W. De Montmorency, J.P.	March 8, 1882	–
Raymond de la Poer, Esq. J.P.	do.	–
J. F. Smithwick, Esq. M.P.	Sept. 13, 1877	4
John Smithwick, Esq. D.L.	May 21, 1883	–
William O'Donnell, Esq. *Mayor*	Jan. 8, 1885	7
The Right Hon. Viscount Clifden	Feb. 18, 1885	–
Right Rev. Dr. Brownrigg	do.	–
KILLARNEY		
The Right Hon. the Earl of Kenmare	April 26, 1852	1
Sir John Blacker Douglas, Esq. D.L.	do.	–
Wm. T. Crosbie, Esq. D.L.	do.	–
D. C. Coltsman, Esq. D.L.	do.	7
Wilson Gunn, Esq. J.P.	do.	–
Denis Shine Lawlor, Esq. J.P.	do.	–
Richard Mahony, Esq. D.L.	do.	–
John M'Carthy O'Leary, Esq. D.L.	do.	–
The O'Donoghue, J.P.	Nov. 13, 1864	–
Henry Arthur Herbert, Esq. D.L.	Jan. 23, 1866	–
Henry Herbert, Esq. J.P.	Feb. 10, 1865	–
Richd. H. Orpen, Esq. J.P.	do.	9
Sir Rowland Blennerhassett, Bart.	Oct. 19, 1867	–
Daniel James O'Connell, Esq. J.P.	May 14, 1869	–
Sir Henry Donovan	Jan. 25, 1870	6
Sir M. J. O'Connell, Bart.	Feb. 16, 1870	5
Sir John F. Godfrey, Bart.	Aug. 16, 1870	–
John Mahony, Esq. J.P.	Nov. 3, 1870	–
Samuel M. Hussey, Esq. J.P.	Nov. 16, 1871	6
Colonel Crosbie, D.L.	Nov. 21, 1876	8
John White Leahy, Esq. J.P.	Dec. 4, 1876	7
Daniel Brennan, Esq. J.P.	do.	–
Edward Morrogh Bernard, Esq. J.P.	April 6, 1877	1
The Right Hon. Lord Headley	Oct. 16, 1878	–
Right Rev. Dr. Higgins	March 7, 1882	6
The MacGillicuddy, J.P.	May 31, 1881	1
Ven. Archdeacon Wynne	do.	11
Wm. C. Hickie, Esq. D.L.	Dec. 12, 1881	1
Very Rev. Dean Coffey	do.	7

* Dead.

No. 24.—Names of Governors and Dates of Appointment, with Number of Meetings attended during the Year ended 31st December, 1885—con.

Name.	Date of Appointment.	Number of Meetings attended.
Letterkenny.		
Viscount Lifford, J.P., D.L.	Jan. 31, 1846	-
Alex. J. R. Stewart, Esq., J.P., D.L.	do.	-
Thomas Ball, Esq., J.P., D.L.	do.	-
John G. Bowen, Esq., J.P.	do.	-
Col. Montgomery, J.P., D.L.	do.	10
Wybrants Olphert, Esq., J.P., D.L.	do.	-
Wm. Sinclair, Esq., J.P., D.L.	do.	-
Marquis of Hamilton,	do.	-
Most Rev. Dr. M'Gettigan	do.	-
Sir W. H. M. Style, Bart.	do.	-
John H. Boyd, Esq., J.P., D.L.	do.	13
Jas. G. Grove, Esq., J.P., D.L.	do.	3
Major Thos. Patterson, J.P.	Nov. 30, 1856	13
T. W. D. Humphreys, Esq., J.P.	May 6, 1864	-
Rev. Robert M'Morris	June 7, 1863	10
Geo. H. Harvey, Esq., J.P.	April 11, 1870	-
William J. Foster, Esq., J.P.	Feb. 14, 1871	-
James M'Cafferty, Esq., J.P.	do.	-
Chas. F. Stewart, Esq., J.P.	Nov. 30, 1871	-
Philip J. Doyne, Esq., J.P.	do.	10
Edmund Murphy, Esq., J.P.	Oct. 19, 1871	-
Colonel Mansfield, J.P.	Dec. 18, 1879	7
Rev. Dr. Kinnear	Feb. 24, 1881	9
R. Sweeney, Esq.	May 28, 1881	-
Jos. Alexander, Esq., J.P.	do.	-
The Most Rev. Dr. Logue	July 29, 1881	4
Rev. Dr. Rolls	Sept. 23, 1882	3
Rev. J. M'Menamin, P.P.	do.	-
Limerick.		
The Right Rev. Dr. Graves, Protestant Bishop (*ex officio*)	-	-
The Rt. Hon. Lord Emly, P.C.	August, 1847	1
William Spaight, Esq.	March, 1849	3
The Most Rev. Dr. Butler, R.C. Bishop	Dec. 31, 1861	4
John T. MacSheehy, Esq., D.L.	do.	-
Sir David V. Roche, Bart.	July 4, 1866	-
Robert Hunt, Esq., J.P.	Oct. 21, 1868	1
John C. Delmege, Esq., J.P.	do.	6
John M'Donnell, Esq.	Dec., 1869	-
Edward J. Synan, Esq., D.L.	do.	-
The Very Rev. Dean Bunbury	August 1, 1874	3
The Very Rev. Dean Cregan, P.P.	do.	-
John R. Tinsly, Esq., J.P.	May 16, 1876	2
James Spaight, Esq., J.P.	do.	1
Chas. B. Barrington, Esq., J.P.	do.	-
The Rt. Hon. Lord Massy, D.L.	Nov. 27, 1871	4
Lt.-Gen. Lord Clarina,	do.	-
Col. Robert Monsell,	Mar. 16, 1877	6
Robert de Ros Rose, Esq.	April 26, 1880	1
Captain Mark Mansell,	April 26, 1880	7
Limerick—continued.		
Thos. R. O'Brien, Esq., D.L.	Mar. 27, 1881	3
The Hon. Gaston Monsell, J.P.	June 29, 1881	-
John J. Cleary, Esq., J.P.	July 3, 1882	4
James Harris, Esq.	May 31, 1882	11
Edward Wm. O'Brien, Esq., D.L.	Aug. 27, 1884	-
Wm. Spillane, Esq., J.P.	do.	5
Jeremiah Coughlan, Esq.	do.	10
Stephen O'Mara, Esq., Mayor	1884	-
Londonderry.		
The Lord Bishop of Derry (*ex officio*)	-	-
J. H. Beresford, Esq., D.L.	Sept. 1, 1825	11
Sir H. H. Bruce, Bart., D.L.	Feb. 13, 1847	1
Rev. D. R. Gough	Dec. 6, 1849	-
Right Rev. Dr. Kelly	do.	-
R. M'Corkell, Esq., J.P.	May 9, 1861	-
Major Browne, D.L.	do.	-
S. M. Alexander, Esq., D.L.	Feb. 1, 1861	-
R. L. Moore, Esq., D.L.	do.	-
C. T. M'Causland, Esq., D.L.	do.	-
J. J. Clarke, Esq., D.L.	do.	-
W. F. Bagot, Esq., J.P.	May 10, 1869	5
William Tillie, Esq., J.P.	do.	1
Sir B. Reid, Knt., J.P.	Feb. 16, 1871	4
Charles O'Neill, Esq., J.P.	do.	8
W. H. Scott, Esq., D.L.	May 18, 1874	4
Rev. D. Babington	do.	13
Wm. Thompson, Esq., J.P.	do.	1
Sir W. F. L. Conyngham, K.C.B., D.L.	Oct. 4, 1876	-
Lieut.-Col. Knox, D.L.	do.	4
Sir R. M'Vicker, Knt., J.P.	Jan. 18, 1880	4
Robt. Hamilton, Esq., J.P.	do.	12
Capt. B. M. Givens, D.L.	April 26, 1880	-
Rev. J. M. Rodgers	Feb. 11, 1882	4
Rev. R. M. Brown, D.D.	do.	1
George Colhoun, Esq., J.P.	do.	-
Henry Tyler, Esq., J.P.	do.	-
Hugh Lyle, Esq., J.P.	do.	7
Alex. Black, Esq., J.P.	do.	10
John Cooke, Esq., J.P.	do.	-
J. S. Mulholland, Esq., J.P.	do.	-
P. T. Rodgers, Esq., J.P.	do.	3
Daniel Taylor, Esq., J.P.	do.	-
The Very Rev. The Dean of Derry	Mar. 24, 1884	8
Rev. Charles M'Faul, P.P.	do.	5
Rev. T. Pettigrew, D.D.	do.	4
Maryborough.		
Edmund G. Dease, Esq., D.L.	Mar. 26, 1862	6
Sir Allen J. Walsh, Bart., D.L.	Dec. 16, 1864	11
William Phillips, Esq., J.P.	April 11, 1864	1

No. 24.—Names of Governors and Dates of Appointment, with Number of Meetings attended during the Year ended 31st December, 1885—*con.*

Name.	Date of Appointment.	Number of Meetings attended.
Maryborough—*con.*		
Right Hon. Earl of Rosse, D.L.	May 24, 1869	-
John V. Cassidy, Esq. J.P.	Jan. 3, 1871	-
Captain R. G. Cosby, D.L.	Oct. 9, 1871	1
Right Hon. Earl of Portarlington, D.L.	do.	1
Thomas Kemmis, Esq. D.L.	do.	4
Lieut.-Col. Ambrose C. W. Cox, J.P.	do.	-
Richard Warburton, Esq. D.L.	Oct. 16, 1874	1
Reginald Digby, Esq. J.P.	May 7, 1875	1
R. H. H. Smyth, Esq. D.L.	Jan. 26, 1876	8
Lt.-Col. H. D. Carden, D.L.	Dec. 4, 1876	9
Right Hon. Viscount de Vesci, D.L.	do.	6
Capt. R. T. Stannus, J.P.	Mar. 31, 1879	5
William Dunne, Esq. J.P.	do.	4
J. L. Bland, Esq. J.P.	do.	5
Capt. J. S. Powell, J.P.	do.	-
Right Hon. Lord Castletown, D.L.	June 14, 1881	-
Charles J. Blake, Esq. J.P.	do.	-
Maj.-Gen. J. P. Mauney, J.P.	do.	1
William Young, Esq. J.P.	do.	1
Toby R. Garvey, Esq. J.P.	do.	7
Rev. Matthew Gaffney, P.P.	do.	-
John Wrafter, Esq. J.P.	do.	4
Rev. Andrew Phelan, P.P.	April 2, 1885	6
Monaghan.		
The Earl of Dartrey, L. and J.P.	Sept. 27, 1868	-
The Marq. of Headfort, L. and J.P.	do.	-
The Hon. Henry Cavendish Butler, J.P. D.L.	do.	2
Lt.-Col. Jesse Lloyd, J.P.	do.	8
R. C. Leslie, Esq. J.P. D.L.	do.	-
John Madden, Esq.	do.	-
Major Saunderson, J.P. D.L. M.P.	do.	1
André Allen Murray-Ker, Esq. J.P. D.L.	do.	5
Mervyn Pratt, Esq. J.P. D.L.	do.	-
W. F. De Vismes Kane, Esq. J.P.	do.	8
Lieut.-Col. H. T. Clements, J.P. D.L.	do.	-
Theophilus Clements, Esq. J.P. D.L.	do.	-
Benjamin B. Adams, Esq. J.P.	do.	-
Most Rev. Jas. Donnelly, D.D. R.C. Bishop, Clogher	March 13, 1869	1
Most Rev. Nicholas Conaty, D.D. R.C. Bishop, Kilmore	do.	-
Plunkett Kenny, Esq. J.P. D.L.	do.	-
Martin N. Wall, Esq. J.P.	do.	9
[illegible] Fitzherbert Filgate, Esq. J.P.	Nov. 1, 1870	-
The Lord Rossmore, D.L.	Oct. 16, 1871	-

Name.	Date of Appointment.	Number of Meetings attended.
Monaghan—*continued.*		
Sir John Leslie, Bart. J.P. D.L.	Oct. 16, 1871	6
Lt.-Col. Gerald R. Dease, J.P.	Nov. 27, 1874	
Thos. A. Cartlan, Esq. J.P.	Jan. 13, 1875	1
Ven. C. M. Stack, D.D. Archdeacon of Clogher	May 7, 1875	12
Henry Gustavus Brooke, Esq. J.P.	June 10, 1875	1
Joseph Wright, Esq.	Mar. 6, 1876	7
Rev. James A. Allison, M.A.	Feb. 17, 1879	14
Rev. John Davidson, M.A.	do.	13
Wm. Henderson, Esq. J.P.	Mar. 7, 1879	16
John Givan, Esq. J.P.	April 1, 1880	8
Rich. John Blakely, Esq. J.P.	do.	14
Surgeon M. G. Bush, J.P.	do.	14
Mullingar.		
Westmeath.		
Sir Benjamin Chapman, Bart.	July 8, 1854	-
G. A. Rochfort-Boyd, Esq. D.L.	do.	4
Thos. J. Smyth, Esq. D.L.	Nov. 10, 1864	2
Right Hon. Earl of Longford, K.C.B.	Mar. 6, 1866	5
Joseph Tuite, Esq. D.L.	do.	-
Lieut.-Col. Nugent, D.L.	do.	8
Richard S. Fetherston H., Esq. D.L.	Feb. 18, 1867	1
Right Hon. Lord Greville, D.L.	do.	7
Right Rev. Dr. Nulty	do.	-
Geo. N. Purdon, Esq. J.P.	Nov. 26, 1868	-
W. B. Smythe, Esq. D.L.	do.	-
Ralph Smyth, Esq. D.L.	Nov. 24, 1871	7
Captain F. Tottenham	do.	-
Walter Pollard-Urquhart, Esq. J.P.	do.	8
Colonel J. Cooper, J.P.	Oct. 19, 1871	3
Lieut.-Gen. Hon. Leicester Smyth, C.B.	Jan. 19, 1875	-
Ambrose More O'Ferrall, Esq. D.L.	do.	1
Sir Walter Nugent, Bart.	Mar. 6, 1866	-
Major-Gen. Meares, D.L.	Oct. 16, 1875	6
F. T. Dames-Longworth, Esq. [illegible]	July 8, 1882	-
Philip O'Reilly, Esq. D.L.	do.	4
T. T. Chapman, Esq. J.P.	June 1, 1883	1
Right Hon. Lord Kilmaine	July 1, 1884	1
Major Hume Kelly, J.P.	June 21, 1881	8
Thomas Maher, Esq.	do.	4
Harry Corbyn Levinge, Esq.	Nov. 2, 1885	1
Meath.		
Edward MacEvoy, Esq. D.L.	July 8, 1861	-
J. L. Naper, Esq. D.L.	do.	1
John A. Farrell, Esq. D.L.	do.	1
Robert Fowler, Esq. D.L.	May 1, 1868	1
James Waldron, Esq. D.L.	do.	1
Marquess of Headfort	Nov. 29, 1870	-
F. H. Langan, Esq. J.P.	do.	7
Right Rev. Lord Plunket	Nov. 17, 1877	-

No. 24.—NAMES of GOVERNORS and Dates of Appointment, with Number of Meetings attended during the Year ended 31st December, 1885—*con.*

Name.	Date of Appointment.	Number of Meetings attended.
Longford.		
Anthony Lefroy, Esq. D.L.	July 5, 1864	-
Hugh Masters, Esq. D.L.	do.	-
John Shuldham, Esq. D.L.	do.	-
Rt. Hon. Earl of Granard	June 24, 1857	-
James W. Bond, Esq. D.L.	Sept. 16, 1863	4
Col. E. Dopping-Hepenstal, D.L.	June 2, 1868	-
Edward More O'Ferrall, Esq. J.P.	Feb. 26, 1873	-
James Wilson, Esq. D.L.	Feb. 16, 1874	-
E. H. King-Harman, Esq. M.P.	Mar. 4, 1874	-
Most Rev. Dr. Woodlock	Dec. 1, 1880	-
Harry M'Cann, Esq.	Mar. 30, 1883	3
T. F. O'Beirne, Esq.	do.	5
OMAGH.		
Tyrone.		
Col. the Hon. W. Stuart Knox	Sept. 10, 1857	-
Earl of Belmore, K.C.M.G.	Sept. 29, 1857	-
William F. Black, Esq. D.L.	do.	7
Sir John M. Stewart, Bart. D.L.	Nov. 19, 1863	-
Col. Geo. P. M'Clintock, D.L.	April 26, 1863	1
Major A. W. Cole Hamilton, D.L.	Nov. 5, 1864	-
James Greer, Esq. J.P.	do.	6
Major Thomas Auchinleck, J.P.	June 23, 1866	3
John S. Galbraith, Esq. J.P.	Nov. 28, 1866	-
Wm. Scott, Esq. M.D. J.P.	do.	1
James Crossle, Esq. J.P.	Jan. 3, 1867	-
Col. Sir W. F. L. Conyngham, K.C.B. D.L.	Feb. 14, 1868	-
A. O. S. M'Causland, Esq.	March 6, 1868	-
Thos. W. D. Humphreys, Esq. J.P.	May 1, 1869	9
Geo. Hall Stack, Esq. J.P.	Dec. 15, 1866	2
Lt.-Col. Irvine Mann, J.P.	do.	7
Rev. Chas. M'Cawley, P.P.	Oct. 31, 1869	3
A. C. Buchanan, Esq. J.P.	Jan. 21, 1870	1
Vaughan Montgomery, Esq. J.P.	do.	-
Sir Wm. M'Mahon, Bart.	May 15, 1871	-
Rev. John Smyth	do.	9
Rev. Leslie A. Lyle	June 23, 1871	4
Robert Wm. Lowry, Esq. J.P.	Nov. 27, 1874	9
William Scott, Esq.	do.	-
Col. James Corry Jones Lowry, J.P.	Oct. 27, 1875	-
Rev. Bernard M'Namee, P.P.	Jan. 24, 1876	11
Rev. Wm. Charters	June 19, 1877	4
The Earl of Ranfurly	Nov. 12, 1877	-
Major G. W. Vesey, D.L.	Mar. 10, 1879	2
Thos. A. Dickson, Esq. J.P.	Dec. 1, 1880	-
James Browne, Esq. J.P.	do.	6
Andrew Sproule, Esq.	Nov. 10, 1881	2
Lt.-Col. L. M. Buchanan	Oct. 5, 1882	7
Robert Harvey, Esq. J.P.	do.	11
Tyrone—continued.		
James Moore, Esq. J.P.	June 11, 1884	8
James Elliott, Esq. J.P.	Jan. 5, 1885	10
Comm. C. R. Cole Hamilton	do.	10
Rev. B. S. O'Loughlin	Aug. 27, 1885	3
Major C. M. Alexander	Dec. 11, 1885	-
Fermanagh.		
Captain Mervyn Archdall	Sept. 10, 1858	-
William H. Archdall, Esq. D.L. M.P.	do.	-
John G. V. Porter, Esq.	do.	1
M. C. Maude, Esq. J.P.	Sept. 22, 1859	-
Edward Smyth, Esq. J.P.	Jan. 13, 1866	-
Colonel J. G. Irvine, D.L.	Nov. 28, 1868	-
John A. Pomeroy, Esq. J.P.	April 10, 1869	-
The Viscount Crichton	May 13, 1874	-
RICHMOND.		
The Rt. Hon. the Earl of Meath, L. Co. Wicklow	Sept. 6, 1850	-
Sir G. F. G. Hodson, Bart. D.L. J.P.	Feb. 15, 1847	-
Sir John Lentaigne, C.B. M.D. J.P. Inspector-General of Reformatory and Industrial Schools in Ireland, and a Commissioner of National Education	do.	3
Sir Jas. W. Mackey, D.L. J.P.	Feb. 10, 1866	1
Alderman John Campbell, J.P.	do.	-
Sir Richard Martin, D.L. J.P.	do.	-
Robert Francis Ellis, Esq. J.P.	Feb. 15, 1870	3
Viscount Powerscourt, K.P. D.L. J.P.	Oct. 17, 1873	6
Lord Annaly, D.L. J.P.	do.	-
Sir John Barrington, D.L. J.P.	do.	16
Ion Trant Hamilton, Esq. D.L. J.P.	do.	-
John Taaffe, Esq. J.P.	do.	-
H. J. MacFarlane, Esq. J.P.	May 17, 1876	1
E. H. Kinahan, Esq. D.L. J.P.	Oct. 28, 1876	8
Sir George B. Owens, M.D. J.P.	Oct. 4, 1876	17
Viscount Gormanston, D.L.	do.	-
H. A. Hamilton, Esq. J.P.	Oct. 18, 1877	1
P. M'Cabe Fay, Esq. J.P.	July 29, 1881	1
J. Casement, Esq. J.P.	April 1, 1882	1
H. Seagrave, Esq. J.P.	do.	3
A. O'Neill, Esq. J.P.	do.	29
Alderman H. Tarpey, J.P.	do.	14
L. A. Lee-Norman, Esq. J.P.	do.	6

No. 24.—NAMES of GOVERNORS and Dates of Appointment, with Number of Meetings attended during the Year ended 31st December, 1885—con.

Name.	Date of Appointment.	Number of Meetings attended.
RICHMOND—continued.		
George O'Neill, Esq., J.P.	July 11, 1843	15
Major Percy E. Gunn, D.L., J.P.	do.	4
*The Right Hon. John O'Connor, M.P. (Lord Mayor)	Jan. 8, 1885	3
*P. Carey Connolly, Esq., J.P. (Mayor of Drogheda)	Jan. 8, 1884	8
Col. H. G. Lindsay, J.P.	Oct. 3, 1885	1
SLIGO.		
C. W. O'Hara, Esq., D.L.	Sept. 10, 1847	7
Richard Brinkley, Esq., J.P.	do.	—
Colonel Ffolliott, J.P.	do.	—
J. A. Holmes, Esq., D.L.	do.	1
F. M. Olpherts, Esq., J.P.	do.	—
Peter O'Connor, Esq., J.P.	do.	10
Edward Smith, Esq., J.P.	do.	10
Wm. Johnston, Esq., D.L.	do.	—
F. A. Le Touche, Esq., J.P.	do.	—
Colonel Whyte, J.P., D.L.	do.	—
Most Rev. Bishop L. Gillooly	Nov. 19, 1860	—
Right Hon. the Earl of Granard, K.P., P.C., Lieut. and C.R. co. Leitrim	Mar. 20, 1863	3
A. L. Tottenham, Esq., M.P.	Mar. 19, 1864	—
Col. E. Cooper, D.L., J.P.	June 24, 1864	—
C. De B. Fox, Esq., J.P.	Feb. 27, 1868	—
Owen Wynne, Esq., D.L.	Nov. 3, 1870	2
C. L'Estrange, Esq., J.P.	do.	6
Roger Parke, Esq., J.P.	do.	—
M. J. Madden, Esq., J.P.	do.	—
J. H. Kinnard, Esq., J.P.	Oct. 16, 1871	—
Capt. Armstrong, D.L., J.P.	Jan. 18, 1876	3
Lewis Algeo, Esq., J.P.	May 7, 1873	—
Col. Edw. King Harman, J.P., M.P.	Mar. 24, 1877	—
Alexander Lyons, Esq., J.P.	do.	2
B. J. Verschoyle, Esq., J.P.	April 26, 1880	—
C. C. R. Whyte, Esq., J.P.	do.	—
Jas. Nelson, Esq. (Mayor of Sligo)	Jan. 8, 1885	1
George Hewson, Esq., J.P.	Aug. 17, 1885	—
Manly M. Palmer, Esq., J.P.	do.	—
SLIGO—continued.		
Hugh Neill O'Donnell, Esq., J.P.	Aug. 17, 1885	1
James Johnston, Esq., J.P., D.L.	do.	—
George Tottenham, Esq., J.P.	do.	—
WATERFORD.		
The Most Noble the Marquess of Waterford, Lieutenant and Custos Rotulorum of the co. and city of Waterford, ex-officio	—	—
Charles Newport, Esq., J.P.	Aug. 1, 1835	—
Sir Robert J. Paul, Bart., D.L., J.P.	Dec. 25, 1841	7
Hon. D. F. Fortescue, D.L., J.P.	do.	6
R. T. Carew, Esq., D.L., J.P.	do.	11
Napoleon B. Wyse, Esq., D.L., J.P.	Jan. 23, 1866	—
Abraham Denny, Esq., D.L., J.P.	June 4, 1867	4
The Most Rev. Dr. John Power, Lord Bishop of Waterford and Lismore	May, 1876	1
The Right Rev. Dr. Day, Lord Bishop of Cashel and Emly	do.	3
Capt. Wm. Armstrong, J.P.	do.	1
A. Congreve, Esq., D.L.	June, 1877	—
Very Rev. Pierse Power, V.G., P.P.	Aug. 1879	1
Pierse Barron-Newell, Esq.	do.	10
Congreve Rogers, Esq., J.P.	do.	12
Captain Geo. Gandy, J.P.	do.	9
Geo. J. Mackesy, J.P., M.D.	do.	10
Very Rev. Dean Morgan	Nov. 1879	7
Very Rev. J. A. Phelan	Sept. 23, 1879	11
David Keat, Esq., J.P.	do.	10
Henry White, Esq.	do.	11
The Right Worshipful the Mayor of Waterford, ex-officio	—	7

* During tenure of office.

No. 23.—Table showing Average Contract Prices paid for the undermentioned Articles of Provisions, &c., consumed in the District Lunatic Asylums of Ireland, during the year ending 31st December, 1885.

Articles.	Beef, per lb.	Mutton, per lb.	Ox Heads, each.	Bread: White, per 4 lb. loaf.	Bread: Brown, per 4 lb. loaf.	Oatmeal, Indian Meal, &c., per cwt.	Flour, per stone.	Potatoes, per stone.	Rice, per cwt.	Tea, per lb.	Sugar, per lb.	Coffee, per lb.	Cocoa, per lb.	Butter, per lb.
	d.	d.	s. d.	d.	d.	s. d.	s. d.	d.	s. d.	s. d.	d.	s. d.	s. d.	s. d.
Armagh,	5	5	1 0	2 1/16	–	1 6	–	–	1 0	1 8	1½	0 8	–	1 1
Ballinasloe,	5½	5½	1 10	2½	–	1 4½	–	1	1 3	2 [illegible]	2½	–	0 1½	1 1
Belfast,	6½	6½	1 7	11½	2¾	9 3½	–	–	2 0	2 [illegible]	2½	–	–	1 6
Carlow,	5½	5½	–	4½	–	1 5½, 10½	–	4½	–	2 0	2½	–	0 2½	1 0
Castlebar,	5½	5½	–	2½	2½	1 4½	–	3½	1 4½	1 11	2	–	0 4½	0 10
Clonmel,	6½	7½	6½ [illegible]	3	–	1 7½	–	½	1 7	2 0	1½	–	0 4	0 11½
Cork,	6½, 7½, 10½, 5 [illegible]	7½, 6½	–	2 [illegible], 2 [illegible], 3 [illegible]	2 [illegible], 2, 2 [illegible]	1 5 [illegible]	1 0	1½	1 6	1 8	2½	0 0	–	1 1
Downpatrick	6½	6	1 6	1½	–	1 9	1 3½	2½	1 8	2 0	3	1 0	1 0	1 2
Ennis,	6	6	1 0	–	–	1 9, 10½	1 8	6	1 9	1 2½	2½	–	0 3½	0 11
Enniscorthy,	7	7	–	–	–	1 7½	1 3½	4	1 4½	2 3	1½	–	0 5	0 11½
Kilkenny,	5½	5½	–	1½	–	1 5	–	–	1 8	1 5½	3	–	0 1½	1 0
Killarney,	6½	8½	–	2½	–	1 5, 1 0½	–	3½	1 3½	1 8	2	1 0	0 5½	0 10½
Letterkenny,	5½	5½	–	2½	–	1 5, 1 6½	1 7	4½	–	2 0	1½	–	0 8½	1 1½
Limerick,	6½	7	–	3	–	1 0, 0 9	1 8	5	1 8	2 0	2½	0 6½	0 11½	1 2
Londonderry,	7, 7½	8½	1 10	2½	–	1 4½, 10½	–	4½, 5½	1 1	1 4	2½	1 3	–	1 3
Maryborough,	5½	5½	1 8	2½	–	1 0	1 3½	1½	3 4½	2 0	3	–	0 2	0 11½
Monaghan,	7½, 7½	8½, 7½	–	2½, 2½	–	1 11, 10½	–	1½	1 5½	2 4	2	1 0	–	1 1½, 1 1½
Mullingar,	5½, 5½	5½, 6½	1 3	2½	–	1 11½	–	–	2 11	2 0	2½	–	0 2	0 11½
Omagh,	5½	5½	–	2½	–	1 4, 9½	1 8	–	1 8	1 5½	2½	–	0 1½	1 1
Richmond,	7½	7½	–	2	–	1 8½	1 8	–	1 1½	1 3	1½	0 3½	0 1	1 3
Sligo,	7	8½	2 0	2½	–	1 5½, 10½	1 7½	3	1 6	1 5½	2	1 3	0 2	1 1½
Waterford,	5½	7½	1 8	2½	–	1 8	–	1	1 4½	2 2	2½	1 0	0 1½	0 11

No. 25.—TABLE showing Average Contract Prices paid for the undermentioned Articles of Provisions &c., consumed in the District Lunatic Asylums of Ireland, during the year ending 31st December, 1883—*continued*.

Asylums.	New Milk, per gallon.	Butter Milk, per gallon.	Eggs, per doz.	Fish, per lb.	Herrings, per doz.	Beer and Porter, per pint.	Wine, per pint.	Whisky, per gallon.	Straw, per cwt.	Coals, per ton.	Barley, per cwt.	Salt, per cwt.	Tobacco, per lb.	Snuff, per lb.
	s. d.	s. d.	s. d.	s. d.	s. d.	s. d.	s. d.	s. d.	s. d.	£ s. d.	s. d.	s. d.	s. d.	s. d.
Armagh,	0 8	–	–	–	–	–	–	–	2 11	0 16 0	8 6	–	8 0	–
Ballinasloe,	0 8	0 4	1 0	0 1½	1 0	0 3	1 4	20 0	1 8½	0 15 6	11 9	1 6	8 7	4 6
Belfast,	0 10½	0 3½	1 0	–	–	0 3, 0 2½	2 6	17 0	–	0 10 11	11 0	1 6	–	–
Carlow,	0 7½	0 4½	1 2	–	–	1 6 [illegible]	20 0 [illegible]	16 6	3 0	1 0 6½ 1 2 6½	–	–	–	–
Castlebar,	0 6½	–	0 10	–	–	0 1½	1 10½	15 0	–	0 18 6	–	–	–	–
Clonmel,	0 7½	–	0 10½	–	17 6 [illegible]	–	0 11½	19 0	3 0	17s. 10d. 18s. 6d.	–	1 8½	–	–
Cork,	7½d., 5½d.	1d., 2d.	1 0	0 8	0 9	0 1½	1 10½	16 9	–	17 3, 16 6	19 6	–	–	–
Downpatrick,	–	0 3	1 0½	–	–	0 1½	17½, 11½	17 0	–	13 8 to 16 6	10 6	–	–	–
Ennis,	0 9½	–	0 10	0 2½	16s. hun.	–	0 11½	16 6	1 9½	0 15 6½ 0 16 3½	–	1 6	8 8	3 10½
Enniscorthy,	0 6½	–	1 0	–	–	0 3	1 10½	16 0	–	0 13 6	2s. 3d. [illegible]	–	–	–
Kilkenny,	0 7½	–	1 0	–	–	0 8	1 4	14 11	–	0 17 1	–	–	8 6	4 2
Killarney,	0 7½	0 4½	0 9½	–	0 8	0 1½	2 0	18 0	1 6	1 1 4, 19 9	–	–	8 4	4 0
Letterkenny,	0 10½	0 4	–	–	–	0 2½	–	–	8 1½	14 5, 12 1	9 8½	–	–	–
Limerick,	0 8½, 0 7½	1d., 3d.	1 0	–	–	0 2	2 0	16 0	–	18 7, 17 11	–	1 4	8 4½	–
Londonderry,	0 11, 10½ 0 10	0 8½	1 0	–	–	1 8 [illegible]	23 6 [illegible]	15 9	–	0 12 4 to 13 5	11 10	1 3	–	–
Maryborough,	0 9½		1 1	–	0 9	0 1½	1 3	18 0	3 0	0 17 5	–	–	–	–
Monaghan,	0 9½ 0 8	–	0 10½	–	–	0 3	1 4	15 0	2 5½	0 17 6	–	–	–	–
Mullingar,	0 3½	–	1 1½	–	–	0 1½	2 0	16 0	2 5	0 18 10 0 18 3	–	–	–	–
Omagh,	0 9	0 8½	0 10½	–	–	0 3	1 8	16 6	–	0 16 10	–	–	–	–
Richmond,	0 7	–	1 8	–	–	0 1	0 9½	11 0	–	0 19 8½	–	–	–	–
Sligo,	0 10	0 4½	–	0 1	1 0	0 2	–	18 0	–	0 16 11 0 13 7	–	–	–	–
Waterford,	0 6½	0 2½	1 0	–		0 1½	2 1	20 0	–	0 16 3 0 15 3	–	–	–	–

No. 26.—DIETARY in each of the District Asylums in Ireland for the year ending 31st December, 1883.

ARMAGH.

Ordinary diet.—Breakfast—8 oz. oatmeal in stirabout, ½ quart new milk; ½ lb. of bread, 1 pint tea. Dinner—Three days in the week, ½ lb. of bread and 1 quart soup, composed of beef, oatmeal, barley, and vegetables; three days in the week, Irish stew, and one day ½ lb. of bread, 1 pint coffee. Supper—½ lb. bread, ½ quart new milk, 1 pint tea.

Extra diet.—Breakfast—8 oz. oatmeal in stirabout, ½ quart new milk, ½ lb. of bread, 1 pint of tea. Dinner—8 oz. of bread and 1 pint soup for working men.

Hospital diet.—Wine, porter, whisky, beef-tea, eggs, fruit, &c., at the discretion of the physicians.

BALLINASLOE.

Ordinary diet.—Breakfast—8 oz. meal made into stirabout, ½ quart milk; 6 oz. bread for working patients; 1 pint tea, 6 oz. bread for females. Dinner—1 quart soup, 6 oz. beef, Scotch barley, and vegetables, and 8 oz. bread, on four days of the week; ¼ stone potatoes and ½ quart milk, on three days of the week. Supper—8 oz. bread and 1 pint cocoa.

Extra diet.—Breakfast—8 oz. bread and 1 pint tea. Dinner—8 oz. bread and 1 pint soup for working patients. Supper—8 oz. bread and 1 pint cocoa.

Hospital diet.—Bread, milk, tea, eggs, wine, or any other article the physicians may deem advisable.

BELFAST.

Ordinary diet.—Breakfast—Males and females, one quart of stirabout, made with 4 oz. coarse meal, and ¾ of a pint of mixed milk, equal parts of new milk and buttermilk, every morning. Dinner—males and females, ½ lb. loaf bread, or 3 lbs. potatoes, 4 oz. solid meat and 1 pint soup, three days a week; males, ½ lb. loaf bread, or 3 lbs. potatoes, and 1 quart soup, made with ox heads and bones cut out of meat, vegetables, oatmeal, barley, peas, &c.; Females, ½ lb. loaf bread, or 3 lbs. potatoes, and 1½ pint soup, three days a week. Males, ½ lb. loaf bread, or 3½ lbs. potatoes, and 1 pint mixed milk; Females, ½ lb. loaf bread or 3 lbs. potatoes, and 1 pint mixed milk, on Fridays. Supper—Males, ½ lb. loaf bread and ¾ of a pint of milk; Females, ½ lb. loaf bread and ½ pint new milk, first six months. Males, 1 quart stirabout and ¾ pint new milk; Females, 1½ pint stirabout and ½ pint new milk, last six months.

Hospital Diet.—Patients who are actively employed are allowed a portion of flesh meat in addition to the soup, five instead of three days in the week. When the state of the patient's health requires it, the diet is changed accordingly, and any other substituted that may be considered requisite by the medical officer.

CARLOW.

Ordinary diet.—Breakfast—4 oz. oatmeal and 2 oz. Indian meal made into 1 quart stirabout, or 8 oz. bread with 1 pint tea or 1 pint new milk. Dinner—males 12 oz. bread; females, 8 oz., with 4 oz. beef made into 1 quart of soup, two days in the week; and on for four days in the week same bread, with 1 pint of mixed milk; on Sundays, each get ½ lb. bacon and vegetables, with 3 lbs. potatoes. Supper—8 oz. bread each, with 1 pint tea, or cocoa or new milk.

Extra diet.—Breakfast—Eggs or mutton chop. Dinner—4 ozs. bread given to some patients employed on the farm, with eggs or mutton chop. Supper—no extras.

Hospital diet.—Beef-tea, arrowroot, eggs, whisky, wine, gin, porter.

CASTLEBAR.

Ordinary diet.—Breakfast—Males, 8 oz. oatmeal in stirabout, 1 pint new milk; females, 6 oz. oatmeal in stirabout, 1 pint new milk. Dinner—Males, three days in the week, 3 lbs. potatoes or 10 oz. bread, 1 quart oatmeal gruel; females, 2½ lbs. potatoes or 8 oz. bread, with gruel, same as males; four days, same allowance, with 6 oz. meat in soup. Supper—Males, 8 oz. bread, 1 pint cocoa; females, 6 oz. bread, 1 pint cocoa.

Extra diet.—Breakfast—Working patients—males, 16 oz. bread, and 1 pint of tea; females, 8 oz. bread, 1 pint of tea. Dinner—Same as ordinary. Supper—Same as ordinary.

Hospital diet.—Eggs, wine, porter, beef-tea, whisky, mutton-chop, or any other article the physicians may deem advisable.

CLONMEL.

Ordinary diet.—Breakfast—8 oz. oatmeal, ½ pint new milk, made into stirabout; 1 pint milk, 8 oz. bread; 1 pint tea, and 8 oz. bread. Dinner—one day, bacon (8 oz.), cabbage, and 3 lbs. potatoes; two days, beef (8 oz.), made into soup, and 8 oz. bread; two days, 1 pint pea soup, same allowance of bread, to both sexes; two days 1 pint new milk, 3 lbs. potatoes. Supper—1 pint cocoa, 8 oz. bread to males, 4 oz. bread to females, 1 pint milk to males, ½ pint to females—same bread.

Extra diet.—Breakfast—butter, eggs, as required. Dinner—chops, 8 oz. to each; beef-tea (1 lb. of beef to each pint of beef-tea), or tea. Supper—extra milk, and tea in lieu of cocoa.

Hospital diet.—Beef-tea, chops, eggs, rice, rice-milk, wine, whisky, tea, chicken, butter, extra milk, arrowroot, &c., as ordered by medical officers.

CORK.

Ordinary diet.—Breakfast—1 pint of stirabout and ½ pint new milk; 1 pint tea and 12 oz. bread; 1 pint tea and 8 oz. bread; on Sundays 8 oz. bread and 1 pint tea. Dinner—6 oz. beef and 4 lbs potatoes; 4 oz. beef and 2½ lbs. potatoes, Tuesdays and Saturdays—6 oz. beef, Sundays and Thursdays, 1 pint new milk and 3 lbs. potatoes, 1 pint new milk and 2½ lbs. potatoes, Mondays and Wednesdays; 12 oz. bread, 1 pint pea soup, Fridays. Supper—1 pint tea and 8 oz. bread, 1 pint tea and 6 oz. bread.

Hospital diet.—Breakfast—1 pint milk and 8 oz. bread. Dinner—1 pint milk and 12 oz. bread. Supper—1 pint milk and 8 oz. bread.

DOWNPATRICK.

Ordinary diet.—Breakfast—1 quart porridge made with 8 oz. oatmeal, and ½ pint milk, five days in the week; tea and ½ lb. bread, two days in the week. Dinner—1 quart soup, made with peas, barley, and vegetables, 4 days in the week; 4 oz. solid meat each, 4 days in the week, or strong soup, made with 50 lbs. meat to the 100 patients; rice, 1 day in the week. Irish stew, 2 days in the week. Supper—1 pint cocoa, with ½ lb. bread.

Extra diet.—Breakfast—Tea, bread and butter, eggs, and beefsteak. Dinner—Soup, beefsteak, rice, potatoes, 1 pint porter. Supper—tea, bread and butter.

Hospital diet.—Tea, bread and butter, broiled meat, mutton chops, wine, spirits, &c., rice, sago, arrowroot.

ENNIS.

Ordinary diet.—Breakfast—6 oz. oatmeal in stirabout, and ½ quart new milk; or 8 oz. bread, with 1 pint milk or tea. Dinner—6 oz. meat and 8 oz. bread, Sundays; 1 pint soup and 8 oz. bread, Tuesdays and Saturdays; 1 pint milk, and 3½ lbs. potatoes, Wednesdays and Fridays; 4 oz. bacon and 3½ lbs. potatoes, Mondays and Thursdays. Supper—8 oz. bread and 1 pint new milk or cocoa.

Extra diet.—Breakfast—Butter and eggs, as ordered by medical officers. Dinner—Workers are allowed 4 oz. bread extra.

Hospital diet.—Chops, beef-tea, eggs, wine, porter, &c., as ordered by medical officers.

ENNISCORTHY.

Ordinary diet.—Breakfast—8 oz. oatmeal, 1 oz. rice in stirabout, ½ quart new milk; or ½ oz. tea, 1 oz. sugar, and 1 noggin new milk, 10 oz. bread for males, 8 oz. for females. Dinner—Mondays, Wednesdays, Fridays, and Saturdays, males, 12 oz. bread or 4 lbs potatoes, 1 pint new milk, females, 10 oz. bread or 3½ lbs. potatoes, 1 pint new milk. Sundays, Tuesdays and Thursdays, males, 12 oz. bread or 3½ lbs potatoes; females, 10 oz. bread or 3 lbs. potatoes, and 1 quart soup. Supper—males and females, 6 oz. bread, ½ oz. tea, 1 oz. sugar and milk, ½ oz. soluble cocoa.

Extra diet.—Breakfast—Males, 10 oz. bread; females, 8 oz. bread, ½ oz. tea, 1 oz. sugar, 1 oz. butter, 1 noggin milk. Dinner—Males and females, ½ lb. meat, bread and potatoes, as ordinary diet. Supper—Males and females, 8 oz. bread, ½ oz. tea, 1 oz. sugar, and milk; any other extras as ordered by the physician.

Hospital Diet.—Whisky, wine, eggs, rice, beef-tea, &c., ordered by the physicians when necessary.

KILKENNY.

Ordinary diet.—Breakfast—6½ oz. oatmeal and 1 oz. rice made into stirabout, with ½ pint new milk, six days—Sundays and holidays, 8 oz. bread and ½ pint new milk. Dinner—8 oz. bread with 1 pint cocoa, four days in the week; 8 oz. bread, with 40 lbs. beef per 100 patients, three days in the week. Supper—6 oz. bread and ½ pint new milk.

Extra diet.—Breakfast—Working diet, same as ordinary, tea diet, 6 oz. bread and 1 pint tea; meat diet, 8 oz. bread and 1 pint tea. Dinner—Working diet, 12 oz. bread, with cocoa and meat, same as ordinary, tea diet, same as ordinary, meat diet, 8 oz. bread and ½ lb. meat. Supper—Working diet, 8 oz. bread and ½ pint new milk; tea diet, same as ordinary; meat diet, 8 oz. bread and 1 pint new milk.

Hospital diet.—Rice, arrowroot, butter, eggs, beef-tea, wine, porter, whisky, &c.

All patients get potatoes occasionally for dinner. A proportion of solid meat is given with the soup, to which rice, oatmeal, and condiments are added, with vegetables.

KILLARNEY.

Ordinary diet.—Breakfast—males, 8 oz. bread, 1 pint tea, cocoa, or coffee; females, 6½ oz. bread, 1 pint tea, cocoa, or coffee, Sundays, Tuesdays, Thursdays and Fridays; males, stirabout, 8 oz. oatmeal, ½ pint new milk, or 8 oz. bread and 1 pint tea or coffee; females, stirabout, 6 oz. oatmeal, and ½ pint new milk, or 6½ oz. bread and 1 pint tea or coffee, Mondays, Wednesdays, and Saturdays. Dinner—males, 7 oz. meat, 4 oz. bread, 1 pint soup, and 1 lb vegetables—double allowance of bread where vegetables cannot be had; females, 6 oz. meat, 1 pint soup, 3½ oz. bread, and 12 oz. vegetables—double allowance of bread where vegetables cannot be had. Sundays, males, 4 oz. bread, or 8 oz. bread, 1 lb vegetables, and 1 pint beef soup, females, 3½ oz. bread, or 3½ oz. bread, 12 oz. vegetables, and 1 pint beef soup, Mondays; males, 5 oz. uncooked meat, 4 oz. bread, and 4 oz. rice; females, 4 oz. uncooked meat, 3½ oz. bread, 3 oz. rice, Tuesdays; males, 4 oz. bread, 1 pint beef soup, and 1 lb. vegetables, or 8 oz. bread, and 1 pint beef soup; females, 3½ oz. bread, and 1 pint beef soup, or 3½ oz. bread, 12 oz. vegetables, and 1 pint beef soup, Wednesdays, males, 5 oz. meat, 4 oz. bread, 1 lb vegetables (8 oz. bread where vegetables cannot be had); females, 4 oz. meat, 1 lb vegetables, 3½ oz. bread (or 6½ oz. bread where vegetables cannot be had),

Thursdays; males, [illegible] lbs. potatoes and 1 pint milk, or [illegible] oz. bread and 1 pint milk; females, [illegible] lbs. potatoes and 1 pint milk. Fridays; males, [illegible] oz. bread, and 1 pint pea soup; females, [illegible] oz. bread, and 1 pint pea soup. Saturdays. *Supper*—Males, [illegible] oz. bread, and 1 pint cocoa, tea, or coffee; females, [illegible] oz. bread, and 1 pint cocoa, coffee, or tea.

In addition to above, male working patients allowed [illegible] oz. bread and ½ pint porter or milk each on working days. Female working patients, [illegible] oz. bread and ½ pint porter or milk. Male and female working patients allowed half pint porter or milk each on Sundays.

Hospital diet.—Wine, arrowroot, whisky, eggs, milk, chops, beef-tea, [illegible], porter, tea, sugar, &c. &c., as ordered by medical officers.

LETTERKENNY.

Ordinary diet.—Breakfast—[illegible] oz. oatmeal made into 1 quart stirabout, with [illegible] pint sweet milk. Dinner—[illegible] oz. meat made into 1 quart soup, with [illegible] oz. barley, [illegible] oz. pea-meal and vegetables, per 100 patients, and [illegible] stone of potatoes each, [illegible] days weekly; [illegible] oz. cocoa, 1 oz. sugar; 1½ oz. milk, 12 oz. bread (males), and [illegible] oz. (females), [illegible] days weekly. *Supper*—[illegible] oz. tea, [illegible] oz. sugar, 1½ oz. milk, [illegible] oz. bread (males), and [illegible] oz. (females).

Extra diet.—Breakfast—[illegible] oz. tea, [illegible] oz. sugar, 1½ oz. milk, and [illegible] oz. bread; [illegible] oz. bread and 1 pint sweet milk. Dinner—[illegible] oz. bread and 1 pint sweet milk. *Supper*—[illegible] oz. bread and 1 pint sweet milk.

Hospital diet.—Regulated according to circumstances of each case.

LIMERICK.

Ordinary diet.—Breakfast—Coffee, four days, cocoa, three days a week; bread, 10 oz. (males), [illegible] oz. (females); or stirabout and 1 pint new milk. Dinner—meat, [illegible] oz., including bone, on five days of week, 1 lb. potatoes or other vegetables, and [illegible] oz. bread; pea-soup or skim-milk on two days, and 10 oz. bread (males), and [illegible] oz. (females). *Supper*—Tea, [illegible] pint; bread, [illegible] oz.

Hospital diet.—As ordered by the medical superintendent.

LONDONDERRY.

Ordinary diet.—Breakfast—[illegible] oz. meal made into porridge, and [illegible] quart of new milk each, or [illegible] oz. bread and ½ quart of new milk each, or [illegible] oz. bread and ½ quart tea each. Dinner—one day in week, 1 quart meat soup; four days in week, 1 quart of soup made with ox heads, or an equivalent of houghs or meat; one day, vegetable soup; one day, pork or bacon, or 1 pint mixed milk; males, 3½ lbs. potatoes, or 12 oz. bread; females, [illegible] lbs. potatoes, or [illegible] oz. bread. *Supper*—[illegible] oz. oatmeal made into porridge, and ½ quart of new milk each, or [illegible] oz. bread and ½ quart of new milk each.

Extra diet.—Dinner—½ lb. beef steak or 1 pint beef-tea (1 lb. beef) each, or ½ quart of new milk each.

Hospital diet.—Specially ordered as may be necessary.

MARYBOROUGH.

Ordinary diet.—Breakfast—[illegible] oz. oatmeal in stirabout, with ½ quart of new milk. Dinner—Four days—12 oz. bread, 1 pint new milk, males; 10 oz. bread, 1 pint new milk, females. Two days—12 oz. bread, [illegible] lb. meat in soup, males; 10 oz. bread, [illegible] lb. meat in soup, females. One day—12 oz. bread, with soup made of [illegible] oz. heads, males; 10 oz. bread, with soup made of [illegible] oz. heads, females; 3½ lb. potatoes, males; 3 lb. potatoes, females, when bread is not given. *Supper*—[illegible] oz. bread and ½ quart of new milk or 1 pint of cocoa, males and females.

Extra diet.—Breakfast—10 oz. bread with ½ quart new milk or 1 pint of tea, males; [illegible] oz. of bread with ½ quart of new milk or 1 pint of tea, females. Dinner—12 oz. bread or 3½ lbs. potatoes with ½ lb. of beefsteak, males; 10 oz. bread or 3 lbs. potatoes with ½ lb. of beefsteak, females. *Supper*—½ lb. rice boiled in 1 quart new milk, males and females.

Hospital diet.—Varies according to prescriptions of physicians.

MONAGHAN.

Ordinary diet.—Breakfast—[illegible] oz. of meal made into stirabout, with ½ quart of sweet milk. Dinner—1 pint of meat soup, with 3 lbs. of potatoes for males, and 2 lbs. for females. When potatoes of good quality cannot be obtained, bread is substituted, viz., 12 oz. for males, and [illegible] oz. for females. *Supper*—[illegible] oz. of meal made into stirabout, with ½ quart of sweet milk.

Extra diet.—Breakfast—Tea, 1 pint; with [illegible] oz. of bread for males, and [illegible] oz. for females. Dinner—Beef-tea, 1 pint, or chop or steak, 12 oz., with 10 oz. of bread for males, and [illegible] oz. for females. *Supper*—Tea, 1 pint; with [illegible] oz. of bread for males and [illegible] oz. for females.

Hospital diet.—Regulated according to the circumstances of each case.

MULLINGAR.

Ordinary diet.—Breakfast—Six days in the week, [illegible] oz. oatmeal made into stirabout, and 1 pint new milk; [illegible] oz. bread and 1 pint tea; one day in the week, [illegible] oz. bread and 1 pint tea. Dinner—Four days in the week, [illegible] oz. bread and [illegible] oz. meat; three days in the week, 10 oz. bread and 1 pint cocoa. *Supper*—[illegible] oz. bread and 1 pint cocoa; [illegible] oz. bread and 1 pint cocoa.

OMAGH.

Ordinary diet.—Breakfast—[illegible] oz. of meal made into stirabout, and ½ quart milk; tea, cocoa, milk, and bread. Dinner—Six days, 1 pint soup, with 12 oz. bread, or ½ stone potatoes, for males; 8 oz. bread, or ½ stone potatoes, for females. On Fridays, tea with bread, as above. Supper—Same as breakfast.

Extra diet.—Dinner—Beefsteak, mutton chop, milk or rice, with bread or potatoes.

Hospital diet.—Regulated by the physicians according to the necessities of each case.

RICHMOND.

Ordinary diet.—Breakfast—Bread, ½ lb.; tea, 1 British pint. Dinner—(two days in week)—Pea soup and coffee, 1 British pint; bread, males, 10 oz.; females, 8 oz. (Five days in week)—Meat, males, 8 oz.; females, 7 oz., and soup, 1 British pint; bread, males, 10 oz., females, 8 oz. Supper—Cocoa, 1 British pint; bread, ½ lb.

Extra diet.—Breakfast—Ordinary. Dinner—Coffee, beer, or porter, 1 British pint; bread, ½ lb. extra. Supper—Tea, 1 British pint; bread, ½ lb. extra.

Hospital diet.—Beef-tea, chops, eggs, porter, beer, wine, whisky, brandy, rice, tea, chickens, butter, extra milk, rice-milk, arrowroot, &c., as ordered by medical officers.

One oz. tea, 2½ oz. sugar, and 3½ naggins milk, allowed to 8 patients. The soup is the liquid in which the meat is boiled, seasoned with salt, spices, and celery. Potatoes are given one day in the week for dinner, 3 lbs. being allowed to each patient without bread. Other vegetables ½ lb. to each patient are given once a week. 1½ stone peas, ½ stone flour, and 3 red herrings allowed to each 100 pints of soup; ½ oz. soluble cocoa, ½ oz. sugar, and ½ naggin milk allowed to each British pint of cocoa.

Lenten and other fast days—dinner to Roman Catholics—coffee, 1 British pint, 1 oz. salt butter, ½ oz. coffee, ½ oz. sugar, and ½ naggin of milk to each pint allowed to each patient; 10 oz. bread to males, 8 oz. to females.

SLIGO.

Ordinary diet.—Breakfast—1 quart stirabout and ½ quart new milk to males; 1½ pint stirabout and ½ quart of new milk to females. Dinner—Sundays and Thursdays, Irish stew; Tuesdays and Saturdays, meat soup; Mondays, Wednesdays, and Fridays, 1 pint rice-milk and 12 oz. bread to males, and 8 oz. bread to females. Supper—1 pint porridge or cocoa and 8 oz. bread to males, and 6 oz. bread to females.

Extra diet.—Breakfast—12 oz. bread to males, 8 oz. to females, with 1 pint of tea, coffee, or new milk. On Sunday all patients get tea. Dinner—12 oz. bread or 4 lbs. potatoes for males; 8 oz. bread or 4 lbs. potatoes for females, with ½ lb. chop or steak, or with a pint of new milk. Supper—8 oz. bread to males, 6 oz. to females, with a pint of tea, coffee, or new milk.

Hospital diet.—Whey, arrowroot, beef-tea, eggs, wine, porter, ale, or other medical comforts as may be ordered by the medical officers, with or without any of the foregoing diets.

WATERFORD.

Ordinary diet.—Breakfast—Stirabout and milk, bread and milk, bread and tea, bread, butter, and coffee on Sunday morning; all on bread, butter, and tea at Christmas and Easter. Bread allowance for breakfast and supper—males, 8 oz.; females, 7 oz. Dinner—Bread, meat, and soup, bread and milk, three days in the week; bread and milk, bread and beef soup, three days in the week; bread and coffee on Fridays. Bread allowance for dinner—males, 10 oz.; females, 7 oz. Supper—Bread and cocoa (shell), bread and milk, bread and tea.

Extra diet.—Breakfast—Extra bread and butter; extra bread (4 oz.) Dinner—Extra bread, mutton chops. Supper—Bread and tea; extra bread (7 oz.)

Hospital diet consists of whatever may be ordered by the resident or visiting physician in each individual case.

No. 27.—Statements of the actual quantities of Food, Medical Stimulants, Coal, &c., consumed in each District Asylum during the year ending 31st December, 1885.

ARMAGH.

Beef, 19,419 lbs.; ox heads, 318; bread, 148,378 lbs.; oatmeal, 1,967 stones; potatoes, 5,183 stones; pepper, 37 lbs.; rice, 11 stones; tea, 1,374 lbs.; sugar, 9,344 lbs.; coffee, 108 lbs.; butter, 871 lbs.; new milk, 11,134 galls.; barley, 1,737 lbs.; eggs, 98 dozen; beer and porter, 11,331 pints; wine, 497 pints; whisky and brandy, 183 pints; straw, 340 cwts.; coal, 647 tons; tobacco, 111 lbs.

BALLINASLOE.

Beef, 33,763 lbs.; mutton, 2,100 lbs.; ox heads, 54; bread, 157,380 lbs.; oatmeal, 4,101 stones; flour, 9 stones; potatoes, 10,806 stones; barley, 709 stones; rice, 11½ stones; tea, 1,173½ lbs.; sugar, 11,901 lbs.; cocoa, 4,470½ lbs.; butter, 6,451 lbs.; new milk, 72,828 gals.; buttermilk, 8,483 gals.; eggs, 1,478 dozen; fish, 183 lbs.; herrings, 60½ dozen; beer and porter, 4,041 pints; wine, 431 pints; whisky and brandy, 334 pints; straw, 1,235 cwts.; coal, 240 tons; salt, 576 stones; tobacco, 320 lbs.; snuff, 20 lbs.; pepper, 43 lbs.; corn flour, 104 lbs.

BELFAST.

Beef, 97,160 lbs.; mutton, 13,341 lbs.; ox heads, 3,676; bread, 101,663 lbs.; oatmeal, 4,131 stones; flour, 10 stones; potatoes, 10,819 stones; barley, 180 stones; pork, 7,671 lbs.; rice, 103 stones; tea, 976 lbs.; sugar, 4,597 lbs.; butter, 1,574 lbs.; new milk, 30,024 gals.; buttermilk, 3,336 gals.; peas, 774 stones; eggs, 300 dozen; beer, 614 pints; porter, 1,363 pints; wine, 173½ pints; whisky, 343½ pints; brandy, 4½ pints; straw, 761 cwts.; coal, 794 tons; gin, 139½ pints.

CARLOW.

Beef, 14,271 lbs.; mutton, 1,839 lbs.; bread, 123,761 lbs.; oatmeal, 1,009 stones; Indian meal, 439 stones; potatoes, 1,997 stones; American bacon, 4,929 lbs.; rice, 6 stones; tea, 671 lbs.; sugar, 7,378 lbs.; cocoa, 2,889 lbs.; butter, 9,028 lbs.; new milk, 33,157 gals.; buttermilk, 3,343 gals.; arrowroot, 159 lbs.; eggs, 473 dozen; beer and porter, 1,163 pints, wine, 17 pints; whisky and brandy, 418 pints; straw, 700 cwts.; coal, 597 tons; pea-meal, 54 stones.

CASTLEBAR.

Beef and mutton, 84,781¾ lbs.; bread, 121,441½ lbs.; oatmeal, 8,738¾ stones; potatoes, 13,341½ stones; rice, 334½ stones; tea, 884¾ lbs.; sugar, 14,048 lbs. 17½ oz.; cocoa, 3,497 lbs. 7 oz.; butter, 1,177 lbs. 13½ oz.; new milk, 14,187 gals.; eggs, 1,331½ dozen; fish, 818 lbs.; beer and porter, 6,831 pints; wine, 486¾ pints; whisky and brandy, 741½ pints; straw, 440 cwts.; coal, 832 tons 13 cwt. 1 stone; tobacco, 343 lbs.; barley, 187½ stones, ale, 21 dozen.

CLONMEL.

Beef, 79,109 lbs. 12 oz.; mutton, 3,343 lbs.; Irish bacon, 16,160 lbs. 12 oz.; bread, 117,033 lbs. 12 oz.; oatmeal, 1,172 stones; pea-meal, 185 stones; flour, 86 stones 10½ lbs.; potatoes, 13,925 stones; rice, 373 stones; tea, 2,780 lbs.; sugar, 31,717 lbs.; loaf sugar, 131 lbs.; cocoa, 3,371 lbs.; butter, 8,101 lbs.; new milk, 30,747 gals.; tobacco, 745 lbs.; eggs, 4,184½ dozen; fish, 440 lbs.; herrings, 133 dozen; beer and porter, 1,440 pints; wine 70 pints; whisky and brandy, 164 pints; straw, 300 cwts.; coal, 460 tons; split peas, 518 stones; pepper, 359 lbs.; soap, 1,110 stones; mustard, 103 lbs.; starch, 886 lbs.; salt, 401 stones; fowls, 76.

CORK.

Beef, 97,083 lbs.; mutton, 11,141 lbs.; bread, 344,934 lbs.; oatmeal, 3,097 stones; flour, 120 stones; potatoes, 48,110 stones; rice, 122 stones; tea, 5,816 lbs.; sugar, 22,769 lbs.; coffee, 119 lbs., butter, 6,033 lbs.; new milk, 37,431 gals.; buttermilk, 720 gals.; eggs, 434 dozen; fish, 4,034 lbs.; herrings, 101 dozen; beer and porter, 107 bottles and 1,756 gals.; ale, 3,100 bottles; wine, 401 pints; whisky and brandy, 53 pints; straw, 900 cwts.; coal, 459 tons. pork, 4,109 lbs.; peas, 4,791 lbs.; barley, 7,793 lbs.

DOWNPATRICK.

Beef, 34,973 lbs.; mutton, 737½ lbs.; ox heads, 440; bread, 109,146 lbs. baked in the Asylum, 4,916 lbs bought; oatmeal, 7,271 stones; pea-meal, 57 stones; flour, 10,914 stones made into bread, &c.; potatoes, 14,209 stones, rice, 216 stones; tea, 7,910 lbs.; sugar, 16,091 lbs.; coffee, 79 lbs.; cocoa, 2,718 lbs., butter, 2,473 lbs.; new milk, 9,197 gals.; buttermilk, 1,183 gals.; eggs, 763 dozen; fish, 230 lbs; herrings, 111 dozen, beer and porter, 7,830 pints; wine, 118 pints; whisky and brandy, 26 pints; straw, 390 cwts.; coal, 373½ tons; barley, 640 stones; arrowroot, 148 lbs., lard, 427 lbs.

ENNIS.

Beef and mutton, 78,877 lbs.; ox and sheep heads, 64; bread, 108,401 lbs.; oatmeal, 111 stones; flour, 103 stones; potatoes, 8,037 stones; rice, 5 stones; tea, 1,534 lbs.; sugar, 9,174 lbs., cocoa, 2,627 lbs; butter, 1,408 lbs; new milk, 18,177 gals.; eggs, 1,098 dozen; fish, 705 lbs.; herrings, 117 dozen beer and porter, 6,679 pints; wine, 67 pints; whisky and brandy, 103 pints; coal, 383 tons; rice flour, 370 stones; pork and bacon, 1,107 lbs.; salt, 303 stones; pepper, 107 lbs; tobacco, 777 lbs; snuff, 16 lbs.

ENNISCORTHY.

Beef, 87,043 lbs.; mutton, 1,345 lbs.; bread, 142,731 lbs.; oatmeal, 2,717 stones; flour, [illegible] stones; potatoes, 17,311 stones; rice, 344 stones; tea, 1,807 lbs.; sugar, 18,470 lbs.; cocoa, 1,871 lbs.; butter, 4,443 lbs.; new milk, 13,[illegible] gals.; eggs, 1,814½ dozen; beer and porter, 3,465 pints; wine, 140 pints; whisky and brandy, 173 pints; straw, 480 cwts.; coal, 180 tons; bacon, 6,341 lbs.; salt, 487 stones; pepper, 70 lbs.

KILKENNY.

Beef, 97,722 lbs.; mutton, 1,616 lbs.; bread, 161,456 lbs.; oatmeal, 1,966 stones; potatoes, 1,257 stones; turf, 60 boxes; rice, 430 stones; tea, 659 lbs.; sugar, 4,176 lbs.; cocoa, 2,000 lbs.; butter, 476 lbs.; new milk, 17,549 gals.; gas, 312,600 cubic feet; eggs, 170 dozen; beer and porter, 1,240 pints; wine, 215 pints; whisky and brandy, 140 pints; straw, 279 cwts.; coal, 760 tons; candles, 640 lbs.

KILLARNEY.

Beef, 88,813 lbs.; mutton, 9,560 lbs.; bread, 103,843 lbs.; oatmeal, 1,380 stones; flour, 181 stones; potatoes, 6,167 stones; bacon, 400 lbs.; peas, 178 stones; rice, 546 stones; tea, 1,110 lbs.; sugar, 10,905 lbs.; coffee, 5 lbs.; cocoa, 4,111 lbs.; butter, 6,410 lbs.; new milk, 12,771 gals.; skim milk, 6,131 gals.; tobacco, 784 lbs.; snuff, 83 lbs.; eggs, 2,963 dozen; herrings, 43 dozen; beer and porter, 7,587 pints; wine, 70 pints; whisky and brandy, 848 pints; straw, 110 cwts.; coal, 630 tons; soap, 360 stones; starch, 436 lbs.

LETTERKENNY.

Beef, 70,099 lbs.; bread, 131,310 lbs.; oatmeal, 3,396 stones; pea meal, 110 stones; potatoes, 16,101 stones; barley, 641 stones; rice, 171 stones; tea, 2,741½ lbs.; sugar, 11,676 lbs.; cocoa, 1,149½ lbs.; butter, 1,344¾ lbs.; new milk, 18,834 gals.; buttermilk, 730 gals.; eggs, 404½ dozen; herrings, 10 dozen; beer and porter, 6,180 pints; wine, 440 pints; whisky and brandy, 373½ pints; straw, 1,170½ cwts.; coal, 619 tons 17 cwts.

LIMERICK.

Beef, 68,750 lbs.; mutton, 3,307 lbs.; pork and bacon, 8,140 lbs.; bread, 251,447 lbs.; oatmeal, 1,173 stones; meal, 516 stones; flour, 73 stones; potatoes, 13,804 stones; split peas, 760 stones; arrowroot, 1,152 lbs.; vinegar, 95 gals.; rice, 50 stones; tea, 3,166 lbs.; sugar, 16,118 lbs.; coffee, 1,085 lbs.; cocoa, 1,920 lbs.; butter, 6,104 lbs.; new milk, 10,277 gals.; buttermilk, 2,041 gals.; salt, 460 stones; chicory, 160 lbs.; tobacco, 483 lbs.; lard, 10½ stones; eggs, 167½ dozen; beer and porter, 6,145 pints; wine, 111 pints; whisky and brandy, 10 pints; straw, 276 cwts.; coal, 463 tons; pepper, 107 lbs.; currants and raisins, 230 lbs.; soda water, 119 bottles.

LONDONDERRY.

Beef, 17,483 lbs.; mutton, 57 lbs.; ox heads, 2,130; bread, 165,820 lbs.; oatmeal, 4,674 stones; meal (Indian), 874 stones; potatoes, 13,446 stones; salt, 106 cwts.; rice, 804 stones; tea 1,899 lbs.; sugar, 4,018 lbs.; coffee, 31 lbs.; butter, 1,653 lbs.; new milk, 27,478 gals.; buttermilk, 1,450 gals.; barley, 118 stones; eggs, 467 dozen; porter, 617 pints; wine, 10 pints; whisky, 84 pints; straw, 297 cwts.; coal, 441 tons; pepper, 128 lbs.

MARYBOROUGH.

Beef, 87,394½ lbs.; mutton, 4,117 lbs.; ox heads, 240; bread, 156,182 lbs. 10 oz.; oatmeal, 2,111 stones; flour, 15 stones; potatoes, 6,648 stones; pepper, 50 lbs.; peas, 473 lbs.; rice, 101 stones; tea, 1,625 lbs. 4½ oz.; sugar, 8,760 lbs. 7 oz.; cocoa, 5,716 lbs.; butter, 3,180 lbs.; new milk, 20,446 gals.; salt, 41 cwt.; eggs, 1,861 dozen; herrings, 234 dozen; beer and porter, 16,880 pints; wine, 61 pints 9 oz.; whisky and brandy, 314 pints 8 oz.; straw, 484 cwts.; coal, 361 tons 8 cwts.; coke, 34½ tons.

MONAGHAN.

Beef, 48,918¾ lbs.; mutton, 6,014½ lbs.; bread, 117,162 lbs.; oatmeal, 7,610¼ stones; Indian meal, 2,974½ stones; flour, 15$\frac{1}{16}$ stones; potatoes, 20,071¼ stones; rice, 441$\frac{1}{16}$ stones; new milk, 78,683 gals.; butter, 2,181½ lbs.; salt, 1,374 lbs.; pepper, 106 lbs.; mustard, 76 lbs.; split peas, 2,191 lbs.; ham, 64½ lbs.; tea, 2,166½ lbs.; coffee, 264½ lbs.; sugar, 18,101¾ lbs.; corn flour, 311 lbs.; wine, 907½ pints; beer and porter, 3,161½ pints; whisky, 464¾ pints; eggs, 1,091 dozen; tobacco, 717¾ lbs.; oat straw, 677¾ cwts.; house coal, 303½ tons; steam coal, 277$\frac{1}{16}$ tons; soap, 4,903½ lbs.; starch, 976½ lbs.; blue, 10 lbs.; washing soda, 1,603 lbs.; candles, 64½ lbs.

MULLINGAR.

Beef, 67,208½ lbs.; mutton, 471 lbs.; ox heads, 181; bread, 237,297½ lbs.; oatmeal, 4,051½ stones; flour, 6 stones; potatoes, 8,946 stones 13 lbs.; loaf sugar, 10 lbs.; rice, 184 stones 1 lb.; tea, 2,633 lbs. 7 oz.; sugar, 10,630½ lbs.; cocoa, 13,976½ lbs.; butter, 2,879½ lbs.; new milk, 17,614¾ gals.; pepper, 109½ lbs.; eggs, 1,609 dozen; fish, 1,118 lbs.; herrings, 137 dozen; beer and porter, 12,063 pints; wine, 617 pints; whisky and brandy, 677 pints; straw, 183 cwts.; coal, 777 tons 17 cwts.; bacon, 6,784 lbs.

OMAGH.

Beef, 41,173½ lbs.; mutton, 3,341¾ lbs.; bread, 198,578 lbs.; oatmeal, 2,677½ stones; meal, 2,061 stones; flour, 16 stones; potatoes, 11,615 stones; split peas, 716½ stones; rice, 35½ stones; tea, 2,771 lbs.; sugar, 16,480½ lbs.; cocoa, 1,054½ lbs.; butter, 2,147½ lbs.; new milk, 70,176 gals.; buttermilk, 4,464 gals.; Scotch barley, 407½ stones; eggs, 646 dozen; herrings, 11½ dozen; beer and porter, 1,119½ pints; wine, 325 pints; whisky and brandy, 114 pints; straw, 326 cwts.; coal, 340 tons; bacon, 240½ lbs.

RICHMOND.

Beef, 146,830 lbs.; mutton, 14,367 lbs.; bread, 445,073 lbs.; oatmeal, 73 stones; flour, 89 stones 6 lbs.; potatoes, 10,846 stones; rice, 111 stones 8 lbs.; tea, 4,331 lbs.; sugar, 34,341 lbs.; coffee, 2,557 lbs.; cocoa, 8,064 lbs.; butter 4,170 lbs. 12 oz.; new milk, 36,970 gals.; buttermilk, 1,080 gals. 3 qrts. 1 pint; eggs, 3,467½ dozen; herrings, 80 dozen and 8; beer and porter, 41,316 pints; wine, 884 pints 19 oz.; whisky and brandy, 297 pints 1 oz.; straw, 765 cwts. 2 qrs.; coal, 1,365 tons 10 cwts.; ham, 815 lbs.; pork, 6,356 lbs.; split peas, 7,300 lbs.; chickens, 765; parsley, 57 bunches; celery, 47½ dozen; celery, 34 bunches; sea kale, 158 dishes; scallions, 167 bunches; leeks, 1,487 bunches; thyme, 171 bunches; lard, 256 lbs.; salt, 911 stones; cabbage, 6,119 dozen; onions, 409½ stones; parsnips, 365½ stones; artichokes, 60 dishes; rhubarb, 897 dishes; spinach, 115 dishes; lettuce, 393½ dozen; peas, 76 dishes; radishes, 38 dozen; pepper, 406 lbs.; tobacco, 733 lbs.; sprouts, 633 dozen; turnips, 2,380½ stones; Brussels sprouts, 65 dishes; cauliflowers, 887 dozen; kidney beans, 79 dishes; beans, 9 dishes.

SLIGO.

Beef, 80,463 lbs.; mutton, 2,612 lbs.; ox heads, 416; bread, 170,009 lbs.; oatmeal, 1,565 stones; meal, 1,383 stones; flour, 165 stones; potatoes, 11,460 stones; pea-meal, 160 stones; rice, 493 stones; tea, 764 lbs.; sugar, 10,647 lbs.; cocoa, 4,148 lbs.; butter, 1,117 lbs.; new milk, 71,640 gals.; buttermilk, 174 gals.; salt, 171 stones; eggs, 36 dozen; fish, 187 lbs.; herrings, 185 dozen; beer and porter, 10 pints; whisky and brandy, 10 pints; straw, 765 cwts.; coal, 168 tons; pepper, 36 lbs.

WATERFORD.

Beef, 88,083 lbs.; beef (foreign), 6,441 lbs.; mutton, 2,019 lbs.; ox heads, 671; pork and pigs heads, 4,930 lbs.; bread, 332,780 lbs.; oatmeal, 1,367 stones; potatoes, 7,894 stones; rice, 376 stones; tea, 1,104 lbs.; sugar, 8,783 lbs.; coffee, 819 lbs.; cocoa, 2,436 lbs.; butter, 8,979 lbs.; new milk, 16,218 gals.; buttermilk, 1,778 gals.; eggs, 1,397 dozen; fish, 1,070 lbs., of salt fish, and fresh fish as it could be procured in the markets weekly, for servants; porter, 11,544 pints; wine, 310 pints; whisky and brandy, 319 pints; straw, 400 cwts.; coal, 365½ tons.

No. 28.—Articles of Clothing, Bedding, &c., made by the Patients during the Year ended 31st December, 1885.

Armagh.

Articles.	Number.
Shirts,	640
Socks (pairs),	366
Dresses,	240
Shifts,	263
Stockings (pairs),	286
Aprons,	644
Caps,	60
Flannel Petticoats,	261
Winsey do.,	64
Flannel Jackets,	6
Bed Gowns,	7
Shrouds	18
Frills,	60
Linen Vests,	11
" Aprons,	13
Bed Ticks,	122
Mattresses,	2
Bolster Ticks,	18
" Cases,	17
Sheets,	310
Hair Bolsters,	3
Table Cloths,	10
Rolling Towels,	17
Dusters,	21
Buttons,	11,000
Flannel Drawers,	9
Canvas Quilts,	2

Ballinasloe.

Men's Clothes.

Articles.	Number.
Jackets,	187
Vests,	174
Trousers,	186
Top Coats,	3
Caps,	713
Bed Stretchers,	53
Shoes (pairs),	320

Ballinasloe—continued.

Articles.	Number.
Women's Clothes.	
Dresses,	309
Petticoats,	779
Stockings (pairs),	304
Aprons,	113
Shirts,	400
Sheets,	182
Bed Ticks,	94
Rollers,	10
Shrouds,	40

Belfast.

Articles.	Number.
Sheets,	208
Chemises,	52
Shirts,	280
Bed Ticks,	146
Bolsters,	145
Aprons,	141
Petticoats,	144
Wrappers,	70
Flannel Vests,	14
Gowns,	101
Neckties,	310
Socks,	140
Table Cloths,	34
Sun-bonnets,	36
Caps,	47
Stockings,	78
Men's Coats,	183
" Trousers,	230
" Vests,	143
" Drawers,	7
Pillow Slips,	197
Towels,	91

Carlow.

Articles.	Number.
Shifts,	133
Petticoats,	142
Gowns,	133
Aprons,	697
Wrappers,	16
Caps,	46
Shirts,	209
Sheets (pairs),	165
Bed Ticks,	80
Bolster Cases,	31
Stockings (pairs),	316
Table Cloths,	20

(Besides a large quantity of clothing and bedding repaired.)

Castlebar.

Articles.	Number.
Men's Jackets,	174
" Trousers,	140
" Vests,	96
" Shirts,	671
" Flannel Vests,	54
" Drawers,	100
" Shoes (pairs),	261
Women's Chemises,	719
" Flannel Petticoats,	71
" " Vests,	18
" Linsey Petticoats,	118
" Gowns,	166
" Shoes (pairs),	73
" Aprons,	311
Bed Ticks,	63
Sheets (pairs),	180

No. 23.—Articles of Clothing, Bedding, &c., made by the Patients during the Year ended 31st December, 1885—*continued.*

CASTLEBAR—*continued.*

Articles.	Number.
Refractory Bags,	25
Refractory Dresses,	10
Canvas Jackets,	11
Men's Caps,	152
Bolster & Pillow Covers,	1[illegible]
Mattress Covers,	17

[Also kept the male and female clothing and all bedding in thorough repair.]

CLONMEL.

Articles.	Number.
Men's Coats,	170
" Vests,	37
" Trousers,	62
" Socks,	770
" Shirts,	481
" Shoes,	60
" Suspenders,	454
" Flannel Vests,	67
" Drawers,	44
Women's Shifts,	485
" Petticoats,	381
" Gowns,	411
" Aprons,	613
" Caps,	48
" Stockings,	311
" Shoes,	112
" Refractory Dresses,	4
Servants' Dresses,	34
" Wrappers,	70
" Caps,	117
" Aprons,	117
Bed Ticks,	163
Bolsters,	136
Single Sheets,	465
Quilted Blankets,	18
Table Cloths,	9
Clothes Bags,	41

[Also the weekly repairs of the male and female patients' clothing, bedding, &c.]

CORK.

Articles.	Number.
Sheets,	673
Pillows,	130
Pillow Slips,	130
Ticks,	34
Jackets,	317
Vests,	43
Trousers,	131
Shirts,	873
Pairs Shoes (Men's),	401
" Socks	1,401
Flannel Vests,	209
Drawers,	140
Gowns,	314
Petticoats,	373
Shifts,	874
Aprons,	352
Pairs Shoes (Women's),	376
" Stockings,	251
Caps,	72
Cloaks,	40
Table Cloths,	70
Pairs Restraint Boots,	44
Restraint Vests,	7
Pairs Clogs,	43
Bonnets,	41

DOWNPATRICK.

Articles.	Number.
Coats,	276
Vests,	341
Trousers,	377
Men's Shoes,	717
Women's "	103
Shirts,	[illegible]
Gowns,	147
Petticoats,	720
Chemises,	754
Wrappers and Jackets,	69
Aprons,	314
Cotton Bonnets,	34
Flannel Vests,	61
Sheets,	152
Pillow Cases,	109
Bed Covers,	60
Coats repaired,	445
Vests "	150
Trousers "	493
Shoes "	98
Chemises "	416
Shirts "	370
Gowns "	766
Socks "	433

ENNIS.

Articles.	Number.
Male Patients' Clothing:	
Jackets,	16
Shirts,	251
Vests,	31
Trousers,	174
Flannel Drawers,	10
" Vests,	43
Shoes (pairs),	10
Slippers "	7
Socks,	307
Locked Boots (pairs),	17
Female Patients' Clothing:	
Chemises,	167
Flannel Petticoats,	44
Coloured "	75
Gowns,	103
Shoes (pairs),	7
Slippers "	16
Stockings "	115
Aprons,	703
Locked Boots (pairs),	2
Refractory Dresses,	8
Bedding, &c.:	
Bed Ticks,	85
Bolsters,	101
Bolster Cases,	179
Sheets (pairs),	59
Refractory Quilts,	5
Hair Mattresses,	9[illegible]
Palliasses,	51
Table Cloths,	17
Towels,	73
Rollers,	179
Male Attendants' Socks (pairs),	64
Male Attendants' Shoes (pairs),	81
Female Attendants' Shoes (pairs),	5
Female Attendants' Boots (pairs),	10

[All repairs of clothing, bedding, &c., were executed by the patients.]

ENNISCORTHY.

Articles.	Number.
Shirts,	434
Shifts,	176
Petticoats,	77
Gowns,	159
Aprons,	230
Day Caps,	49
Pairs Socks,	80
" Stockings,	86
Refractory Dresses,	35
Bed Ticks,	17
Pairs Sheets,	71
Table Cloths,	18
Rollers,	6
Towels,	7
Bolster Cases,	83
Jackets,	165
Vests,	148
Trousers,	178
Chemises,	15
Flannel Drawers,	15
" Vests,	61
Pairs Boots,	34
Pairs Men's Shoes,	46
Pairs Women's "	75
Canvas Petticoats,	1

KILKENNY.

Articles.	Number.
Shirts,	309
Socks (pairs),	618
Chemises,	373
Petticoats,	179
Gowns,	119
Stockings (pairs),	130
Check Aprons,	301
Bed Ticks,	47
Bolster Cases,	[illegible]
Sheets (pairs),	61
Mattresses,	114
Round Towels,	14

KILLARNEY.

Articles.	Number.
Coats and Jackets,	177
Trousers,	311
Vests,	163
Caps,	98
Flannel Drawers,	88
" Vests,	179
Socks,	63
Shirts,	279
Shifts,	166
Petticoats,	33
Gowns,	113
Night-wrappers,	36
Aprons,	379
Stockings,	134
Caps,	136
Stays,	87
Bolster Ticks,	113
" Cases,	70
Rollers,	46
Table Cloths,	101

No. 28.—Articles of Clothing, Bedding, &c., made by the Patients during the Year ended 31st December, 1885—*continued*.

KILLARNEY—*continued*.

Articles.	Number.
Sheets,	319
Quilts,	40
Men's Shoes,	201
Women's Shoes,	64

LETTERKENNY.

Articles.	Number.
Jackets,	167
Vests,	114
Trousers, pairs,	175
Flannel Shirts,	113
" Drawers, pairs,	100
Socks, pairs,	275
Stockings, pairs,	174
Canvas Shoes, pairs,	102
Leather Boots, pairs,	103
Shirts,	[illegible]
Aprons,	570
Chemises,	217
Flannel Petticoats,	157
Winsey Skirts,	110
" Wrappers,	97
Linsey Petticoats,	60
Day Caps,	58
Towels,	40
Bed Ticks,	171
Sheets, single,	332
Bolster Cases,	211
Shrouds,	63
Winding Sheets,	73

LIMERICK.

Articles.	Number.
Leather Boots, pairs,	[illegible]
Canvas " "	307
Brogues,	746
Men's Caps,	319
Flannel Drawers,	15
Frieze Jackets,	14
Cloth "	19
Tweed "	61
Handkerchiefs,	531
Neckties,	367
Day Shirts,	607
Night Shirts,	71
Socks, pairs,	1,730
Corduroy Trousers,	55
Moleskin "	47
Waistcoats,	117
Aprons,	604
Hoods,	60
Caps,	79
Chemises,	278
Gowns,	203
Pinafores,	46
Dresses,	81
Petticoats,	164
Winter Shawls,	73
" Stockings,	404

LONDONDERRY.

Articles.	Number.
Coats,	31
Vests,	55
Patients' Trousers, pairs,	61
Attendants' Trousers, pairs,	9

LONDONDERRY—*continued*.

Articles.	Number.
Patients' Caps, dozen,	12
Shirts,	531
Socks,	780
Flannel Vests,	34
" Drawers, pairs,	53
Shifts,	313
Winsey Petticoats,	207
Flannel "	103
Winsey Wrappers,	153
Sun Bonnets,	10
Aprons,	460
Stockings,	460
Flannel Vests,	14
Turkey Dresses,	11
Winsey "	85
Hospital Wrappers,	5
Ticks,	60
Bolsters,	67
Pillow Covers,	19
Sheets,	148
Quilted Blankets,	15
Twill Sheets,	18
Table Cloths,	3
Towels,	41
Rollers,	27
Clothes Bags,	30
Attendants' Wrappers,	76
" Aprons,	20
" Chemises,	74
" Petticoats,	18

MARYBOROUGH.

Articles.	Number.
Shirts,	241
Shifts,	706
Petticoats,	102
Gowns,	117
Bed Ticks,	117
Bolsters,	45
Aprons,	271
Caps,	157
Bonnets,	92
Cloaks,	73
Coverlets,	6
Sheets, pairs,	183½
Stockings, "	160
Socks, "	677½
Table Cloths,	4
Refractory Dresses,	15
Wrappers,	12
Men's Shoes, pairs,	17
" Boots, "	9
Women's Shoes, pairs,	57
" Boots, "	13
(Other boots and shoes got by Contract.)	
Men's Jackets,	144
" Vests,	130
" Trousers,	95

MONAGHAN.

Articles.	Number.
Shirts,	470
Flannel Vests,	91
" Drawers,	134
Cotton "	60

MONAGHAN—*continued*.

Articles.	Number.
Socks, pairs,	731
Chemises,	484
Petticoats,	178
Dresses,	129
Aprons,	181
Jackets,	128
Bodices,	53
Caps,	130
Stockings, pairs,	109½
Bonnets,	24
Neckties,	45
Window Blinds,	70
Mats,	2
Shawls,	150
Bed Ticks,	231
Bolster Covers,	111
Pillow "	45
Quilted Rugs,	91
Mattress Covers,	53
Palliasses,	4
Table Cloths,	10
Towels,	60
Napkins,	33
Shrouds,	41
(Bedding and male and female clothing kept in repair.)	

MULLINGAR.

Articles.	Number.
Chemises,	268
Petticoats,	315
Shirts,	457
Mattress Cases,	17
Bed "	147
Women's Caps,	217
Coverlets,	9
Women's Dresses,	294
Sheets,	440
Bolster Cases,	71
Stockings, pairs,	75
Socks "	187
Blinds,	1
Pillow Cases,	105
Refractory Dresses,	3
Drawers,	7
Flannel Jackets,	51
Aprons,	702
Lock Suits,	8

OMAGH.

Articles.	Number.
Coats,	104
Vests,	86
Trousers,	171
Shirts,	642
Socks,	1,143
Shoes,	104
Slushers,	87
Flannel Vests,	19
Flannel Drawers,	60
Twilled "	100
Shifts,	281
Petticoats,	165
Wrappers,	31
Gowns,	179
Aprons,	493
Stockings,	451

No. 29.—Articles of Clothing, Bedding, &c., made by the Patients during the Year ended 31st December, 1885—*continued.*

Omagh—*continued.*

Articles.	Number.
Boots, Women's,	85
Jackets, Flannel,	47
Bed Ticks,	81
Sheets,	144
Quilts,	23
Pillows,	47
Pillow Covers,	47
Refractory Rugs,	30

Richmond.

Articles.	Number.
Frieze Jackets,	717
Vests,	78
Trousers,	910
Shirts,	1,313
Coats,	15
Flannel Vests,	123
" Drawers,	71
Shoes, pairs,	707
Slippers,	80
Lock Suits,	13
Boots, pairs,	11
Tweed Coats,	6
" Vests,	6
" Trousers,	6
Shifts,	1,379
Linsey Petticoats,	610
Flannel "	670
Gowns, Winsey,	593
" Calico,	270
" Gingham,	480
" Refractory,	3
Night Wrappers,	173
Wincey Jackets,	1,957
Cloaks,	4
Women's Shoes, pairs,	371
" Slippers,	67
" Lock Boots, pairs,	18
" Soft Lock Boots, pairs,	78
Hessian Aprons,	724
Check "	1,336
Refractory Quilts,	5
Shrouds,	70

Richmond—*continued.*

Articles.	Number.
Flannel Shirts,	19
Bolster Cases,	816
" Blay,	619
Sheets (pairs),	760½
Mattress Covers, Ticken,	373
" Blay,	87
Bolsters,	840
Table Cloths,	32
Roller Towels,	340
Forehead Bands,	91
Bolster Covers, Ticken,	1
Mattresses re-made,	541
Men's Socks, pairs,	24
" Lock Boots, pairs,	16
" Soft Lock Boots, pairs,	17
Window Curtains,	93
Hessian Bags,	100
Canvas Suits,	37

Sligo.

Articles.	Number.
For Males:	
Shirts,	364
Vests,	207
Trousers,	149
Coats,	160
Shoes, pairs,	235
Stockings, pairs,	190
For Females:	
Chemises,	358
Flannel Petticoats,	164
Linsey "	67
Gowns,	6
Wrappers,	133
Shoes, pairs,	167
Stockings, pairs,	210
Aprons,	464
Hoods,	48
Bedding, &c.:	
Bed Ticks,	376
Bolster Ticks,	352
" Cases,	60
Sheets, pairs,	608½

Sligo—*continued.*

Articles.	Number.
Quilts,	16
Pillows,	24
Towels,	14
Rollers,	6

Waterford.

Articles.	Number.
Jackets,	49
Trousers,	111
Vests,	51
Shirts,	274
Shifts,	373
Pillow Covers,	18
Wrappers,	251
Petticoats,	157
(Calico used in repairs and lining of wrappers, pillow covers, petticoats, 716½ yards slight blay.)	
Flannel Drawers,	78
" Vests,	67
Table Covers,	25
Towels,	101
Round Towels,	7
Aprons,	345
Caps,	163
Aprons for Servants,	71
Sheets,	220
Socks,	864
Stockings,	179
(With repairs in which 36 lbs. of cotton were used.)	
Men's Shoes, pairs,	174
Women's Shoes,	111
Repairs to Shoes, pairs,	623
(With sundry work at leathering of refractory drawers, camisoles, putting on locks, &c., on same.)	
Bolsters,	26
Ticks,	21
Mattresses,	9
Refractory Jackets,	4
" Dresses,	3

APPENDIX D.

Return of the Number of Persons who were Confined in Gaols as "*Criminal*
31st December, 1885, and of the Number of Lunatics so Confined who were

Gaols.	Remaining in Custody from previous Year.			Committed during the Year.			Total Number in Custody.			Removed to District Asylums by Warrant of Lord Lieutenant.			Removed to Central Asylum by Order of Lord Lieutenant.		
	M.	F.	T.	M.	F.	T.	M.	F.	T.	M.	F.	T.	M.	F.	T.
Armagh,	–	–	–	2	–	2	2	–	2	–	–	–	2	–	2
Belfast,	–	–	–	2	2	4	2	2	4	2	2	4	–	–	–
Castlebar,	–	–	–	2	1	3	2	1	3	2	1	3	–	–	–
Cavan,	–	–	–	1	–	1	1	–	1	1	–	1	–	–	–
Clonmel,	–	–	–	2	–	2	2	–	2	1	–	1	1	–	1
Cork City,	–	–	–	–	3	3	–	3	3	–	3	3	–	–	–
Cork County,	–	–	–	2	–	2	2	–	2	2	–	2	–	–	–
Downpatrick,	–	–	–	1	–	1	1	–	1	1	–	1	–	–	–
Dundalk,	–	–	–	2	–	2	2	–	2	2	–	2	–	–	–
Galway,	–	–	–	4	4	8	4	4	8	4	4	8	–	–	–
Grangegorman,	–	–	–	–	13	13	–	13	13	–	11	11	–	1	1
Kilmainham,	–	–	–	4	–	4	4	–	4	4	–	4	–	–	–
Limerick City,	–	–	–	–	1	1	–	1	1	–	1	1	–	–	–
Limerick County,	–	–	–	5	–	5	5	–	5	5	–	5	–	–	–
Londonderry,	–	–	–	3	–	3	3	–	3	2	–	2	1	–	1
Mullingar,	1	–	1	5	–	5	6	–	6	3	–	3	3	–	3
Omagh,	–	–	–	5	2	7	5	2	7	4	2	6	–	–	–
Richmond,	–	–	–	10	–	10	10	–	10	9	–	9	–	–	–
Sligo,	–	–	–	3	2	5	3	2	5	3	2	5	–	–	–
Tralee,	–	–	–	2	–	2	2	–	2	–	–	–	2	–	2
Waterford,	–	–	–	2	1	3	2	1	3	2	1	3	–	–	–
Wexford,	–	–	–	2	2	4	2	2	4	2	2	4	–	–	–

Discharged by Order of Lord Lieutenant.			Otherwise Removed from Gaol.			Died.			Total Removed, Discharged, and Dead.			Remaining in Gaols on 31st December, 18[illegible].			Gaols.
M.	F.	T.	M.	F.	T.	M.	F.	T.	M.	F.	T.	M.	F.	T.	
–	–	–	–	–	–	–	–	–	2	–	2	–	–	–	Armagh.
–	–	–	–	–	–	–	–	–	2	2	4	–	–	–	Belfast.
–	–	–	–	–	–	–	–	–	2	1	3	–	–	–	Castlebar.
–	–	–	–	–	–	–	–	–	1	–	1	–	–	–	Cavan.
–	–	–	–	–	–	–	–	–	2	–	2	–	–	–	Clonmel.
–	–	–	–	–	–	–	–	–	–	3	3	–	–	–	Cork City.
–	–	–	–	–	–	–	–	–	2	–	2	–	–	–	Cork County.
–	–	–	–	–	–	–	–	–	1	–	1	–	–	–	Downpatrick.
–	–	–	–	–	–	–	–	–	2	–	2	–	–	–	Dundalk.
–	–	–	–	–	–	–	–	–	4	4	8	–	–	–	Galway.
–	–	–	–	1	1	–	–	–	–	13	13	–	–	–	Grangegorman.
–	–	–	–	–	–	–	–	–	4	–	4	–	–	–	Kilmainham.
–	–	–	–	–	–	–	–	–	–	1	1	–	–	–	Limerick City.
–	–	–	–	–	–	–	–	–	5	–	5	–	–	–	Limerick County.
–	–	–	–	–	–	–	–	–	3	–	3	–	–	–	Londonderry.
–	–	–	–	–	–	–	–	–	6	–	6	–	–	–	Mullingar.
–	–	–	–	–	–	1	–	1	5	2	7	–	–	–	Omagh.
1	–	1	–	–	–	–	–	–	10	–	10	–	–	–	Richmond.
–	–	–	–	–	–	–	–	–	3	2	5	–	–	–	Sligo.
–	–	–	–	–	–	–	–	–	2	–	2	–	–	–	Tralee.
–	–	–	–	–	–	–	–	–	2	1	3	–	–	–	Waterford.
–	–	–	–	–	–	–	–	–	2	2	4	–	–	–	Wexford.
–	–	–	–	–	–	–	–	–	1	–	1	–	–	–	Wicklow.

SUMMARY of all classes of Lunatics who were confined in Gaols during the Year ended 31st December, 1883, and of the number of Lunatics so confined who were removed to Asylums, Discharged, or who Died during the same period.

Classification of Lunatics.	Number Remaining in Custody on 31st December, 1882.			Number Committed during the Year ended 31st December, 1883.			Total Number in Custody during the Year 1883.			Removed, Discharged, and Died. Removed to District Asylums by Warrant of the Lord Lieutenant.			Removed to the Central Asylum by order of the Lord Lieutenant.			Discharged by order of the Lord Lieutenant.			Otherwise removed from Gaol.			Died.			Total Removed, Discharged, or Died in the Year.			Remaining in Gaols on 31st December, 1883.		
	M.	F.	T.	M.	F.	T.	M.	F.	T.	M.	F.	T.	M.	F.	T.	M.	F.	T.	M.	F.	T.	M.	F.	T.	M.	F.	T.	M.	F.	T.
Persons acquitted of offences on the ground of insanity,	–	–	–	7	3	10	7	3	10	4	2	6	2	1	3	1	–	1	–	–	–	–	–	–	7	3	10	–	–	–
Persons found insane on arraignment, and incapable of pleading,	1	–	1	19	2	21	20	2	22	14	2	16	6	–	6	–	–	–	–	–	–	–	–	–	20	2	22	–	–	–
Persons under sentence of imprisonment or transportation, who became insane in gaol,	–	–	–	20	20	40	20	20	40	27	19	46	1	–	1	–	–	–	–	1	1	1	–	1	29	20	49	–	–	–
Persons committed in default of surety to keep the peace, who were insane on, or who became insane subsequent to committal,	–	–	–	4	5	9	4	5	9	4	5	9	–	–	–	–	–	–	–	–	–	–	–	–	4	5	9	–	–	–
Persons committed under the Vagrancy Act, who were insane on, or who became insane subsequent to committal,	–	–	–	1	1	2	1	1	2	1	1	2	–	–	–	–	–	–	–	–	–	–	–	–	1	1	2	–	–	–
Total,	1	–	1	60	31	91	61	31	92	50	29	79	9	1	10	1	–	1	–	1	1	1	–	1	61	31	92	–	–	–

APPENDIX E.

Criminal Lunatics.

Return of the Number of Persons confined in Convict Prisons, who were or became insane during the year ending 31st December, 1885, and of the Number of Lunatics so confined who were removed to Asylum, Discharged, or who Died during the same period.

—	Convicts.		
	Male.	Female.	Total.
Remaining in custody on 31st December, 1884, . .	–	–	–
Became insane during the year ended 31st December, 1885, ...	6	3	9
Total number in custody during the year, . . .	6	3	9
Removed, Discharged, Died.			
Removed to Dundrum Asylum by warrant of Lord Lieutenant, ...	6	3	9
Discharged by order of Lord Lieutenant, or on expiration of sentence, ...	–	–	–
Otherwise removed from Prisons, ...		-	-
Died, ...	–	-	-
Total Removed, Discharged, and Died, ...	6	3	9
Remaining in Prisons on 31st December, 1885, . .	-	–	–

Note.—Mountjoy Prison is now exclusively for Male Convicts. The Female Convicts formerly there have been transferred to Grangegorman Prison.

APPENDIX F.

Private Licensed Houses.

No. 1.—Table showing the Numbers Licensed for, the Number of Admissions, Discharges, Deaths, and Escapes during the Year ending 31st December, 1885.

Asylums.	Number Licensed for.			Number remaining in Asylums on 31st December, 1884.			Admitted during the Year 1885. Relapsed Cases.			Cases of First Attack.			Total Number Admitted.			Total Number under treatment during the Year 1885.			Discharged during the Year 1885. Recovered.			Improved.		
	M.	F.	T.	M.	F.	T.	M.	F.	T.	M.	F.	T.	M.	F.	T.	M.	F.	T.	M.	F.	T.	M.	F.	T.
Allen Retreat, Co. Armagh,	20	15	35	21	13	34	2	2	4	6	3	9	8	5	13	29	18	47	3	8	11	2	–	2
Bloomfield Retreat, Co. Dublin,	15	35	50	13	26	39	–	1	1	2	2	4	2	3	5	15	29	44	–	–	–	1	–	1
Citadella, Co. Cork,	7	11	18	6	13	19	1	–	1	4	2	6	5	2	7	11	15	26	1	2	3	1	–	1
Course Lodge, Co. Armagh,	–	15	15	–	9	9	–	–	–	–	1	1	–	1	1	–	10	10	–	–	–	–	–	–
Elm Lawn, Co. Dublin,	–	10	10	–	4	4	–	1	1	–	1	1	–	2	2	–	6	6	–	1	1	–	–	–
Esker House, do.,	–	6	6	–	3	3	–	–	–	–	–	–	–	–	–	–	3	3	–	–	–	–	–	–
Farnham House, do.,	35	25	60	29	21	53	1	1	2	4	3	7	5	4	9	34	28	62	6	1	7	–	–	–
Hampstead House, do.,	28	2	30	22	1	23	1	–	1	5	–	5	6	–	6	28	1	29	3	–	3	2	–	2
Hartfield House, do.,	30	–	30	27	–	27	5	–	5	4	–	4	9	–	9	36	–	36	4	–	4	2	–	2
Highfield House, do.,	–	18	18	–	13	13	–	1	1	–	2	2	–	3	3	–	16	16	–	2	2	–	–	–
Lindville, Co. Cork,	16	14	30	12	11	23	3	–	3	3	1	4	6	1	7	18	12	30	2	1	3	2	–	2
Lisle House, Co. Dublin,	–	10	10	–	3	3	–	–	–	–	–	–	–	–	–	–	3	3	–	–	–	–	–	–
Midland Retreat, Queen's Co.,	10	10	20	5	4	9	1	1	2	3	–	3	4	1	5	9	5	14	3	2	5	–	–	–
Mount Alton, Co. Dublin,	–	6	6	–	1	1	–	2	2	–	1	1	–	3	3	–	4	4	–	1	1	–	–	–
Orchardstown House, Co. Dublin,	6	6	12	2	6	8	–	–	–	–	–	–	–	–	–	2	6	8	–	–	–	–	–	–
St. John of God, do.,	20	–	20	–	–	–	2	–	2	21	–	21	23	–	23	23	–	23	9	–	9	1	–	1
St. Patrick's (Belmont), Co. Waterford,	18	–	18	3	–	3	1	–	1	3	–	3	4	–	4	7	–	7	2	–	2	–	–	–
St. Patrick's (Swift's), Dublin City,*	–	–	–	36	58	94	–	2	2	8	10	18	8	12	20	44	70	114	1	3	4	3	4	7
Spring Lawn House, King's Co.,	1	2	3	1	2	3	–	–	–	–	–	–	–	–	–	1	2	3	–	–	–	–	–	–
Stewart Institution, Co. Dublin,	–	–	–	68	72	140	1	1	2	10	15	25	11	16	27	79	88	167	2	3	5	3	–	3
Verville, do.,	–	23	23	–	20	20	–	4	4	–	5	5	–	9	9	–	29	29	–	2	2	–	2	2
St. Vincent's, do.,	–	–	–	–	107	107	–	2	2	–	16	16	–	18	18	–	125	125	–	8	8	–	2	2
Woodbine Lodge, do.,	–	10	10	–	4	4	–	–	–	–	1	1	–	1	1	–	5	5	–	1	1	–	–	–
Total,	206	230	436	245	394	639	18	18	36	73	63	136	91	81	172	336	475	811	38	33	71	17	8	25

* In the Annual Report for the year ending 31st December, 1884, the number of patients in St. Patrick's (Swift's) Private Asylum at the end of that year was 35 males and 59 females. When preparing the tables for last year it was discovered that the number of males was 36, and females 58.

No. 1.—TABLE showing the Numbers Licensed for, the Number of Admissions, Discharges, Deaths, and Escapes during the Year ending 31st December, 1883—*continued.*

ASYLUMS.	Discharged during the Year 1883.						Died during the Year 1883.									Escapes.			Total No. Discharged, Died, and Escaped, during the year 1883.			Number Remaining in Asylums on 31st December, 1883.		
	Unrecovered or Incurable.			Total Number Discharged.			Natural Causes.			Accidental Causes.			Total Number Died.											
	M.	F.	T.	M.	F.	T.	M.	F.	T.	M.	F.	T.	M.	F.	T.	M.	F.	T.	M.	F.	T.	M.	F.	T.
Allen Retreat, Co. Armagh,	3	–	3	10	6	16	1	–	1	–	–	–	1	–	1	–	–	–	11	6	17	18	12	30
Bloomfield Retreat, Co. Dublin,	1	–	1	2	–	2	3	3	6	–	–	–	3	3	6	–	–	–	5	3	8	10	26	36
Cittadella, Co. Cork,	–	–	–	2	2	4	–	1	1	–	–	–	–	1	1	–	–	–	2	3	5	9	12	21
Course Lodge, Co. Armagh,	–	2	2	–	2	2	–	–	–	–	–	–	–	–	–	–	–	–	–	2	2	–	8	8
Elm Lawn, Co. Dublin,	–	–	–	–	1	1	–	1	1	–	–	–	–	1	1	–	–	–	–	2	2	–	4	4
Esker House, do.,	–	–	–	–	–	–	–	–	–	–	–	–	–	–	–	–	–	–	–	–	–	–	5	5
Farnham House, do.,	–	–	–	6	1	7	2	1	3	1	–	1	3	1	4	–	–	–	9	2	11	25	26	51
Hampstead House, do.,	1	–	1	6	–	6	–	–	–	–	–	–	–	–	–	–	–	–	6	–	6	22	1	23
Hartfield House, do.,	–	–	–	6	–	6	2	–	2	–	–	–	2	–	2	–	–	–	8	–	8	29	–	29
Highfield House, do.,	–	–	–	–	2	2	–	2	2	–	–	–	–	2	2	–	–	–	–	4	4	–	12	12
Lindville, Co. Cork,	2	–	2	6	1	7	2	–	2	–	–	–	2	–	2	–	–	–	8	1	9	10	11	21
Lisle House, Co. Dublin,	–	–	–	–	–	–	–	1	1	–	–	–	–	1	1	–	–	–	–	1	1	–	2	2
Midland Retreat, Queen's Co.,	–	3	3	5	3	8	1	–	1	–	–	–	1	–	1	–	–	–	6	3	9	5	–	5
Mount Alton, County Dublin,	–	–	–	–	1	1	–	–	–	–	–	–	–	–	–	–	–	–	–	1	1	–	3	3
Orchardstown House, do.,	–	1	1	–	1	1	–	1	1	–	–	–	–	1	1	–	–	–	–	2	2	2	4	6
St. John of God, do.,	1	–	1	11	–	11	–	–	–	–	–	–	–	–	–	–	–	–	11	–	11	12	–	12
St. Patrick's (Belmont), Co. Waterford,	–	–	–	2	–	2	1	–	1	–	–	–	1	–	1	–	–	–	3	–	3	4	–	4
St. Patrick's (Swift's), Dublin City,	–	1	1	4	8	12	5	4	9	–	–	–	5	4	9	–	–	–	9	12	21	35	58	93
Spring Lawn House, King's Co.	–	–	–	–	–	–	–	–	–	–	–	–	–	–	–	–	–	–	–	–	–	1	2	3
Stewart Institution, Co. Dublin,	4	4	8	9	7	16	8	10	18	–	–	–	8	10	18	–	–	–	17	17	34	62	71	133
Verville, do.,	–	–	–	–	4	4	–	2	2	–	–	–	–	2	2	–	–	–	–	6	6	–	23	23
St. Vincent's, do.,	–	1	1	–	11	11	–	6	6	–	–	–	–	6	6	–	–	–	–	17	17	–	106	106
Woodlawn Lodge, do.,	–	–	–	–	1	1	–	1	1	–	–	–	–	1	1	–	–	–	–	2	2	–	3	3
Total,	12	13	21	67	53	120	25	33	58	1	–	1	26	33	59	–	–	–	93	86	179	243	386	629

No. 2.—Table showing the Number of Patients in Private Asylums on 31st December, 1885.

Asylums.	Curable.			Incurable.			Idiots.			Epileptics.			Total.		
	M.	F.	T.	M.	F.	T.	M.	F.	T.	M.	F.	T.	M.	F.	T.
Allen Retreat, County Armagh,	12	9	21	5	3	8	–	–	–	1	–	1	18	12	30
Bloomfield Retreat, Co. Dublin,	–	2	2	9	24	33	1	–	1	–	1	1	10	26	36
Citadella, Co. Cork,	4	5	9	5	7	12	–	–	–	–	–	–	9	12	21
Course Lodge, Co. Armagh,	–	2	2	–	6	6	–	–	–	–	–	–	–	8	8
Elm Lawn, Co. Dublin,	–	1	1	–	2	2	–	1	1	–	–	–	–	4	4
Esker House, County Dublin,	–	–	–	–	3	3	–	–	–	–	–	–	–	3	3
Farnham House, do.,	3	2	5	20	22	42	–	–	–	–	2	2	23	26	51
Hampstead House, do.,	7	–	7	15	1	16	–	–	–	–	–	–	22	1	23
Hartfield House, do.,	6	–	6	22	–	22	–	–	–	–	–	–	28	–	28
Highfield House, do.,	–	1	1	–	11	11	–	–	–	–	–	–	–	12	12
Lindville, Co. Cork,	–	3	3	10	8	18	–	–	–	–	–	–	10	11	21
Lisle House, Co. Dublin,	–	–	–	–	2	2	–	–	–	–	–	–	–	2	2
Midland Retreat, Queen's Co.,	3	–	3	2	–	2	–	–	–	–	–	–	5	–	5
Mount Alton, Co. Dublin,	–	1	1	–	2	2	–	–	–	–	–	–	–	3	3
Orchardstown House, Co. Dublin,	–	1	1	1	3	4	–	–	–	1	–	1	2	4	6
St. John of God, Co. Dublin,	8	–	8	3	–	3	1	–	1	–	–	–	12	–	12
St. Patrick's (Belmont), Co. Waterford,	–	–	–	3	–	3	1	–	1	–	–	–	4	–	4
St. Patrick's (Swift's), Dublin City,	2	2	4	31	53	84	2	1	3	–	–	–	35	56	91
Spring Lawn House, King's Co.,	–	–	–	1	2	3	–	–	–	–	–	–	1	2	3
Stewart Institution, Co. Dublin,	–	–	–	29	37	66	36	31	67	–	3	3	65	71	136
Verville, Co. Dublin,	–	6	6	–	17	17	–	–	–	–	–	–	–	23	23
St. Vincent's, do.,	–	11	11	–	96	96	–	–	–	–	1	1	–	108	108
Woodbine Lodge, do.,	–	–	–	–	3	3	–	–	–	–	–	–	–	3	3
Total,	43	54	97	155	297	452	41	33	74	2	7	9	212	[illegible]	[illegible]

No. 3.—Table showing the Social Condition of Patients in Private Asylums on 31st December, 1885.

Asylums.	Married.			Single.			Widowers or Widows.			Unknown.			Total.		
	M.	F.	T.	M.	F.	T.	M.	F.	T.	M.	F.	T.	M.	F.	T.
Allen Retreat, County Armagh,	2	4	6	16	8	24	–	–	–	–	–	–	18	12	30
Bloomfield Retreat, Co. Dublin,	1	10	11	9	15	24	–	1	1	–	–	–	10	26	36
Citadella, Co. Cork,	3	1	4	6	11	17	–	–	–	–	–	–	9	12	21
Course Lodge, County Armagh,	–	–	–	–	7	7	–	1	1	–	–	–	–	8	8
Elm Lawn, Co. Dublin,	–	–	–	–	2	2	–	2	2	–	–	–	–	4	4
Esker House, County Dublin,	–	–	–	–	2	2	–	1	1	–	–	–	–	3	3
Farnham House, do.,	5	2	7	17	21	38	3	3	6	–	–	–	25	26	51
Hampstead House, do.,	7	1	8	11	–	11	4	–	4	–	–	–	22	1	23
Hartfield House, do.,	–	–	–	25	–	25	3	–	3	–	–	–	28	–	28
Highfield House, do.,	–	2	2	–	9	9	–	1	1	–	–	–	–	12	12
Lindville, Co. Cork,	–	2	2	7	7	14	3	2	5	–	–	–	10	11	21
Lisle House, Co. Dublin,	–	1	1	–	1	1	–	–	–	–	–	–	–	2	2
Midland Retreat, Queen's County,	–	–	–	5	–	5	–	–	–	–	–	–	5	–	5
Mount Alton, Co. Dublin,	–	–	–	–	2	2	–	1	1	–	–	–	–	3	3
Orchardstown House, County Dublin,	–	–	–	2	3	5	–	1	1	–	–	–	2	4	6
St. John of God, Co. Dublin,	2	–	2	10	–	10	–	–	–	–	–	–	12	–	12
St. Patrick's (Belmont), Co. Waterford,	–	–	–	4	–	4	–	–	–	–	–	–	4	–	4
St. Patrick's (Swift's), Dublin City,	3	2	5	30	51	81	2	5	7	–	–	–	35	58	93
Spring Lawn House, King's Co.,	–	–	–	1	1	2	–	1	1	–	–	–	1	2	3
Stewart Institution, County Dublin,	–	7	7	62	57	119	–	7	7	–	–	–	62	71	133
Verville, Co. Dublin,	–	3	3	–	16	16	–	4	4	–	–	–	–	23	23
St. Vincent's, do.,	–	11	11	–	85	85	–	12	12	–	–	–	–	108	108
Woodbine Lodge, do.,	–	–	–	–	3	3	–	–	–	–	–	–	–	3	3
Total,	23	46	69	203	301	504	15	42	57	–	–	–	243	390	633

No. 4.—Table showing Form of Lunacy in the several Cases in Private Asylums on the 31st December, 1885.

Asylums.	Mania.										Melancholia.												Monomania.		Hypochondriasis.	
	Mania.		With Epilepsy.		With Paralysis.		Hysteria.		Chorea.		Melancholia.		With Epilepsy.		With Paralysis.		With occasional Violence.		With Suicidal.		With Suicidal with Epilepsy.					
	M.	F.	M.	F.	M.	F.	M.	F.	M.	F.	M.	F.	M.	F.	M.	F.	M.	F.	M.	F.	M.	F.	M.	F.	M.	F.
Allen Retreat, Co. Armagh,	14	5	1	–	–	–	–	–	–	1	–	–	–	–	–	–	–	–	–	–	–	–	–	1	–	–
Bloomfield Retreat, Co. Dublin,	3	8	–	1	–	–	–	2	–	–	1	7	–	–	–	–	–	–	–	–	–	–	1	2	–	3
Citadella, Co. Cork,	9	11	–	1	–	–	–	–	–	–	–	–	–	–	–	–	–	–	–	–	–	–	–	–	–	–
Course Lodge, Co. Armagh,	–	–	–	–	–	–	–	5	–	1	–	–	–	–	–	–	–	–	–	–	–	–	–	1	–	1
Elm Lawn, County Dublin,	–	–	–	–	–	–	–	1	–	–	–	–	–	–	–	–	–	–	–	–	–	–	–	–	–	–
Esker House, do.,	–	–	–	–	–	–	–	–	–	–	–	–	–	–	–	–	–	1	–	–	–	–	–	–	–	–
Farnham House, do.,	20	18	–	–	–	–	–	4	–	–	2	1	1	1	1	–	–	–	–	–	–	–	–	–	–	–
Hampstead House, do.,	7	–	–	–	–	–	–	–	–	–	1	–	–	–	–	–	–	–	1	1	–	–	1	–	1	–
Hartfield House, do.,	14	–	–	–	–	–	–	–	–	–	1	–	–	–	–	–	2	–	2	–	–	–	3	–	–	–
Highfield House, do.,	–	4	–	1	–	–	–	–	–	–	–	1	–	–	–	–	–	–	–	–	–	–	–	–	–	–
Lindville, Co. Cork,	9	9	–	–	–	–	–	–	–	–	–	1	–	–	–	–	–	–	–	–	–	–	–	–	–	–
Lisle House, Co. Dublin	–	–	–	–	–	–	–	–	–	–	–	–	–	–	–	–	–	–	–	1	–	–	–	–	–	–
Midland Retreat, Queen's Co.,	2	–	–	–	–	–	–	–	–	–	–	–	–	–	–	–	–	–	–	–	–	–	1	–	–	–
Mount Alton, Co. Dublin,	–	1	–	–	–	–	–	–	–	–	–	–	–	–	–	–	–	–	–	–	–	–	–	–	–	1
Orchardstown House, Co. Dublin,	–	–	–	–	–	–	–	–	–	–	–	1	–	–	–	–	–	–	–	–	–	–	–	–	–	–
St. John of God, do.,	–	–	–	–	–	–	1	–	–	–	3	–	–	–	–	–	–	–	–	–	–	–	–	–	–	–
St. Patrick's (Belmont), County Waterford,	–	–	–	–	–	–	–	–	–	–	–	–	–	–	–	–	–	–	–	–	–	–	2	–	–	–
St. Patrick's (Swift's), Dublin City,	17	24	–	–	–	–	–	–	–	3	5	15	–	–	–	–	3	5	1	1	–	–	1	–	–	–
Spring Lawn House, King's Co.,	–	2	–	–	–	–	–	–	–	–	–	–	–	–	–	–	1	–	–	–	–	–	–	–	–	–
Stewart Institution, Co. Dublin,	5	6	–	–	–	–	–	–	–	–	8	11	–	–	–	–	–	–	–	–	–	–	3	17	–	–
Verville, do.,	–	9	–	–	–	–	–	3	–	–	–	1	–	–	–	–	–	–	–	2	–	–	–	2	–	–
St. Vincent's, do.,	–	76	–	1	–	–	–	–	–	1	–	1	–	–	–	–	–	–	–	–	–	–	–	–	–	–
Woodbine Lodge, do.,	–	1	–	–	–	–	–	–	–	–	–	–	–	–	–	–	–	2	–	–	–	–	–	–	–	–
Total,	100	174	1	4	–	–	1	15	–	6	24	45	1	1	1	–	6	8	4	5	–	–	14	23	1	4

No. 4.—Table showing Form of Lunacy in the several Cases in Private Asylums on the 31st December, 1885—*continued*.

Asylums.	Incoherence.								Imbecility.										Slight Impairment of the Faculties.		Idiocy.		Total in Asylums on 31st December, 1885		
	Inco-herence.		With Epilepsy.		With Paralysis.		With occasional Violence.		Imbe-cility.		With Epilepsy.		With Paralysis.		With occasional Violence.		Tending to Dementia.								
	M.	F.	M.	F.	M.	F.	M.	F.	M.	F.	M.	F.	M.	F.	M.	F.	M.	F.	M.	F.	M.	F.	M.	F.	T.
Allen Retreat, Co. Armagh,	–	–	–	–	–	–	–	–	1	1	–	–	–	–	2	2	–	2	–	–	–	–	18	12	30
Bloomfield Retreat, Co. Dublin,	–	–	–	–	–	–	–	–	1	–	–	–	–	–	–	–	–	1	2	1	1	1	10	26	36
Citadella, Co. Cork,	–	–	–	–	–	–	–	–	–	–	–	–	–	–	–	–	–	–	–	–	–	–	9	12	21
Course Lodge, Co. Armagh,	–	–	–	–	–	–	–	–	–	–	–	–	–	–	–	–	–	–	–	–	–	–	–	8	8
Elm Lawn, County Dublin,	–	1	–	–	–	–	–	–	–	1	–	–	–	–	–	–	–	–	–	1	–	–	–	4	4
Esker House, do.,	–	2	–	–	–	–	–	–	–	–	–	–	–	–	–	–	–	–	–	–	–	–	–	3	3
Farnham House, do.,	–	1	–	–	–	–	–	–	–	1	–	–	–	–	–	–	–	–	1	–	–	–	25	26	51
Hampstead House, do.,	–	–	–	–	1	–	–	–	2	–	–	–	–	–	1	–	1	–	6	–	–	–	22	1	23
Hartfield House, do.,	–	–	–	–	–	–	–	–	2	–	–	–	–	–	–	–	1	–	–	–	–	–	28	–	28
Highfield House, do.,	–	–	–	–	–	–	–	–	–	1	–	–	–	–	–	3	–	–	–	2	–	–	–	13	13
Lindville, Co. Cork,	–	–	–	–	–	–	–	–	1	–	–	–	–	–	–	1	–	–	–	–	–	–	10	11	21
Lisle House, Co. Dublin,	–	–	–	–	–	–	–	–	–	1	–	–	–	–	–	–	–	–	–	–	–	–	–	3	3
Midland Retreat, Queen's Co.,	–	–	–	–	–	–	–	–	2	–	–	–	–	–	–	–	–	–	–	–	–	–	5	–	5
Mount Alton, Co. Dublin,	–	–	–	–	–	–	–	–	–	–	–	–	–	–	–	–	–	1	–	–	–	–	–	3	3
Orchardstown House, Co. Dublin,	–	–	–	–	–	–	–	–	–	1	–	1	–	–	1	1	–	1	–	–	–	–	2	4	6
St John of God, do.	–	–	–	–	1	–	2	–	2	–	–	–	–	–	–	–	–	–	3	–	–	–	12	–	12
St. Patrick's (Belmont), County Waterford,	–	–	–	–	1	–	–		1	–	–	–	–	–	–	–	–	–	–	–	–	–	4	–	4
St Patrick's (Swift's), Dublin City,	–	–	–	–	–	–	–	1	3	6	–	–	–	–	1	–	2	–	–	–	2	1	33	60	93
Spring Lawn House, King's Co.,	–	–	–	–	–	–	–	–	–	–	–	–	–	–	–	–	–	–	–	–	–	–	1	2	3
Stewart Institution, Co. Dublin,	1	1	–	–	–	–	–	–	4	3	–	–	–	–	–	–	3	–	–	1	36	30	62	71	133
Verville, do.,	–	–	–	–	–	–	–	2	–	–	–	–	–	–	–	–	–	1	–	3	–	–	–	23	23
St. Vincent's, do.,	–	5	–	–	–	–	–	–	–	14	–	–	–	–	–	–	–	7	–	–	–	–	–	103	103
Woodbine Lodge, do.,	–	–	–	–	–	–	–	–	–	–	–	–	–	–	–	–	–	–	–	–	–	–	–	3	3
Total,	1	10	–	–	3	–	2	3	19	30	–	–	–	–	5	7	7	13	9	8	39	32	243	389	632

No. 5.—Table showing the Ages of Patients in Private Lunatic Asylums, on 31st December, 1885.

Asylums.	Under 20 years.			20 to 40 years.			40 to 60 years.			Over 60 years.			Total.		
	M.	F.	T.	M.	F.	T.	M.	F.	T.	M.	F.	T.	M.	F.	T.
Allen Retreat, County Armagh,	–	–	–	6	5	11	7	6	13	3	3	6	16	14	30
Bloomfield Retreat, Co. Dublin,	–	–	–	1	5	6	6	13	19	3	8	11	10	26	36
Citadella, Co. Cork,	–	–	–	5	5	10	2	7	9	2	–	2	9	12	21
Course Lodge, County Armagh,	–	–	–	–	2	2	–	4	4	–	2	2	–	8	8
Elm Lawn, Co. Dublin,	–	–	–	–	2	2	–	1	1	–	1	1	–	4	4
Esker House, do.,	–	–	–	–	–	–	–	1	1	–	2	2	–	3	3
Farnham House, do.,	1	–	1	5	5	10	12	13	25	7	8	16	25	26	51
Hampstead House, do.,	–	–	–	2	–	2	10	–	10	10	–	10	22	1	23
Hartfield House, do.,	1	–	1	4	–	4	16	–	16	7	–	7	28	–	28
Highfield House, do.,	–	–	–	–	2	2	–	5	5	–	5	5	–	12	12
Lindville, Co. Cork,	–	–	–	2	2	4	7	7	14	1	2	3	10	11	21
Lisle House, Co. Dublin,	–	–	–	–	–	–	–	1	1	–	1	1	–	2	2
Midland Retreat, Queen's County,	–	–	–	2	–	2	2	–	2	1	–	1	5	–	5
Mount Alton, Co. Dublin,	–	–	–	–	2	2	–	–	–	–	1	1	–	3	3
Orchardstown House, do.,	–	–	–	1	–	1	1	1	2	–	3	3	2	4	6
St. John of God, do.,	2	–	2	4	–	4	6	–	6	–	–	–	12	–	12
St. Patrick's (Belmont), County Waterford,	1	–	1	1	–	1	–	–	–	2	–	2	4	–	4
St. Patrick's (Swift's), Dublin City,	–	–	–	16	20	36	12	21	33	7	15	22	35	56	91
Spring Lawn House, King's County,	–	–	–	–	1	1	–	–	–	1	1	2	1	2	3
Stewart Institution, Co. Dublin,	28	20	48	23	16	39	12	25	37	1	10	11	64	71	135
Verville, County Dublin,	–	–	–	–	6	6	–	10	10	–	5	5	–	23	23
St. Vincent's, do.,	–	1	1	–	26	26	–	59	59	–	22	22	–	108	108
Woodbine Lodge, do.,	–	–	–	–	1	1	–	2	2	–	–	–	–	3	3
Total,	31	21	52	74	109	183	93	177	270	45	89	134	243	389	632

No. 6.—Table showing the Educational Condition of Patients in Private Lunatic Asylums on 31st December, 1885.

Asylum.	Well Educated.			Can Read and Write well.			Can Read and Write indifferently.			Can Read only.			Cannot Read or Write.			Unknown.			Total.		
	M.	F.	T.	M.	F.	T.	M.	F.	T.	M.	F.	T.	M.	F.	T.	M.	F.	T.	M.	F.	T.
Allen Retreat, Co. Armagh,	13	8	21	–	3	3	–	1	1	–	–	–	–	–	–	–	–	–	13	12	25
Bloomfield Retreat, County Dublin,	10	26	36	–	–	–	–	–	–	–	–	–	–	–	–	–	–	–	10	26	36
Citadella, County Cork,	9	12	21	–	–	–	–	–	–	–	–	–	–	–	–	–	–	–	9	12	21
Course Lodge, Co. Armagh,	–	8	8	–	–	–	–	–	–	–	–	–	–	–	–	–	–	–	–	8	8
Elm Lawn, Co. Dublin,	–	4	4	–	–	–	–	–	–	–	–	–	–	–	–	–	–	–	–	4	4
Esker House, do.,	–	2	2	–	1	1	–	–	–	–	–	–	–	–	–	–	–	–	–	3	3
Farnham House, do.,	25	26	51	–	–	–	–	–	–	–	–	–	–	–	–	–	–	–	25	26	51
Hampstead House, do.,	21	1	22	–	–	–	1	–	1	–	–	–	–	–	–	–	–	–	22	1	23
Hartfield House, do.,	23	–	23	6	–	6	–	–	–	–	–	–	–	–	–	–	–	–	29	–	29
Highfield House, do.,	–	12	12	–	–	–	–	–	–	–	–	–	–	–	–	–	–	–	–	12	12
Lindville, County Cork,	8	9	17	1	2	3	1	–	1	–	–	–	–	–	–	–	–	–	10	11	21
Lisle House, Co. Dublin,	–	2	2	–	–	–	–	–	–	–	–	–	–	–	–	–	–	–	–	2	2
Midland Retreat, Queen's County,	3	–	3	1	–	1	–	–	–	–	–	–	1	–	1	–	–	–	5	–	5
Mount Alton, Co. Dublin,	–	3	3	–	–	–	–	–	–	–	–	–	–	–	–	–	–	–	–	3	3
Orchardstown House, do.	2	4	6	–	–	–	–	–	–	–	–	–	–	–	–	–	–	–	2	4	6
St. John of God, do.	10	–	10	–	–	–	–	–	–	1	–	1	1	–	1	–	–	–	12	–	12
St. Patrick's (Belmont), County Waterford,	3	–	3	–	–	–	–	–	–	–	–	–	1	–	1	–	–	–	4	–	4
St. Patrick's (Swift's), Dublin City,	33	51	84	2	7	9	–	–	–	–	–	–	–	–	–	–	–	–	35	58	93
Spring Lawn House, King's County,	1	2	3	–	–	–	–	–	–	–	–	–	–	–	–	–	–	–	1	2	3
Stewart Institution, Co. Dublin,	23	40	63	6	5	11	7	7	14	–	3	3	26	16	42	–	–	–	62	71	133
Verville, Co. Dublin,	–	23	23	–	–	–	–	–	–	–	–	–	–	–	–	–	–	–	–	23	23
St. Vincent's, do.,	–	87	87	–	14	14	–	7	7	–	–	–	–	–	–	–	–	–	–	108	108
Woodlawn Lodge, do.,	–	3	3	–	–	–	–	–	–	–	–	–	–	–	–	–	–	–	–	3	3
Total,	189	324	513	15	32	47	9	15	24	1	3	4	29	16	45	–	–	–	239	390	629

No. 7.—TABLE showing the Number of Patients in Private Lunatic Asylums on 31st December, 1885, classified as to Professions, Trades, &c., &c.

ASYLUMS.	Married.			Single.			Total, Married and Single.			Previous Professions or Occupations.									
										Army.		Navy.		Church.		Law.		Medicine.	
	M.	F.	T.	M.	F.	T.	M.	F.	T.	M.	F.	M.	F.	M.	F.	M.	F.	M.	F.
Allen Retreat, Co. Armagh,	2	4	6	16	5	21	16	12	30	–	–	–	–	2	–	–	–	–	–
Bloomfield Retreat, Co. Dublin,	1	11	12	9	15	24	10	26	36	–	–	–	–	–	–	–	–	–	–
Cittadella, Co. Cork,	3	1	4	6	11	17	9	12	21	1	–	–	–	–	–	–	–	–	–
Course Lodge, Co. Armagh,	–	1	1	–	7	7	–	8	8	–	–	–	–	–	–	–	–	–	–
Elm Lawn, Co. Dublin,	–	2	2	–	2	2	–	4	4	–	–	–	–	–	–	–	–	–	–
Esker House, do.,	–	1	1	–	3	3	–	3	3	–	–	–	–	–	–	–	–	–	–
Farnham House, do.,	8	5	13	17	21	38	25	26	51	5	–	–	–	3	–	–	–	–	–
Hampstead House, do.,	7	1	8	15	–	15	22	1	23	7	–	–	–	1	–	2	–	1	–
Hartfield House, do.,	3	–	3	23	–	23	26	–	26	3	–	1	–	2	–	4	–	2	–
Highfield House, do.,	–	2	2	–	10	10	–	12	12	–	–	–	–	–	–	–	–	–	–
Lindville, Co. Cork,	3	4	7	7	7	14	10	11	21	–	–	–	–	2	–	–	–	–	–
Lisle House, Co. Dublin,	–	1	1	–	1	1	–	2	2	–	–	–	–	–	–	–	–	–	–
Midland Retreat, Queen's Co.,	–	–	–	5	–	5	5	–	5	–	–	–	–	–	–	1	–	–	–
Mount Alton, County Dublin,	–	1	1	–	2	2	–	3	3	–	–	–	–	–	–	–	–	–	–
Orchardstown House, do.,	–	1	1	2	3	5	2	4	6	–	–	–	–	–	–	–	–	–	–
St. John of God, do.,	2	–	2	10	–	10	12	–	12	–	–	–	–	2	–	–	–	–	–
St. Patrick's (Belmont), County Waterford,	–	–	–	4	–	4	4	–	4	–	–	–	–	3	–	–	–	–	–
St. Patrick's (Swift's), Dublin City,	3	2	5	32	56	88	35	58	93	4	–	1	–	2	–	1	–	1	–
Spring Lawn House, King's Co.,	–	1	1	1	1	2	1	2	3	–	–	–	–	–	–	–	–	–	–
Stewart Institution, Co. Dublin,	–	14	14	62	57	119	62	71	133	1	–	–	–	–	–	1	–	–	–
Verville, do.,	–	6	6	–	17	17	–	23	23	–	–	–	–	–	–	–	–	–	–
St. Vincent's, do.,	–	11	11	–	97	97	–	108	108	–	–	–	–	–	–	–	–	–	–
Woodbine Lodge, do.,	–	–	–	–	3	3	–	3	3	–	–	–	–	–	–	–	–	–	–
Total,	22	69	101	211	320	531	214	[illegible]	632	20	–	2	–	17	–	9	–	3	–

No. 7.—Table showing the Number of Patients in Private Lunatic Asylums on 31st December, 1883, classified as to Professions, Trades, &c., &c.—*continued.*

Asylums.	Previous Professions or Occupations. Student.		In Trade.		Other Occupations.		Farmers.		No occupation.		Total.			Found Lunatics by Inquisition.			Sent by authority of Relatives or Friends.			Total remaining in Asylums on 31st December, 1883.		
	M.	F.	M.	F.	M.	F.	M.	F.	M.	F.	M.	F.	T.	M.	F.	T.	M.	F.	T.	M.	F.	T.
Allen Retreat, Co. Armagh,	1	–	6	–	–	1	4	–	3	11	18	12	30	–	–	–	18	12	30	18	12	30
Bloomfield Retreat, Co. Dublin	1	–	3	–	2	2	–	–	4	21	10	26	36	–	1	1	10	25	35	10	25	35
Cittadella, Co. Cork,	–	–	–	–	5	–	3	–	–	12	9	12	21	1	2	3	8	10	18	9	12	21
Course Lodge, Co. Armagh,	–	–	–	–	–	–	–	–	–	8	–	8	8	–	–	–	–	8	8	–	8	8
Elm Lawn, Co. Dublin,	–	–	–	–	–	1	–	–	–	3	–	4	4	–	–	–	–	4	4	–	4	4
Esker House, do.,	–	–	–	–	–	–	–	–	–	3	–	3	3	–	–	–	–	3	3	–	3	3
Farnham House, do.,	–	–	–	–	5	–	–	–	19	36	25	36	51	9	5	14	16	21	37	25	26	51
Hampstead House, do.,	2	–	3	–	1	–	2	–	8	1	22	1	23	4	–	4	18	1	19	22	1	23
Hartfield House, do.,	3	–	3	–	2	–	4	–	3	–	28	–	28	10	–	10	18	–	18	28	–	28
Highfield House, do.,	–	–	–	–	–	–	–	–	–	12	–	12	12	–	–	–	–	12	12	–	12	12
Lindville, Co. Cork,	1	–	2	–	–	–	1	–	4	11	10	11	21	–	–	–	10	11	21	10	11	21
Lisle House, Co. Dublin,	–	–	–	–	–	–	–	–	–	2	–	2	2	–	–	–	–	2	2	–	2	2
Midland Retreat, Queen's Co.,	–	–	–	–	–	–	2	–	2	–	5	–	5	3	–	3	2	–	2	5	–	5
Mount Alton, County Dublin,	–	–	–	–	–	–	–	–	–	3	–	3	3	–	–	–	–	3	3	–	3	3
Orchardstown House, do.,	–	–	–	–	–	–	–	–	2	4	2	4	6	–	–	–	2	4	6	2	4	6
St. John of God, do.,	1	–	2	–	4	–	1	–	2	–	12	–	12	–	–	–	12	–	12	12	–	12
St. Patrick's (Belmont), County Waterford,	–	–	–	–	–	–	–	–	1	–	4	–	4	–	–	–	4	–	4	4	–	4
St. Patrick's (Swift's), Dublin City,	1	–	2	–	12	8	3	–	8	50	35	58	93	5	5	10	30	53	83	35	58	93
Spring Lawn House, King's Co.,	–	–	–	–	–	–	–	–	1	2	1	2	3	–	–	–	1	2	3	1	2	3
Stewart Institution, Co. Dublin,	2	–	1	3	10	3	–	1	47	64	62	71	133	–	–	–	62	71	133	62	71	133
Verville, do.,	–	–	–	–	–	–	–	–	–	23	–	23	23	–	7	7	–	16	16	–	23	23
St. Vincent's, do.,	–	–	–	–	–	–	–	–	–	108	–	108	108	–	13	13	–	95	95	–	108	108
Woodbine Lodge, do.,	–	–	–	–	–	–	–	–	–	3	–	3	3	–	–	–	–	3	3	–	3	3
Total	12		22	8	42	15	20	1	94	370	243	380	623	30	33	63	211	346	567	213	380	623

No. 8.—Table showing the Number of Patients who were Discharged or who Died in Private Lunatic Asylums, and their respective Ages, during the Year ending 31st December, 1885.

Asylums.	Cured.												Total Cured.			Not Cured.												Total not Cured.		
	Under 20 Years of age.			20 Years and under 40.			40 Years and under 60.			60 Years and upwards.						Under 20 years of age.			20 Years and under 40.			40 Years and under 60.			60 Years and upwards.					
	M.	F.	T.	M.	F.	T.	M.	F.	T.	M.	F.	T.	M.	F.	T.	M.	F.	T.	M.	F.	T.	M.	F.	T.	M.	F.	T.	M.	F.	T.
Allen Retreat, Co. Armagh,	–	–	–	2	1	3	3	5	8	–	–	–	5	6	11	–	–	–	1	–	1	3	–	3	–	–	–	4	–	4
Bloomfield Retreat, Co. Dublin,	–	–	–	–	–	–	–	–	–	–	–	–	–	–	–	–	–	–	1	–	1	1	–	1	–	–	–	2	–	2
Citadella, Co. Cork,	–	–	–	–	1	1	1	1	2	–	–	–	1	2	3	–	–	–	1	–	1	–	–	–	–	–	–	1	–	1
Course Lodge, Co. Armagh,	–	–	–	–	–	–	–	–	–	–	–	–	–	–	–	–	–	–	–	–	–	–	–	–	–	–	–	–	–	–
Elm Lawn, Co. Dublin,	–	–	–	–	–	–	–	–	–	–	1	1	–	1	1	–	–	–	–	–	–	–	–	–	–	–	–	–	–	–
Esker House, do.,	–	–	–	–	–	–	–	–	–	–	–	–	–	–	–	–	–	–	–	–	–	–	–	–	–	–	–	–	–	–
Farnham House, do.,	1	–	1	3	1	4	1	–	1	1	–	1	6	1	7	–	–	–	–	–	–	–	–	–	–	–	–	–	–	–
Hampstead House, do.,	–	–	–	2	–	2	1	–	1	–	–	–	3	–	3	1	–	1	–	–	–	1	–	1	–	–	–	2	–	2
Hartfield House, do.,	–	–	–	3	–	3	–	–	–	1	–	1	4	–	4	–	–	–	–	–	–	2	–	2	–	–	–	2	–	2
Highfield House, do.,	–	–	–	–	–	–	–	–	–	–	–	–	–	–	–	–	–	–	–	–	–	–	2	2	–	–	–	–	2	2
Lindville, Co. Cork,	–	–	–	1	1	2	3	–	3	–	–	–	4	1	5	–	–	–	–	–	–	–	–	–	–	–	–	–	–	–
Lisle House, Co. Dublin,	–	–	–	–	–	–	–	–	–	–	–	–	–	–	–	–	–	–	–	–	–	–	–	–	–	–	–	–	–	–
Midland Retreat, Queen's Co.,	–	–	–	3	1	4	–	1	1	–	–	–	3	2	5	–	–	–	–	–	–	–	–	–	–	–	–	–	–	–
Mount Alton, Co. Dublin,	–	–	–	–	1	1	–	–	–	–	–	–	–	1	1	–	–	–	–	–	–	–	–	–	–	–	–	–	–	–
Orchardstown House, do.,	–	–	–	–	–	–	–	–	–	–	–	–	–	–	–	–	–	–	–	–	–	–	–	–	–	–	–	–	–	–
St. John of God, do.,	–	–	–	6	–	6	2	–	2	1	–	1	9	–	9	–	–	–	2	–	2	–	–	–	–	–	–	2	–	2
St. Patrick's (Belmont), Co. Waterford,	–	–	–	2	–	2	–	–	–	–	–	–	2	–	2	–	–	–	–	–	–	–	–	–	–	–	–	–	–	–
St. Patrick's (Swift's), Dublin City,	–	–	–	1	3	4	–	–	–	–	–	–	1	3	4	–	–	–	2	1	3	1	4	5	–	–	–	3	5	8
Spring Lawn House, King's County,	–	–	–	–	–	–	–	–	–	–	–	–	–	–	–	–	–	–	–	–	–	–	–	–	–	–	–	–	–	–
Stewart Institution, Co. Dublin,	–	–	–	1	1	2	–	2	2	1	–	1	2	3	5	2	–	2	–	–	–	1	–	1	–	–	–	3	–	3
Verville, Co. Dublin,	–	–	–	–	2	2	–	–	–	–	–	–	–	2	2	–	–	–	–	1	1	–	1	1	–	–	–	–	2	2
St. Vincent's, do.,	–	1	1	–	3	3	–	2	2	–	–	–	–	6	6	–	–	–	–	2	2	–	1	1	–	–	–	–	3	3
Woodlawn Lodge, do.,	–	–	–	–	–	–	–	–	–	–	1	1	–	1	1	–	–	–	–	–	–	–	–	–	–	–	–	–	–	–
Total,	1	1	2	24	17	41	11	11	22	4	2	6	40	31	71	3	–	3	7	4	11	9	8	17	–	–	–	19	13	34

No. 8.—TABLE showing the Number of Patients who were Discharged or who Died in Private Lunatic Asylums, and their respective Ages, during the Year ended 31st December, 1883—*continued.*

ASYLUMS	Incurable.												Total Incurable.			Died.												Total Died.			Grand Total Discharged and Died		
	Under 20 years of age.			20 Years and under 40.			40 Years and under 60.			60 Years and upwards.						Under 20 Years of age			20 Years and under 40.			40 Years and under 60			60 Years and upwards.								
	M.	F.	T.	M.	F.	T.	M.	F.	T.	M.	F.	T.	M.	F.	T.	M.	F.	T.	M.	F.	T.	M.	F.	T.	M.	F.	T.	M.	F.	T.	M.	F.	T.
Allen Retreat, Co. Armagh,	–	–	–	1	–	1	–	–	–	–	–	–	1	–	1	–	–	–	–	–	–	1	–	1	–	–	–	1	–	1	11	6	17
Bloomfield Retreat, Co. Dublin,	–	–	–	–	–	–	–	–	–	–	–	–	–	–	–	–	–	–	2	–	2	1	2	3	–	1	1	3	3	6	5	3	8
Cittadella, Co. Cork,	–	–	–	–	–	–	–	–	–	–	–	–	–	–	–	–	–	–	–	–	–	–	–	–	–	1	1	–	1	1	2	3	5
Course Lodge, Co. Armagh,	–	–	–	–	1	1	–	1	1	–	–	–	–	2	2	–	–	–	–	–	–	–	–	–	–	–	–	–	–	–	–	3	3
Elm Lawn, Co. Dublin,	–	–	–	–	–	–	–	–	–	–	–	–	–	–	–	–	–	–	–	–	–	–	–	–	–	1	1	–	1	1	–	2	2
Esker House, County Dublin,	–	–	–	–	–	–	–	–	–	–	–	–	–	–	–	–	–	–	–	–	–	–	–	–	–	–	–	–	–	–	–	–	–
Farnham House, do.,	–	–	–	–	–	–	–	–	–	–	–	–	–	–	–	–	–	–	–	1	1	2	–	2	1	–	1	3	1	4	8	3	11
Hampstead House, do.,	–	–	–	1	–	1	–	–	–	–	–	–	1	–	1	–	–	–	–	–	–	–	–	–	–	–	–	–	–	–	6	–	6
Hartfield House, do.,	–	–	–	–	–	–	–	–	–	–	–	–	–	–	–	–	–	–	1	–	1	1	–	1	–	–	–	2	–	2	8	–	8
Highfield House, do.,	–	–	–	–	–	–	–	–	–	–	–	–	–	–	–	–	–	–	–	–	–	–	–	–	–	2	2	–	2	2	–	4	4
Lindville, Co. Cork,	–	–	–	2	–	2	–	–	–	–	–	–	2	–	2	–	–	–	1	–	1	–	–	–	1	–	1	2	–	2	5	1	6
Lisle House, Co. Dublin,	–	–	–	–	–	–	–	–	–	–	–	–	–	–	–	–	–	–	–	–	–	–	–	–	–	1	1	–	1	1	–	1	1
Midland Retreat, Queen's Co.,	–	–	–	–	–	–	–	2	2	–	1	1	–	3	3	–	–	–	–	–	–	–	–	–	1	–	1	1	–	1	4	5	9
Mount Alton, Co. Dublin,	–	–	–	–	–	–	–	–	–	–	–	–	–	–	–	–	–	–	–	–	–	–	–	–	–	–	–	–	–	–	–	1	1
Orchardstown House, do.	–	–	–	–	1	1	–	–	–	–	–	–	–	1	1	–	–	–	–	–	–	–	1	1	–	–	–	–	1	1	–	2	2
St. John of God, do.	–	–	–	–	–	–	–	–	–	–	–	–	–	–	–	–	–	–	–	–	–	–	–	–	–	–	–	–	–	–	11	–	11
St. Patrick's (Belmont), County Waterford,	–	–	–	–	–	–	–	–	–	–	–	–	–	–	–	–	–	–	–	–	–	–	–	–	1	–	1	1	–	1	3	–	3
St. Patrick's (Swift's), Dublin City,	–	–	–	–	–	–	–	–	–	–	–	–	–	–	–	–	–	–	–	1	1	3	1	4	2	2	4	5	4	9	9	12	21
Spring Lawn House, King's County,	–	–	–	–	–	–	–	–	–	–	–	–	–	–	–	–	–	–	–	–	–	–	–	–	–	–	–	–	–	–	–	–	–
Stewart Institution, Co. Dublin,	2	1	3	1	3	4	1	–	1	–	–	–	4	4	8	5	2	7	–	4	4	1	1	2	2	3	5	8	10	18	17	17	34
Verville, Co. Dublin,	–	–	–	–	–	–	–	–	–	–	–	–	–	–	–	–	–	–	–	–	–	–	–	–	–	2	2	–	2	2	–	6	6
St. Vincent's, do.,	–	–	–	–	–	–	–	–	–	–	–	–	–	–	–	–	–	–	–	1	1	–	–	–	–	5	5	–	6	6	–	17	17
Woodbine Lodge, do.,	–	–	–	–	–	–	–	–	–	–	–	–	–	–	–	–	–	–	–	–	–	–	–	–	–	1	1	–	1	1	–	2	2
Total,	2	1	3	5	5	10	1	3	4	–	1	1	8	10	18	5	2	7	4	7	11	9	5	14	8	19	27	26	33	59	93	86	179

APPENDIX G.

Letter from Dr. Ashe, Resident Physician and Governor, Central Asylum, Dundrum.

Central Asylum,
4th June, 1886.

"Gentlemen,—I have the honour herewith to transmit my annual report of the above asylum, to accompany the statistical and financial tables, the former of which are made up as usual to the end of the calendar year 1885, and the latter to the end of the financial year 1885–6.

"There has, fortunately, been little in the history of the asylum during the past year calling for special notice, apart from the records presented by the figures in the tables.

"The death-rate has been higher during the past year than during the preceding one, in which it had been only 2·5 per cent. on the total number resident; but this is a casual increase only, and not due to any special outbreak of disease. The house has, on the whole, indeed, been remarkably healthy.

"The admissions on the male side were exactly the same in 1885 as in the preceding year, viz., twenty-six; and on the female side four, as against three. The total population of the asylum has, therefore, slightly diminished during the period comprised in the tables.

"I am happy to be able to report that no escape of a permanent character has occurred in the past year; in one case a patient crossed the wall of the airing-court, having been undoubtedly helped over by some of his fellow-patients, notwithstanding that six attendants and some of the Constabulary guard were on duty in the court at the time. That there was negligence on the part of the attendants and Constabulary alike on this occasion, there can be, in my opinion, no possible doubt; and it is in reference to such cases as this that I have expressed the wish that I was empowered to inflict a somewhat heavier penalty than the trifling fine of five shillings now within my competence. The patient referred to was, however, discovered and brought back within three hours, not having crossed any public road in the meantime, but having remained concealed in an adjoining shrubbery. The structural additions to the boundary walls and gateway, so long urged on the attention of the Executive, were finished during the past year, and have undoubtedly materially aided the safe keeping of the prisoners.

"The staff of warders on the male side has also been increased under the authority of the Treasury, by the addition of two permanent, and two temporary members; the two latter, however, being sanctioned up to the 30th September, prox. My experience of the difficulties which occasionally, very frequently, occur, even with this augmented staff, lead me to the conviction that, on the dismissal of the two temporary attendants at present employed, grave difficulties will again present themselves in regard of the safe-keeping of the prisoners, and that serious disaster may again result. In my opinion, the staff as it stands at present is the smallest with which efficiency can be maintained, the smallest with which such contingencies as the casual illness of two or more warders at once, the detail of two, three, or even four on escort duty, funeral duty, &c., can be met without incurring an immediate dislocation of all arrangements, and grave risk of outbreaks, escapes, &c., among the inmates, who of course are well aware of the opportunity presented to them by such a reduction of the staff available to cope with them, and fully prepared to seize it. On one occasion during the past year one attendant was sick, another had been dismissed for misconduct, and just at this juncture I was called upon to provide an escort of two to proceed to Broadmoor and bring a prisoner from thence. The staff of warders was thus reduced at once from fourteen to ten, or by about 30 per cent., and it is obvious that such a reduction must be more severely felt in proportion as the actual numbers of attendants is smaller. A large staff can bear such a reduction of its relative strength better than a small one. On the occasion above mentioned a severe struggle occurred between the men in charge of the airing yard and a group of prisoners, sane or approximately so, who obviously took advantage of the opportunity to combine for aggressive purposes. Two of the attendants were knocked down and kicked, and incurred considerable risk of having their keys wrested from them: this would have resulted in a rush of all the sane and many of the insane prisoners through the airing-yard door, and to the boundary walls in an attempt to escape, and in this attempt several would undoubtedly have been successful with the aid one of another, and these would have been chiefly the sane, who are, of course, the most difficult to recapture. There were but four men in charge of about one hundred prisoners in the yard at the time, every other member of the staff being definitely and satisfactorily accounted for. Had the two temporary attendants, whose services it is proposed to dispense with, not been on the staff on that occasion it is more than probable that a grave disaster would have occurred.

"The presence of these sane prisoners, capable as they are of combination, organization, and conspiracy, is a source of constant anxiety and danger here, where our arrangements, and the architectural structure of the building, are designed for the safe-keeping of the insane only, these being accorded an amount of freedom and indulgence unsuited for sane and dangerous convicts. A group of such prisoners has lately been confined here, and, as you are aware, I have been disappointed in an endeavour to have their ringleader, the notorious W. M. of prison history, again secluded within the walls of a prison, the only proper place for such a character, undoubtedly sane as he is. It was discovered that this man was actually swearing in his comrades, sane and insane alike, to resist discipline and take the lives of the warders and others, myself included, who might have to enforce discipline among them. If such persons are to be confined here it will be a matter of urgency to make special structural provision for their safe-keeping.

"There have been several changes in the staff during the past year. The assistant storekeeper retired from ill-health, after a service of upwards of thirty four years; she was a valuable and trustworthy officer; in consequence of the decision of the Government to that effect, her post has not been filled up. It has consequently been necessary to call upon other members of the staff, viz., the assistant laundress and the stoker, to aid the storekeeper in the discharge of his duties in her stead. Three male attendants were dismissed for misconduct, and two others resigned. The various contracts were satisfactorily discharged during the year.

"I subjoin herewith notes of the cases admitted in the course of the year.

"I am, gentlemen,
"Your obedient servant,

"ISAAC ASHE, M.D., F.C.D.
Resident Physician and Governor

"The Inspectors of Lunatics,
"Dublin Castle."

NOTES OF THE CASES ADMITTED DURING THE YEAR 1885.

MALES.

Reg. No. 681.—M. D., aged 19. Single. Sentenced at Roscommon Quarter Sessions to six months hard labour for indecent assault. Was convicted on 14th October, 1884, certified as insane while undergoing his imprisonment in Mullingar gaol, and transferred here on the 2nd January, 1885. His sentence having expired during the year he was transferred to Ballinasloe Asylum on the 14th April, 1885.

682.—J. B., aged 50. Brought up at Monaghan Assizes on the 6th March, 1885, for the murder of his own child. Found insane and incapable of pleading. Removed to Armagh gaol, and transferred from thence to this asylum on the 12th March, 1885, under warrant of detention during His Excellency's pleasure. He had cut his own throat after murdering his child. He is a case of utter dementia.

683.—P. G., aged 37. Shopkeeper, married. Found guilty at Roscommon Assizes on 11th March, 1885, of the murder of his own child while in a state of insanity. Remitted to Mullingar prison and transferred thence under warrant of detention during His Excellency's pleasure on the 18th March, 1885. It is stated that his insanity is due to delirium tremens. Observation since his admission shows that it is recurrent mania of a very violent character and accompanied occasionally by epilepsy. A note by the Governor of Mullingar prison states that this man was admitted to bail on the 11th February, and surrendered to his bail on the 11th March. It would, therefore, appear that a man who was the subject of delirium tremens, violent recurrent mania, and epilepsy, and who while so affected had actually murdered his own child, was considered a proper person to be at large in the world. This case must be regarded as incurable.

684.—P. M., aged 47. Grocer. Indicted at Roscommon Assizes, 11th March, 1885, for felonious wounding. Found incapable of pleading. Remitted to Mullingar gaol accordingly, and transferred thence on 18th March, 1885, under warrant of detention during His Excellency's pleasure. This is a case of religious mania with delusions. He had been an inmate of Mullingar District Asylum for three months previous to his trial.

685.—J. C., aged 35. Butcher. Tried at Clonmel Assizes, on 10th March, 1885, for murder. Found guilty, but insane. Remitted to Clonmel prison, and thence transferred here on 30th March, 1885, under warrant of detention during His Excellency's pleasure. This is a case of violent mania with long lucid intervals.

686.—W. M., aged 26. Married. Indicted at Londonderry Assizes, on 21st March, 1885, for the murder of one Robert Smith. Found incapable of pleading, and transferred from Londonderry gaol here on 1st April, 1885, under warrant of detention during His Excellency's pleasure. A prisoner of violent temper and manners.

687.—D. K., aged 51. Sawyer. This prisoner was committed to Cork gaol for a grievous assault causing the death of one Anthony Canty; the offence was committed on the 19th March, 1882. His trial having been postponed from the Cork July Assizes on the ground of insanity he was removed to Cork District Asylum by direction of the Lord Lieutenant on 29th July, 1882. He was subsequently indicted at the Cork Spring Assizes of 1885, and found incapable of pleading. The warrant for his reception here, dated 31st March, 1885, states that he was then confined in Cork Male Prison, but he would appear to have been remitted to the Cork Asylum under some order not received among his papers here; and from Cork District Asylum he was transmitted here on the 17th April, 1885, to be detained during His Excellency's pleasure. The case is one of dementia with religious delusions.

688.—J. M., aged 70. Indicted at Monaghan Assizes, 10th July, 1885, for murder of one John Niel; found guilty, but of unsound mind. He was received here accordingly from Armagh Prison on the 18th July, 1885, under warrant of detention during His Excellency's pleasure. The surgeon of the county gaol emphatically certified him as "not insane" on the day preceding his transmission. On his reception here the next day he was undoubtedly in a state of chronic melancholic dementia.

689.—P. B., aged 30. Single. Labourer. This prisoner was convicted at the Galway Assizes on 23rd March, 1885, of violent assault; his brother, the next case, being tried and convicted along with him. They were both sentenced to five years' penal servitude, and removed accordingly to Mountjoy Convict Prison on 27th March. They having both been certified as insane on the 14th July, they were transferred here on the 20th. They are both suffering under delusional mania, and are badly conducted and violent men. P. B. has previously been in Ballinasloe Asylum, and a sister is there at present.

690.—M. B., aged 25. Single. Labourer. Brother of the preceding, tried and convicted of the same offence, and at the same time. Sentenced to five years' penal servitude. Certified as insane at Mountjoy Prison on same date, and removed here along with him. Is much the worse case of the two in mental condition and violence, and has been in Ballinasloe Asylum two or three times.

691.—J. M'C., aged 64. Single. Tailor. Convicted of larceny at Enniskillen Quarter Sessions on 15th January, 1883, and sentenced to seven years penal servitude. Certified as insane on 25th July, 1885 while undergoing sentence in Mountjoy Convict Prison, and transferred here on 31st July, accordingly. He has been frequently convicted under different aliases. He was under a fixed delusion of long standing that there was a conspiracy against him among the officials of Mountjoy Prison to poison his food, or in some other manner take away his life; and he is under the same delusion regarding the officials and prisoners here.

694.—M. S., aged 27. This prisoner was convicted at the Kerry Summer Assizes of an attempt to commit suicide, and ordered to be detained during His Excellency's pleasure. He was transferred here from Tralee Gaol on 10th August, 1885, by letter from the Under-Secretary pending issue of warrant, and again transferred to his district asylum of Killarney on the 28th of the same month. The governor and surgeon of Tralee Gaol certified him as "not insane," though weak and debilitated; but he appeared to be suffering under melancholia when admitted here, and his hand and arm were atrophied from the self-inflicted wound.

695.—B. N., aged 46. Indicted at Kerry Assizes in July, 1885, for the murder of his wife on the 6th July, and found insane and incapable of pleading; certified by the Governor and Surgeon of the gaol as labouring under "moral insanity." The term, perhaps, is not misplaced in a case presenting such marked intellectual aberration and delusions as this patient exhibits. Admitted on the 10th August under the same authority, and along with the preceding case. He is under the delusion that his wife is still alive, and is an inmate of this asylum, and constantly begs to be allowed to see her.

696.—T. M'C., aged 28. This prisoner was convicted at Belfast Quarter Sessions in April, 1877, of burglary and assault, and was sentenced to seven years' penal servitude, with two months for assault. He was liberated under licence on the 25th October, 1882, but this licence having been revoked on the 7th September, 1883, he was sent to Mountjoy Convict Prison. Here he was certified as insane on the 12th August, 1885, labouring under a delusion that the prison officials had conspired to take his life. He was accordingly admitted here on the 15th August, 1885, presenting the symptoms of maniacal dementia. His sentence having expired, according to information received from the Prisons Department, on the 12th March, 1886, he was then transferred under His Excellency's warrant to the Belfast District Asylum.

697.—T. B., aged 27. Convicted of burglary at Nenagh Quarter Sessions, and sentenced to five years' penal servitude. Transferred to Mountjoy Convict Prison. There certified as insane on account of occasional outbreaks of violence and passion, and transferred here under His Excellency's warrant on 13th August, 1885. This man is a habitual criminal of very low moral type, but we failed to find any evidence of intellectual aberration. He was one of a party of nine prisoners engaged in combination to resist authority and discipline here, and in conspiracies of various kinds, extending even to the length of taking the lives of the officials. Since the termination of the year we certified him as sane, and he was retransferred accordingly under His Excellency's warrant to Mountjoy, to serve out the remainder of his sentence there.

698.—J. K., aged 30. This prisoner was convicted of larceny at the Kilkenny Assizes in March, 1885, and sentenced to five years' penal servitude. Having been transferred to Mountjoy, he was there certified as insane with delusions on monetary and religious subjects, the mania of exaltation, believing that he is the Saviour, &c. He was accordingly admitted here on the 19th November. After any excitement, such as walking quickly, &c., his speech presented a slight defect in power of utterance. This, along with the above-mentioned circumstances, led me to the conclusion that this will prove to be a case of general paralysis. Since his admission the defect in his utterance has become much worse.

He had been butler in a family of position and formerly of good character; no doubt his crime was one of the early symptoms of his disease. From private information I have learned that a historical interest attaches to one of the articles stolen, which was nothing less than the watch worn by the Duke of Wellington at the battle of Waterloo.

700	B. C.	Aged	45	Admitted	20th November, 1885.
702	J. R.	"	42	"	24th December, 1885.
703	H. K.	"	45	"	" "
704	J. L.	"	86	"	" "
705	W. T. P.	"	61	"	" "
706	T. C.	"	47	"	" "
707	T. K.	"	46	"	" "
708	J. H.	"	45	"	" "
709	J. C.	"	44	"	" "
710	M. O'H.	"	31	"	" "

The above ten prisoners were admitted from Broadmoor Asylum by warrant of one of the Under Secretaries of State, under the Criminal Lunatics Act, 1884, their periods of imprisonment having terminated, and they having become removable to their district asylums in Ireland accordingly; they were admitted here *in transitu* merely, and have all been since transferred to their respective district asylums.

FEMALES.

692.—A. C., aged 38. Single. Pleaded guilty of larceny, at Dublin Commission Court, in October, 1884, and was sentenced to five years penal servitude. Certified as insane while undergoing sentence in Grangegorman Prison, July, 1885, and admitted here on 1st August; a patient labouring under dementia, of noisy behaviour, foul language, and filthy habits.

693.—W. K., aged 40. Single. Convicted of stealing a cow, at Sligo Assizes, in December, 1882, and sentenced to seven years penal servitude. Certified as insane while undergoing sentence in Grangegorman Prison in July, 1885, and admitted here on 1st August. She is a quiet and well-conducted patient, though noisy in her conversation; a case of chronic mania.

698.—M. R., aged 22. Single. Convicted of larceny, at Dublin Commission Court, in October, 1884, and sentenced to five years penal servitude. Certified as insane while undergoing sentence in Grangegorman Prison in September, 1885, and admitted here on 18th September. A troublesome case of mania, noisy, passionate, and of an incurable grumbling habit; always imagining herself the subject of ill-usage and conspiracy.

701.—B. D., aged 42. Married. A respectable woman, who murdered her own child and attempted to commit suicide while suffering under melancholia due to over-nursing. She was found guilty, but insane at Wicklow Assizes, in December, 1885, and admitted here on the 22nd of that month, still suffering under melancholia. She has been always quiet and well-conducted, and will soon, probably, be a fully recovered case.

ISAAC ASHE.

www.ingramcontent.com/pod-product-compliance
Lightning Source LLC
Chambersburg PA
CBHW030618270326
41927CB00007B/1228

* 9 7 8 3 7 4 2 8 1 0 3 6 6 *